THE JEWISH CALENDAR, HOLIDAYS & FESTIVALS

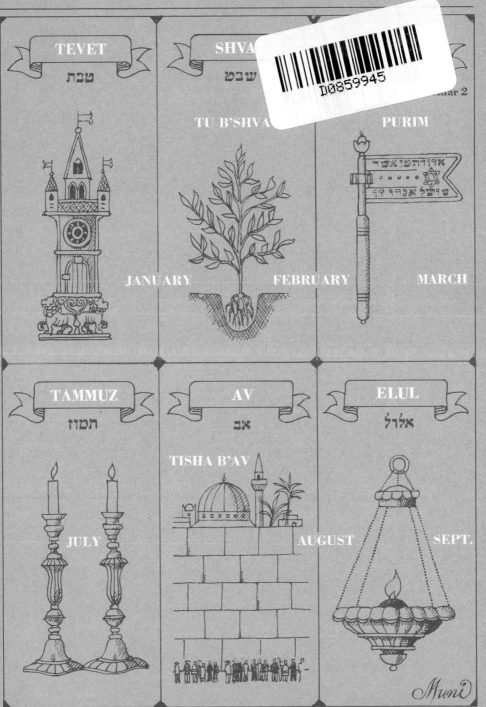

TEVET
טבת

SHVA[T]
שבט

[...]dar 2

TU B'SHVA[T]

PURIM

JANUARY

FEBRUARY

MARCH

TAMMUZ
תמוז

AV
אב

ELUL
אלול

TISHA B'AV

JULY

AUGUST

SEPT.

Muni

1,001 QUESTIONS
AND ANSWERS
ABOUT JUDAISM

By David C. Gross

1,001 QUESTIONS AND ANSWERS ABOUT JUDAISM
A DICTIONARY OF THE JEWISH RELIGION (ED.),
with Ben Isaacson
LOVE POEMS FROM THE HEBREW (ED.)
SHALOM CALENDAR FOR YOUNG PEOPLE

1,001 QUESTIONS AND ANSWERS ABOUT JUDAISM

DAVID C. GROSS

Doubleday & Company, Inc.
Garden City, New York
1978

ISBN: 0-385-11137-1
Library of Congress Catalog Card Number 76–42330
Copyright © 1978 by David C. Gross
Printed in the United States of America
First Edition

FOR MY PARENTS,

who taught me all about Judaism . . .
by the simple method of living by its tenets

PREFACE

The study of Judaism—or more specifically, the study of Bible and Talmud—has traditionally been a lifelong pursuit. In the *shtetl* of pre-World-War-I (and to a lesser extent pre-World-War-II) Europe, it was traditional for most adolescent and adult males to set aside a given period of time every day for Jewish study. This same intensive quest for knowledge and understanding of Judaic subjects permeates the lives of Orthodox Jews today. In recent years, there has evolved an enormous growth of adult Jewish study courses among Conservative, Reform, Reconstructionist, and secular Jews; virtually every synagogue, every Jewish community center, and every Jewish organization is involved with one form or another of Jewish education.

Of approximately 400,000 boys and girls under the age of sixteen or seventeen who attend a Jewish religious school in the United States and Canada, fully one fourth are enrolled in intensive all-day schools, affording them a maximal Jewish education.

Nevertheless, the vast majority of the American Jewish community are still painfully ignorant of fundamental Jewish knowledge. Despite the proliferation of college Judaica courses, the sad truth is that as many as 90 per cent of all Jewish collegians, totaling some 450,000 currently, do not really know the basic data of the great Jewish heritage.

Since the impact of the Holocaust in Europe, which saw

six million Jews murdered in Nazi-run European death camps; and since the establishment of Israel in 1948, when a new dawn seemed to presage a hopeful new chapter in Jewish history; and since the historic promulgations of Vatican II, when the Christian world appeared to be saying loudly and clearly that anti-Jewish sentiments were a thing of the past and belonged to the ignoble Dark Ages, Christians have manifested a deep and sincere interest in knowing more about Judaism and the Jews.

For Jews, the study of Judaism is regarded as a prerequisite of Jewish life. To do it justice, one must devote many years of concentrated learning—and then one will find that there is still much more to know and to understand. This book was conceived as a work that will answer 1,001 questions about Judaism most likely to occur to a great number of people—both Jews and non-Jews—and that the end result will be a ready-reference volume to which one can turn when the occasion arises. It is also hoped that this book will encourage and stimulate one to delve deeper into the sources of Jewish knowledge in order to broaden one's knowledge and understanding of what Judaism is all about.

The Jewish religion has been around for some four thousand years. Jews have lived their lives according to its tenets and mores in nearly every part of the world, and continue to do so today. In a world that seems to be searching for spiritual guidelines, and cognizant of the fact that mankind has attained a potential for universal destructiveness that staggers the imagination, it behooves all of us to know of a way of life that for centuries on end has persistently sought to create a world of peace, justice, and freedom for all.

D.C.G.

CONTENTS

Contents

LIST OF ILLUSTRATIONS

AUTHOR'S NOTE

It is the author's intention to present—through 1,001 questions and answers—a kaleidoscopic view of Judaism.

Although the Jewish community includes both religious and secular Jews, and among the former there are Orthodox, ultra-Orthodox, Conservative, Reform, and Reconstructionist Jews, there is no desire on my part to emphasize one viewpoint or belittle another.

There is a beautiful Hassidic story of a father who came running to his rabbi, begging for help with his son.

"Rabbi," the distraught father cried out, "what shall I do? My son has just told me he does not believe in God! Tell me, what shall I do?"

"Love him more than ever," was the rabbi's quick rejoinder.

I confess to a deep and abiding love for Judaism. It is a way of life that I believe brings in its wake peace of mind, serenity, even wisdom. But it is at one and the same time an activist faith—ever striving for a better life for all people, for universal peace, for justice, for brotherhood.

If this book succeeds in illuminating the truth and beauty of Judaism for even only one reader, the effort in producing it will have been worthwhile.

And if it turns some readers, one would hope many, toward a deeper study of Judaism, it will have been a profound success.

The Glossary, the Index, and the Suggested List of Readings, at the end of the book, are self-explanatory aids to the reader. The transliteration of Hebrew terms follows the modern, Sephardi style.

Two abbreviations used throughout should be explained now: B.C.E., before the common era, and C.E., common era. These are respectively equivalent to the better-known B.C. and A.D. designations.

D.C.G.

Chapter 1

JUDAISM: BASIC BELIEFS

"The Torah can be interpreted in forty-nine different ways, God
told Moses. Decide according to the majority."

— TALMUD

◄1► What is Judaism? Strictly speaking, Judaism is the Jewish religion. There are, however, many Jews who are not observant of the Jewish religious laws and rites and yet profess to believe in "Judaism." To them, the word encompasses the whole Jewish heritage—history, culture, values, a sense of community with Jews everywhere and especially with Israel.

◄2► How is God defined in Jewish thinking? The concept of God as being omniscient, omnipresent, and all-powerful is fundamental to Judaism, as is God's oneness. Put another way, the Jewish vision of God is that He is the source of ethical monotheism. The Bible talks of creating man in God's image; by this is meant that people should emulate God's attributes of mercy, loving-kindness, and holiness. On a par with the basic Jewish conception of God is the sharp antagonism to any idea of an anthropomorphic, or humanlike, God. The great Jewish philosopher Maimonides, in his Thirteen Principles of Faith, stressed that God has no form. The Jewish people, on the other hand, whose origins date back some four thousand years, have been described as a people ever in search of God. Since the idea of a set dogma is alien to Jewish belief, one may assume that there are wide variations by Jews, now and throughout history, of the concept of God.

◄3► What is monotheism? The concept of one God, generally considered to have originated in Judaism with Abraham, the first of the patriarchs. The concept has been taken over by all religious groups in the West, notably Christianity and Islam. Judaism sees God as the one, unifying creator of the universe, who wishes to see all peoples living in peace, harmony, justice, and plenty, and who is ever ready to punish the wicked. He is also seen to be compassionate beyond measure, with profound insights into the weaknesses and foibles of human beings. The belief in God's oneness is so strong in Judaism that the well-known six-word prayer *Shma Yisrael, Adonai Eloheinu, Adonai Echad* (Hear, O Israel, the Lord Our God, the Lord is One) is taught to children at a tender age, and forms the traditional declaration of a person who feels he is dying. It is also a high point of the Jewish liturgy.

◄4► Does Judaism believe in free will, or predestination? Although God is considered to know everything that will befall man beforehand, Judaism nevertheless takes an unequivocal stand maintaining that people have complete freedom of choice. The Jewish sages and rabbis explained this seeming contradiction by asserting that God's knowledge of all events that will transpire does not remove the choice that confronts each and every person: to live ethically or to lead a life of sinfulness. A Talmudic saying sums it up best: "Everything is in God's hands, except the fear of God." The Talmud also noted that "man has the power to defile himself and to keep himself pure."

◄5► What are some typical Jewish values? Fundamentally, Judaism and morality are considered by Jews to be one and the same. One cannot be Jewish and immoral. Nor can a person profess his great love for God and simultaneously be inconsiderate of his fellow man. Judaism is a very down-to-earth religion, or way of life, that sees the kingdom of God nearing only after the elimination of injustice, inequality, suffering, and strife. A Jew who is brought to court on charges of a crime must be found guilty not only by the prosecutor's legal case but also in the hearts and minds of his own community. When worshipers recite the confessional prayers on the Day of Atonement, they do so in the plural, as a community, since the life of each person is considered to be interwoven with the life of his fellows.

◄6► Why are there no monks or nuns in Judaism? Because of the basic belief that withdrawing from the community—even for so noble a purpose as leading a hallowed life—is contrary to Jewish tradition. Judaism insists that true holiness can best be achieved by those who participate fully in the life around them, seeking to support the fallen, succoring the ill and needy, ameliorating the conditions of life that prevail.

◄7► Does Judaism consider people basically sinful? No, but Jewish tradition does recognize that people are born with two opposing life forces: the inclination to do good (*yetzer tov*) and the equally powerful inclination to commit evil (*yetzer ra*). By obeying the laws of Judaism, which encompass every aspect of a person's life, from morning through the night, every day of the year, a person can be helped to avoid evil and do good.

◄8► How do Jews regard the Bible? The Jewish Bible (i.e., the Old Testament) is believed by most Orthodox Jews to have been given to Moses on Mount Sinai by God. (The reference here is to the first third of the Bible, the Pentateuch, or Five Books of Moses, also known as the

Torah.) Most other Jews either believe that the Bible was divinely inspired or that it represents a collective compilation of writings by religious thinkers and leaders going back some three millennia. Put in another way, the Bible is looked upon by Jews as a record of the Jewish experience in ancient days and a moral guide for all time.

◄9► What is the Oral Law? After the Torah, or Five Books of Moses, became the basic source of Judaism, there began a period of commentaries and interpretations of the Torah on the part of rabbis, sages, scholars, and judges. This growing literature of commentary was organized and edited by Rabbi Judah Ha-Nassi (the prince) in the third century and was called the Mishna. Some three centuries later, a commentary on the Mishna known as the Gemara was assembled, and together they form the Talmud, which is the Oral Law, as distinct from the Mosaic Torah.

◄10► Some people believe that Judaism teaches revenge, citing the biblical exhortation of an eye for an eye. Is this true? No. Despite the biblical reference, the rabbis taught that anyone who actually carries out this command literally is risking the life of the person involved. Hence, the ruling was amended to a monetary fine, and only when the attack on the victim was deliberate.

◄11► Do the Jews consider themselves a race, a religious group, a nationality, or what? By and large, Jews think of themselves as a people or a community, encompassing a common heritage of religious, historical, cultural, and national traditions. The founder of an America-oriented wing of Judaism, Rabbi Mordecai Kaplan, said that his movement, Reconstructionism, considers Judaism an evolving civilization, a view that seems to be gaining increasing numbers of adherents. Throughout history, there have been small groups of Jews who tried to call themselves a religious group only, most notably some German Jews in pre-Hitler Germany, but to all intents and purposes Jews are thought of as a combination religious-nationality grouping. They are certainly not a race, if by that term is meant a racially pure stock. A cursory visit to Israel will reveal Israeli Jews who come in all sizes, shapes, and shades.

◄ 12 ► Why are Jews so opposed to intermarriage? Marrying out of the faith has traditionally been a source of grief to Jews, who look upon Jewish life and the Jewish community as a model to be emulated and enjoyed, and who see no better way of life around them. This is not to say that Jews feel superior to other groups, although undoubtedly some do. Since the Holocaust of the Nazi era, when fully one third of the world's Jewish population, some 6 million Jews, were murdered, there is even a greater urgency than ever not to see the Jewish community eroded still further through intermarriage with non-Jewish partners. An additional factor is the traditional low birth rate among Jews: Jews fear that intermarriage coupled with a low birth rate will shrink the size of the Jewish community.

◄ 13 ► What about non-Jews who convert to Judaism? A non-Jew who undergoes formal conversion to Judaism is regarded as a full-fledged Jew, just as if he or she had been born to Jewish parents. Over the centuries, there has been a strong tradition against encouraging conversions, but to a limited extent this feeling has been supplanted today. Most rabbis, if confronted by a non-Jew who wishes to convert to Judaism, after ascertaining that the motives are genuine and positive, will offer encouragement. In fact, there are special conversion classes in a number of synagogues, and there is even a proselytizing organization, dedicated to seeking out prospective converts.

◄14► Speaking of synagogues, is there any difference between a synagogue, a temple, and a Jewish center? A Jewish house of worship is a synagogue, and can be a magnificent edifice seating more than one thousand congregants or a modest, one-room affair. Most Reform synagogues are called temples, but there is no hard and fast rule. The term Jewish center for a synagogue has evolved in recent years, notably in the suburbs, since many synagogues have extended their scope and are in fact communal centers, where people come to worship, children to attend classes, and adults for social and educational purposes; most synagogues also offer catering facilities for the celebration of weddings and Bar and Bat Mitzvahs. Major fund-raising functions are often held in the synagogue too. Separate and apart, there are also YM-YWHAs and Jewish community centers, which offer cultural, educational, and recreational programs but generally are not used for religious services.

◄15► Do Jews believe in the hereafter? There is wide divergence on this question. When a person dies, the prayer that accompanies him includes a reference that his soul will rest in the Garden of Eden, i.e., in heaven. Hebrew and Yiddish curses include a wish that the person being castigated will wind up in hell. Nevertheless, it is fair to state that most Jews do not believe in a physical hereafter but share a belief that their souls, once released from their earthly remains, will ascend heavenward and join the infinite cosmos. Jewish tradition, recognizing that in this world not all the saints are rewarded and not all the sinners are punished, voices the hope that "in the next world" the virtuous will be suitably acclaimed and the wicked properly chastised.

◄16► What is the Jewish attitude toward immortality? Jews who have deep religious faith believe that a person's death is not the end of his life—that he lives on in his children and in the memory of his good deeds. Judaism traditionally separates a man's soul from his body, maintaining that the soul lives on eternally.

◄17► What about resurrection? Here you have two widely differing views. Traditionalist, fundamentalist Jews accept the Jewish doctrine that there will be a resurrection in the Messianic era. It is one of the thirteen Principles of Faith enunciated by Maimonides. Modern Jews, however, including modern theologians, take a differing view, interpreting the sketchy biblical references differently from the traditionalists. They hold that the soul remains after death but that the concepts of resurrection and immortality are foreign to Jewish belief. Contemporary thinkers point out that for many centuries Judaism did not even discuss these concepts, and that they were in a sense forced to consider them after the emergence of Zoroastrianism, which taught about resurrection, and Hellenism, which developed the notion of immortality. The modern Jew feels that Judaism existed quite effectively without the incursion of these foreign ideas and can do so in the future.

◄18► Exactly how is the Halachah defined? The term encompasses Jewish law, both biblical and talmudic (oral), and includes the religio-judicial decisions handed down by great rabbinic scholars and commentators. The word itself literally means "the path"—referring to the laws Jews must follow if they are to abide by Jewish teaching.

Those laws that emanate from the Bible are virtually unchangeable, while those deriving from the rabbis may, under given circumstances, be modified. Halachah covers nearly every conceivable event and activity, ranging from ritual and religious duties to ethical questions and including also civil and criminal law. Orthodox and Conservative Judaism, two of the three major wings of American Judaism, accept the Halachah as the code of behavior their adherents follow; Reform Judaism does not accept Halachah *in toto,* although Reform Jews are free to select certain of its teachings.

◄19► Is it possible, in view of the lack of a formal credo in Judaism, to summarize its basic tenets? Attempts to do so have been going on for centuries, but most Jews today take the view that to know and understand Judaism it is necessary first to study the Bible and Talmud, to live a Jewish life, observing the commandments, and only then will true comprehension of what Judaism is, follow. Nevertheless, some two thousand years ago the great sage Hillel was asked by a pagan to tell him all about Judaism while he remained on one foot. Hillel responded: "That which is hurtful to you, do not do to your neighbor. Everything else is commentary. Now go and study." The same problem confronted the saintly Rabbi Akiva two centuries later, and he cited the sentence in the Book of Leviticus "Love your neighbor as yourself."

◄20► Is it true that there are 613 commandments in Judaism that a Jew must obey? Yes, but a great many of these are no longer in force, because they refer to temple worship service, and both the first and second Holy Temples in Jerusalem have been destroyed. One rabbi taught that David, in Psalm 15, summarized the basic Jewish tenets, reducing the total number of the essential ones to eleven. Psalm 15 reads:

Lord, who shall sojourn in Thy tabernacle?
Who shall dwell on Thy holy mountain?
He that walketh uprightly, and worketh righteousness,
And speaketh truth in his heart;
That hath no slander upon his tongue,
Nor doeth evil to his fellow
Nor taketh up a reproach against his neighbor;
In whose eyes a vile person is despised,
But he honoreth them that fear the Lord;
He that sweareth to his own hurt and breaketh not his word;
He that putteth not out his money on interest,
Nor taketh a bribe against the innocent.
He that doeth these things shall never be moved.

◄ **21** ► What is meant by the duality of Judaism? Simply, the foundation stone of Jewish belief is that faith in and reverence for God must go hand in hand with compassionate kindness to people. An act of goodness is seen as revealing the divine spark present in each person; a person who observes all the ritual commandments but does not possess a genuine compassion for his fellow man is, in the Jewish view, an empty shell. Thus, duality refers to the concept of a simultaneous love by each person for God and for man.

◄ **22** ► What is the Covenant between God and the Jewish people? Genesis records God's promise to Abraham (considered the first Jew although the Torah had not yet been given to the Jews by Moses) in which the land of Canaan—modern Israel—was pledged to "you and your offspring to come . . . as an everlasting possession." The Hebrew word for covenant is brith, and the well-known or-

11

ganization B'nai B'rith, or Sons of the Covenant, is a reference to this phrase.

◄23► How can an educated person accept the biblical account of creation? Jewish tradition holds that the world was created by God and did not spring into being through sheer accident. Indeed, everything in the world around us is the handiwork of God, and if we do not fathom the meaning of certain phenomena, it is merely because we are mortal humans. Judaism stresses the purposefulness of all life and therefore must reject any notion that the world as we know it came about by happenstance. There are deeply devout Jews who are skilled physicists, chemists, biologists, astronomers, who see no contradiction in their professional work and their religious faith. They, and others, maintain that the deeper they probe the mysteries of the universe, the deeper grows their faith at the miraculousness of it all. Although not a religious Jew, Einstein said on a number of occasions that he believed in the existence of what he called a Supreme Intelligence. With regard to the biblical account of six days of creation, most modern Jews do not interpret the words and time spans literally—and simply accept the narrative as only a small part of the whole sum and substance of Judaism.

◄24► How do you explain the Jewish concept that the Jews are, or should strive to be, "a kingdom of priests"? Judaism holds that God chose the Jewish people to be a "light unto the nations"—not a chosen people for purposes of domination but an exemplary people whose moral code will set a standard for all peoples. Jews today may feel that in many ways they have achieved part of this goal; they can point to the disproportionately low crime rate among Jews, their high degree of charity, the emphasis on family life, education, and the like. However, most Jews would quickly concede that there is still a long road ahead before the Jewish people could properly be described as a kingdom of priests. Jewish teaching also stresses that righteous living is not an objective for Jews alone, and cites the talmudic dictum that "the righteous of all nations have a share in the world to come."

◄ 25 ► Does Judaism encourage intellectual dissent? Yes, so long as it stems from committed Jews who are genuinely desirous of a deeper understanding of the tenets of the Jewish religion. The reason for the huge literature of commentaries on the Bible is that in every generation scholars and rabbis debated some of the age-old questions that trouble man to this day, and sought at the same time to interpret Judaism as a living, pragmatic, and viable way of life. Although reverence for God is a cardinal principle of Judaism, intellectual understanding and thorough knowledge of each and every facet of Judaism are equally important. In some synagogues today, during or after formal services, congregants will confront the rabbi with probing questions of why and how come, and not infrequently the rabbi may be forced to admit he does not know. To summarize, Judaism has a set of rules determining how people should conduct themselves, but not how to think.

◄ 26 ► Has Judaism ever sought to "prove" the existence of God? Not really, although for centuries some tried to show His grandeur by citing the beauty and orderliness of the world. Since Judaism is not dogmatic, Jews have differing views of God, ranging from the mystical to the highly personal. The Book of Proverbs sums it up best perhaps by declaring, "In all thy ways know Him." The first sentence of the Bible assumes a belief in God, as does the first of the Ten Commandments. Jewish tradition comments that no matter how hard one tries, one cannot know God completely.

◄27► How does Judaism describe God? In many ways, of course, but chief among these are: God is one; He is infinite; He is the creator of everything through all time; He is the Lawgiver, including the natural law and moral law; He guides the history of the world, in the sense that history is an ever-unfolding drama; He is mankind's helper, aiding human beings in their daily lives.

◄28► If God is all-powerful, why is there so much suffering in the world? The question obviously is as old as Judaism itself. Every generation has struggled with this fundamental challenge to faith, and as might be expected, there are no simple, ready answers. Some explanations of evil point to a possible prior sin of a sufferer, to the need for teaching a moral lesson for all, to showing the sharp differences between good and evil, to the need for a test of man's faith. One traditional explanation among many is that evil itself is inexplicable; this is to be seen in Job's final act, when he contritely confesses his ignorance. A rabbinical epigram admits that "it is not in our power to explain the tranquillity of the wicked or the sufferings of the upright."

◄29► Does the rabbi or the cantor intercede in behalf of the congregation? No. Judaism has no interceders; each person must confront God in his own way; each must do his own praying and perform his own deeds. A rabbi can only show the way, teach, act as a model, as can a cantor, or for that matter any righteous person, but the ultimate responsibility must fall on each person's shoulders individually. The cantor, who actually conducts the service under the rabbi's tutelage, is referred to as a *shaliach tzibur* —the public's emissary—but that is really meant as a tribute to his ability to lead a beautiful, melodious service.

◄ 30 ► What is Judaism's attitude toward physical pleasure? As might be expected, the Jewish view is opposed to the sensual, hedonistic approach to life and is equally opposed to the ascetic stance. The biblical command to "rejoice before the Lord, thy God" is interpreted to mean the spiritual joys that follow worship, study, and the performance of good deeds, but also the mundane pleasures of food, clothes, and comradeship. A man who sees a legitimate source of joy and does not take advantage of it, one rabbi taught, "is an ingrate against God," from whom the joy came. Judaism recognizes that the body, regarded as holy a creation of God as the soul, has certain irrepressible needs, and tries to teach Jews to utilize and enjoy the body in an ambience of sanctity. In brief, Jewish tradition believes it is obligatory to pursue happiness and enjoy one's life.

◄ 31 ► What is the Jewish view of such negative attributes of a person as selfishness, pride, lust? Recognizing that these traits exist, Judaism seeks to channel them into positive directions or at the least modify them. A talmudic scholar noted that if not for the "evil inclination" no man would get married, have children, or establish a business to make money. Hillel recognized selfishness as a basically destructive characteristic, but taught: "If I am not for myself, who will be for me?" He modified this, however, with an additional, significant touch: "If I am only for myself, what good am I?"

◄ 32 ► Is it true that when a Jewish family sits down to a meal, the table is regarded as an altar? Yes. Judaism realizes that everyone must eat to live but wants the simple act of consuming food clothed in some form of sanctity. Thus, traditionally, before the family members sit down to eat, they are obligated to wash and recite an appropriate blessing, recite still another benediction for the food on the table, intersperse the meal with suitable talk of a spiritual nature, and conclude the repast with a recitation of grace, often chanted, by the entire family.

◄33► Why is an unmarried Jewish male regarded with disdain in Judaism? There are four reasons: first, the Bible commands a young man of eighteen to get married; second, the rabbis felt that abstinence from marriage was physically harmful; third, it denies the man an opportunity to complete his soul; and finally, it is inimical to society's future. Unwed Jewish women were traditionally regarded with more compassion, on the theory that virtually every girl wanted to get married, and if she remained unwed it was not of her own volition.

◄34► If Jews do not believe in "turning the other cheek," what do they believe? The Jewish view is that accepting a blow is tantamount to acquiescing in an injustice. Judaism vigorously believes that justice and fair play must be pursued and fought for, and no innocent victim should be advised to stand idly by when an unfair blow is struck— even if the victim is oneself. The only exception to the rule is when an innocent third party is in danger of being injured; a man must choose death rather than commit murder against an innocent bystander.

◄35► How can the concept of loving thy neighbor as thyself be carried out, practically? The idea of not getting involved when one sees a fellow human being in distress is abhorrent to the basic Jewish teachings. The Bible admonishes us: "Righteousness, righteousness shalt thou pursue." In Jewish tradition, this means *action*—going out of one's way to extend a helping hand, a kind word, a friendly smile. The rabbis centuries ago taught that the best way to make kindness almost instinctive is to behave toward all people kindly at all times.

◄ 36 ► Is there a special significance to Jews being unusually generous philanthropists? Judaism regards charity, i.e., the giving of financial and other support to the poor, underprivileged, and handicapped, as much more than a religious commandment. In the Jewish view, charity is an effort to rectify something that has gone wrong with society. Interestingly, the Hebrew term for charity, *tzedakah,* comes from the same word used for justice, *tzedek,* and is related to the word for a righteous person, *tzadik.*

◄ 37 ► How does Judaism look upon other religions? Broadly speaking, with special reference to Christianity and Islam, both of which are derived from Judaism, the Jewish attitude toward other faiths is positive and warm. The feeling in the Jewish tradition is that so long as people live righteously, it is not important if they seek to attain an understanding of God through their own religious paths. During the past two millennia, Jews were attacked and murdered in the name of religious movements; understandably, those groups and their defenders were both hated and feared by Jews. Whenever Jews and Christians or Jews and Moslems have lived together in peace, there has never been any hatred on the part of Jews toward the other religions. As for the religions of the East, they were as little known to Jews as they were to other Westerners, and by and large there has been little contact between them. A good example of interreligious tranquillity is modern

17

Jerusalem, where synagogues, Christian churches of various denominations, and Moslem mosques coexist amicably, each group pursuing its individual path to God.

◄38► What is Judaism's attitude toward the Messiah? Judaism believes that the Messiah, who will usher in an era of universal peace and brotherhood, has not yet arrived. One of the Thirteen Principles of Faith, enunciated by Maimonides in the twelfth century, is that Jews believe in the coming of the Messiah, "and even if he tarry, I will nonetheless wait for him." Jesus is considered by Jews to have been a unique personality—like other historic figures of antiquity—but not the Messiah. There was an outbreak of false messiahs among the Jewish communities of Europe during the last one thousand years, and although the hopes of many of the impoverished and endangered Jews were raised for a while that at long last their wandering and suffering would come to an end, these hopes were quickly dashed when the claimants' true colors were exposed.

Chapter 2

PERSONAL LIFE

"You shall be holy unto me."

— EXODUS

◄ 39 ► What is a Bris (sometimes pronounced, in the Israeli fashion, Brit)? The word itself means a covenant, and the full term for the ceremony is *Bris (or Brit) Milah*, the covenant of circumcision. The Bible commands every male Jewish child of eight days to be "circumcised throughout the generations," a sign of the covenant between God and the Jewish people. It adds: "The uncircumcised male shall be cut off from his people." The ceremony has been stringently adhered to by Jews throughout history, long before there was growing medical evidence that the operation is beneficial hygienically. The carefully trained and pious Jew who performs the rite is known as a *mohel*. In recent years, some Jewish families have utilized the services of surgeons, a practice frowned upon by the traditionalists. The ceremony generally takes place in the morning and is followed by a festive meal. The infant is formally named during the ceremony. The person who holds the infant during the operation and ceremony is called a *sandak* (roughly translated, a godfather); the honor usually goes to the grandfather of the child. A Bris Milah is performed on the eighth day after birth, even if it falls on the Sabbath or on Yom Kippur, the holiest day of the Jewish calendar.

◄ 40 ► How does an infant girl get named? A brief naming ceremony takes place in the synagogue on the Sabbath following her birth, at the time that the father is called to the reading of the Torah. The naming includes a special prayer for the health and welfare of the mother and the newborn child.

◀ 41 ▶ Are there prescribed rules for child naming? Generally, a child is named as follows: his first name in Hebrew, e.g., Moshe, *ben* (son of) Shaul. Throughout that boy's lifetime he will carry that Hebrew name, one that is required when called to the reading of the Torah in synagogue or when a congregant is honored in synagogue in some other way. If the father is a member of the Kohen, or priestly tribe, the appellation "ha-Kohen" is appended; if he belongs to the Levites, the term "ha-Levi" is added.

◀ 42 ▶ Are Jewish children named for the deceased members of the family? This custom developed in the Eastern European communities in recent centuries and is still quite prevalent in the United States and other Western countries. The purpose of naming a child for a deceased close relative is to honor and perpetuate the decedent's memory. Sometimes, for example, a child will be called Francine in her daily life, even though her Jewish name is *Fruma,* in memory of a departed relative.

◀ 43 ▶ Do Jews ever change their names? When someone is critically ill, it is customary for the next of kin to add the name of "Chayim" (which means life) to the patient's own name in the hope that the appendage will pull him through. In the case of a woman, the additional name is "Chaya."

◀ 44 ▶ Is that the only time Jews change their names? No. In Israel, for example, the typical Jewish name of Goldberg might well be Hebraized to Golan, which has a more generic Middle Eastern ring. On the other hand, a Goldberg who wished to disguise his Jewish background might change it to Montor—the French equivalent (*mont d'or*) of the name's meaning, "golden mountain." When a non-Jew (male) converts to Judaism, he is generally given the Hebrew name Avraham (Abraham, the first patriarch); a woman convert customarily takes the name of Sarah, the first matriarch.

◄45► Do Israeli Jews and American Jews have basically the same names? Not really. For first names, many Israelis select little-known and seldom-used biblical names for their children, while most other Jews stick to the popular names such as David, Solomon, and the like.

◄46► How is it possible that a boy is named Pesach (Passover)? Customarily, if a boy is born on Passover, he is named Pesach; if he is born on another holiday, he might well be called Yomtov (holiday); some children born on the Sabbath have been called Shabtai.

◄47► What is a Pidyon ha-Ben? Literally, redemption of the first-born. By biblical precept, the first-born male child was to be consecrated to the priesthood. In order to "redeem" the child from this obligation, a ceremony is held a month after the infant's birth, "freeing" the child from the duty to serve as a priest and allowing him to lead a normal life. The ceremony, usually a festive one, does not take place, however, if the infant's father is a "Kohen" or a "Levi" or if the mother's father belongs to either group.

◄48► What does a Jewish child do immediately on awakening? He is expected to recite a brief prayer, known

23

as the *modeh ani,* or "I give thanks," after which he may begin the day's activities. A brief and simple prayer, it has been especially popular with small children since it was first introduced, some three hundred years ago. The practice is in force today among Orthodox and some Conservative Jews.

◄ **49** ► Photos of Jews at morning prayers show them wearing what looks like a fringed shawl, and a little box on the head and another on the arm. What are these things? The shawl is a prayer shawl, known as a *tallit,* and the boxes, attached to the head and arm respectively by leather thongs, are known as *tefillin,* or phylacteries. A biblical command orders Jews to attach fringes on the corners of their clothes as reminders of the need to obey the laws of Judaism. Most Jewish worshipers today observe the command by wearing a *tallit,* to which are attached *tzitzith,* or fringes, during morning services. (The *tallit* is also worn on the eve of Yom Kippur, the Day of Atonement, and all through the day on Rosh Hashanah and Yom Kippur.) Some extreme Orthodox Jews, including members of Hassidic sects, wear a small *tallit,* under a shirt, known as an *arba kanfot,* which lets the fringes hang loose and be seen. The *tefillin* are a pair of small leather boxes containing brief biblical excerpts written on parchment, which are used at morning prayer services (except on the Sabbath and holidays). A Bar Mitzvah boy (when he reaches the age of thirteen) is usually presented with a set of *tefillin* and a *tallit,* since he has now reached an age when he may be counted in a *minyan* (a religious quorum). The daily donning of *tefillin* and *tallit* for morning services is obligatory from the age of thirteen on. The morning service, known as *shacharit,* may be said at home singly or in the synagogue.

◀ 50 ▶ Is a blessing recited before each meal, when the hands are washed? What does it say? Jews are commanded to wash their hands before each meal and to recite the following: "Blessed art thou, Lord our God, King of the Universe, who has sanctified us with thy commandments and commanded us regarding the washing of hands."

◀ 51 ▶ After the morning prayers and the washing of hands, can breakfast now be eaten? Traditionally, after reciting the blessing over the washing of hands, no word is spoken until a piece of bread is broken off and the *hamotzi lechem* blessing is pronounced. At most public functions, as well as at festive occasions such as weddings and Bar Mitzvah celebrations, the actual meal does not begin until after the *hamotzi* blessing has been recited.

◀ 52 ▶ How does Judaism regard the education of children? The purpose of Jewish religious education, as distinct from general schooling, is to implant in the child the basics of ethical behavior, to encourage observance of the Jewish religious laws and customs, to lay the groundwork for the lifetime study of the Bible and Talmud, the foundations of Judaism, and to instill in the child a strong sense of identity with the Jewish heritage and the Jewish people. This over-all goal is considered by religious Jewish families to be more important than secular training, including the preparation for a career.

◀ 53 ▶ But if the stress is on religious education, how will a youngster learn to earn a livelihood? The Talmud dictum makes it clear that a father must instruct his child in a gainful occupation. He who does not teach his son a skill, the sages said, "teaches him to steal."

◄ 54 ► The Bible warns that to spare the rod is to spoil the child. Does this mean that Judaism approves of corporal punishment? A child may be punished if his misbehavior justifies such action, but in Jewish teaching a parent must never do so in anger or with cruelty. Each act of punishment must be carefully weighed and considered, and under no circumstance may the child's dignity be destroyed. Thus, the punishment must become a true learning experience. A grown child, i.e., past the age of maturity (thirteen years of age) may not be physically punished but may be verbally chastised, if the occasion warrants.

◄ 55 ► Up to what age is a parent liable for his child's actions? Parental responsibility for a child's deeds ceases at the age of thirteen, when the youngster's actions are considered his own doing. This refers primarily to a child's religious or ethical behavior. Legal responsibility is quite another thing.

◄ 56 ► Is it a religious duty for a male to wear a head covering at all times? Orthodox Jews wear a hat or a skullcap (known as a *yarmulke* in Yiddish and a *kipah* in Hebrew) at all times. Conservative Jews usually don a skullcap at services, and at the table either on Sabbath and on holidays or at all meals. Reform Jews usually are bareheaded, even at services. The donning of a head covering is a custom dating back a few thousand years, but it is not a formal obligation. Young Jewish men seen today wearing small skullcaps do so because of religious convictions or to demonstrate their allegiance to the Jewish community. Skullcaps come in many shapes, sizes, and colors. On the High Holy Days, worshipers usually wear a white *yar-*

mulke, denoting the sense of purity that permeates these special and awesome days.

◄57► Do beards have special significance in Judaism? The Bible specifically stipulates: Jews should not "destroy the corners of your beard." In ancient times, pagans cut off their beards and tattoed themselves, and the prohibition against both actions may well have derived from that era. Nowadays, Orthodox Jews are permitted to use an electric razor but not a straight-edged blade when shaving. With the proliferation of beards in recent years among young men, the image of the typical Jew as a hat-wearing, bearded man seems to have waned.

◄58► Why are Jews forbidden to wear the clothes of the opposite sex? The Bible clearly warns that "a woman shall not wear that which pertains to a man, neither shall a man put on a woman's garment." Doing so, the Bible continues, is "an abomination." The rabbis interpreted this law as seeking to establish codes of behavior that will preclude wanton actions. Among Orthodox Jews today, for example, women are not permitted to wear slacks, unless they are specifically designed for women and cannot possibly be mistaken for men's apparel (they usually come with buttons or a zipper on the side).

◄59► What is the Jewish attitude toward abortion? The only time abortion is permissible in Jewish law is in order to save the life of the mother, and only when the fetus is not considered a valid person, i.e., prior to emerging from the womb. Since such cases are rare today, and most abortions take place in order to terminate an unwanted pregnancy, the Jewish view is that although this is not homicide, it is in fact feticide and should be done only after the most careful consideration. Scholars and rabbis are divided on what reasons constitute valid grounds for abortion, some maintaining that if the birth of the child would lead to the mother's insanity, this would be reason enough. Others feel that the birth of a deformed or imbecilic child is ample ground for aborting the pregnancy. The rape of a woman, particularly a married woman, is another possible ground for permitting abortion. No other reasons, especially economic circumstances or the mere wish not to have the baby, are considered justification for abortion.

◄ 60 ► How does Judaism view artificial insemination? Most contemporary authorities argue that if the donor is the husband, it is permissible, but if the semen comes from a stranger, it is not. The feeling is that this is adultery even if it is not technically one of the prohibitions listed in the Decalogue. (If the woman is unmarried, however, there is a more lenient attitude toward her receiving artificial insemination by a stranger.) What modern rabbinical authorities fear might result from artificial insemination is a situation of lax sexual practices.

◄ 61 ► What is the Jewish view of birth control? Generally, Conservative and Reform rabbis take a lenient stand and permit contraceptives, while Orthodox rabbis take a more stringent view against it. However, in recent years even the Orthodox rabbis have leaned toward use of the oral contraceptive, noting that the biblical injunction against the "wasting of seed" does not technically apply when the "Pill" is used.

◄ 62 ► What is Judaism's attitude toward homosexuality? Dating from biblical times, Jews have cited the law in Leviticus that asserts that homosexual relations between two men is "an abomination" and "they shall be put to death." The reason for the destruction of Sodom was because its male residents practiced homosexuality, although rabbinic scholars insisted later that the city was destroyed primarily for its cruelty and injustice. Jewish tradition warns against two males sleeping together, and a talmudic ruling even precludes two males being alone together. The prohibition against homosexuality is extended to non-Jews too, since it is included in the seven special sins for the sons of Noah (the Noachian Laws), aimed at gentiles. Female homosexuality is also condemned in Jewish teaching but not quite as severely as the male version. Maimonides ruled, for example, that if a husband is aware of his wife's Lesbian inclinations, he should prevent her from meeting with other women of a similar nature.

◄ 63 ► How does Judaism view the practice of cremation? Orthodox and most Conservative Jews oppose it, but Reform Jews do not. The traditional Jewish view is that a corpse is not to be mutilated, and cremation is interpreted to fall in that category.

◄ 64 ► Is there a Jewish viewpoint on nudism? Basically, Judaism believes that clothing the human body adds dignity to the person and that people should always strive for modesty in dress. Thus, Orthodox women will seldom be seen wearing short skirts, plunging necklines, or sleeveless dresses. The talmudic sages strictly forbade the enunciation of the sacred *Shema Yisrael* prayer if a man was naked from the waist down. A woman criminal who is to be executed must, according to a talmudic ruling, remain clothed so as not to add embarrassment to her punishment. All branches of Judaism are opposed to any form of nudism, primarily because clothing separates people from the animal kingdom.

◄ 65 ► How does Judaism regard gambling? Occasional gambling is permissible, but the habitual gambler is disqualified as a witness in a Jewish court of law. Although lotteries and games of chance on such festivals as Purim and Hanukkah are acceptable, the Jewish view of regular, frequent gambling is definitely negative.

◄ 66 ► How does Judaism view polygamy? Although the Bible sanctioned it, most authorities are convinced that even in ancient times—long before the outlawing of polygamy among Jews some one thousand years ago—it was not widely practiced. The principal reason for its being legally sanctioned apparently was the feeling that a woman who did not have the protection of a husband was in grave peril. Practically none of the two thousand rabbis and sages mentioned in talmudic works ever practiced polygamy, and one need merely look at the famous line in Proverbs where "a woman of valor" is extolled to see the ideal state as being monogamy. Although the ban on polygamy never reached some small, distant Jewish communities, notably in the Islamic world, all Jews in Israel today, including the remnants of those isolated communities, are enjoined from practicing polygamy.

◄ 67 ► What about pornography? Judaism was never confronted with the kind of open pornography prevalent in the Western world today, but it long ago took a firm stand against any manifestation of wanton talk or any sexual activity outside of marriage. Rabbinic authorities forbade a man to stare at a beautiful woman, even if she was unmarried, or at a married woman even if she was homely. Animals engaged in mating were not to be looked at. Snide comments about a bride entering the bridal chamber were strictly forbidden. The Hebrew language was always considered a holy vehicle, and for that reason, although the Bible is amazingly frank and open about sexual relations between men and women, there is widespread use of euphemisms to describe the acts of physical love. There is nevertheless ample evidence that off-color jokes circulated among Jews, including scholars, but putting them down on paper never entered anyone's mind. Judaism looks upon life as a struggle for holiness and dignity, which rules out any hint of pornography.

◄ 68 ► Is it true that in Judaism divorce proceedings may be instituted only by the husband? There are a few exceptions in Jewish religious law permitting the wife to institute divorce proceedings, but in the majority of cases the initiative must be the husband's. Various rabbinic rulings and customs have eased the woman's situation, making it almost but not quite equally possible for both to start any action for a *get*, a religious divorce. (Most Reform rabbis nowadays rely solely on a civil divorce.) The rabbis of the Talmud, in their various probings as to the kinds of grounds that would constitute acceptable reasons for divorce, said that only unfaithfulness on the wife's part was ample reason (Shammai), if a woman "spoiled a dish for" her husband (Hillel), or if the husband "found another fairer" than his wife (Akiva). The latter explanation has been seen in modern times as meaning that if the marriage was foundering, whatever the cause, the marriage could be dissolved by divorce. Most rabbis and Jewish family agencies nevertheless do their utmost to patch things up between a couple before taking the ultimate step of a divorce action.

◄ 69 ► Is faith healing permitted in Judaism? There are many reports of Jews, particularly in the small villages of Eastern Europe a century or two ago, who would, when stricken with illness, beseech the so-called wonder rabbis for amulets to help cure them. There was a lenient attitude toward this practice, the feeling being that hanging an amulet on the neck of an ill person could not hurt and perhaps would help. In quite a few cases they did help, further bolstering the psychosomatic theory of many diseases. Modern rabbis tend to shun the whole question, although a Jewish Science movement sprang up some decades ago in the United States as a kind of Jewish version of Christian Science. If a Jew, however, turns to a non-Jewish faith healer for help, there is generally a negative attitude on the part of contemporary rabbis. To a very limited extent, a form of faith healing is still practiced among Hassidic and other Orthodox Jews.

◄ 70 ► Does Judaism have a special view on friendship? The value of a good friend is stressed in biblical and talmudic texts, the former citing the friendship of David and Jonathan, and the latter advising every person to have a teacher and a friend. The principal basis for friendship has always, in Jewish teaching, included a common bond through the study of Torah. Rabbi Judah Ha-Nassi said: "I have learned much from my teachers, more from my friends, and most of all from my students."

◄ 71 ► How does Judaism regard sinfulness? Realistically, i.e., Judaism believes in the enormous moral potential of all people but at the same time recognizes that each person is capable of the most horrendous acts of cruelty. The Bible teaches that man's "heart is deceitful above all things and exceedingly weak." Sin is regarded as anything that is diametrically opposite of good; this can be by omission or by commission. The Bible, however, believes in man's ability to resist sin and assures him that "thou mayest rule over it." The traditional "defenses" against a sinful way of life, in the Jewish view, are prayer, Torah study, performance of good deeds, being in the company of wise and saintly people, and most of all will power. What's more, Judaism believes that a person who has transgressed can always repent and start anew, provided the penitent recognizes his past shortcomings and makes a valiant, sincere effort to achieve a new way of life. By and large, Judaism takes the view that people are far from perfect and that the very best that can be achieved in the vast majority of people is a continuing battle for a righteous way of life.

◄72► If, as the Bible says, man was created in God's image, why are most people not Godlike? The rabbis of old explained that it was beneficial to each person to know he was created in the divine image and that he should therefore strive to attain Godlike qualities. Put another way, the feeling in Jewish thought is that a divine spark exists in each person, and it is the duty of each human being to develop a strong sense of self-esteem and to conduct himself with dignity throughout his lifetime as a result of this inner spark. The sages further taught that it is the duty of each person to nurture and develop that spark by living his own life individually, uniquely, so as to reach the highest possible plateaus toward Godlikeness.

◄73► Wouldn't this concept of having the divine spark make most people arrogant? Yes, and for that reason rabbinic authorities through the centuries taught that although it is true that most people are a little lower than the angels, it is equally true that they are only a little higher than the beasts. Consequently, Jews have been instructed to be humble, and the greatest attribute of Moses himself is listed as his humility.

◄ 74 ► Does Judaism believe that the soul is more important than the body? Not really. The Jewish view is that both the spirit and the flesh, as it were, are to be gratified on an equal basis. Judaism is opposed to wanton sensuality as it is to asceticism, maintaining that both courses are not normal modes of behavior. Judaism says that marriage, for example, is not a human weakness but a beautiful, soul-fulfilling link between a man and a woman. Life must be enjoyed, in the Jewish view, and people must not cut themselves off from the community but must share in its trials and tribulations in full and work for the betterment of mankind.

◄ 75 ► Haven't there in the past been Jews who lived monastic lives? Yes, but they were not part of the mainstream of the Jewish community or of Jewish history. There have been Jews who lived physically among their fellow Jews but consecrated all of their time and energies to Torah study, cutting themselves off from the world around them. There have also been some who sought to isolate themselves physically and lead the lives of recluses—and both trends have always been strongly condemned by Jewish thinkers.

◄ 76 ► What is the Jewish formula for happiness? The Bible cites a number of examples for attaining true inner happiness: Those who support wisdom, those who trust in God, people who do not sin, people who do not associate with transgressors, people who practice justice, people who aid the poor, people who earn their livelihood by honest labor, those who observe the Sabbath, and those who fear God. One talmudic description sums it up as follows: "This is the way of the Torah: eat bread with salt, drink water by measure, sleep on the ground, and live a life of pain while you toil in the Torah. By so doing, 'happy shalt thou be and it shall be well with thee.'"

◄77► Which is more important in Judaism, compassion or justice? Without question, justice. The Bible says, "Neither shalt thou favor a poor man in his cause." A judge may not sit in a case where he is prejudiced either against or for the defendant. Nevertheless, there is a great stress in Jewish tradition on the need for compassion. God is described as "merciful," and people are to be merciful; He is described as "compassionate—be thou compassionate." A Jew who lacks a sense of compassion is considered as not being a true descendant of Abraham. Women arc generally seen as being more compassionate. Indeed, the Hebrew word for compassion, *rachamim*, is related etymologically to the Hebrew word for womb, *rechem*. Nevertheless, the Talmud cautions: "They may not show pity in a legal suit"—signifying the greater importance of justice.

◄78► Flogging is listed in the Bible as suitable punishment. Do Jews still practice this? No. No inmates in Israeli prisons are flogged, nor would a rabbinic court today decree flogging as a form of punishment. It is true that there was a harsh discipline in some of the religious schools centuries ago, but as a routine form of punishment flogging has all but disappeared from Jewish life. Public flogging in the Eastern European Jewish villages was still known as late as the latter part of the eighteenth century. Proverbs speaks of corporal punishment for a child as follows: "As a man chastiseth his son, so the Lord thy God chastiseth thee" and "Correct thy son, and he will give thee rest, he will give delight unto thy soul."

◄79► Is heredity a primary factor in Jewish life? Traditionally, most Jews always felt that a child is a direct reflection of his parents, and pointed to long generations of rabbis, proving that the qualities of Torah devotion and study can be transmitted. Choosing a marriage partner was to include careful consideration of the spouse's parental background, in Jewish teaching. Rabbi Akiva taught that a "father endows his sons with handsomeness, strength, riches, wisdom, and length of years."

Chapter 3

FAMILY LIFE

"The object of the whole Torah is that man shall become a
Torah himself."

—BAAL SHEM TOV

◄ 80 ► What does the term *shalom bayit,* referring to the family atmosphere, signify? Literally, the term means "home peace" but it connotes a good deal more: a loving, peaceful, harmonious ambience that permeates the family at all times.

◄ 81 ► Most Jewish families seem to have fewer breakups than non-Jewish families. Is this true, and if so, why? Although the younger Jewish families are not as stable and long-lived as the older ones, it is true that, by and large, Jewish families experience fewer cases of divorce, abandonment, child abuse, and related problems than non-Jewish families. There is a strong tradition in the Jewish family of togetherness, of mutual respect and support, of understanding of the role of each member at varying ages, and of the dependability of the parental role. The humorous and sometimes caustic comments on the so-called Jewish mother as being a domineering personage are based on the innate sense of commitment on the parents' part to the children's welfare.

◄ 82 ► Can a Jewish family remain childless and still be traditionally Jewish? No. In addition to the biblical command "be fruitful and multiply," Jews are expected to look upon marriage as a step toward procreation. Rabbinical traditions differ as to how many children a couple should have, with most disputants favoring at least one of

39

each sex. Nevertheless, it should be stressed that having children is not the sole goal of marriage; Judaism sees companionship, the joining of two people in a lifetime contract with its concomitant results of love and spiritual growth, as the chief purpose of the marital state. As the Talmud puts it, "He who does not marry lives without blessing, goodness, or peace." A man is complete only, the sages wrote, when he is married.

◀ 83 ▶ Does a wife have any sexual rights in a Jewish marriage? The Bible looks upon sexual relations in a marriage as the husband's responsibility. Exodus puts it straightforwardly, referring to a wife: "Her food, her clothing, and her conjugal rights shall not be withheld." While the marital ties, including the sexual relationship of the husband and wife, are described affirmatively and warmly, Judaism takes pains to condemn all forms of sexual license, including promiscuity, prostitution, adultery, and any display of lewd behavior. Scientific proof may be lacking, but the sages of the Talmud insisted that children's health, character, and appearance were influenced directly by the quality of their parents' sex life.

◀ 84 ▶ Are there restrictions on the sexual aspects of family life? There is virtually a whole literature on how to maintain the purity of family life for Jews, including the woman's observance of a time of abstinence during her menstrual period and the ritual self-cleansing by immersing herself in a *mikvah* (a special ritual bath) before resuming marital relations. A husband is also forbidden to force himself on his wife against her will, nor may he approach her while under the influence of alcohol or while they are in the midst of an argument. Maimonides, the great Jewish philosopher, who was a physician and scholar as well, put it simply: "Sexual union should be consummated only out of desire, and as a result of joy of the husband and the wife."

◄85► Are there special rules for husbands' treatment of their wives? The Talmud declared that a "man must love his wife at least as much as himself, but honor her more than himself." A husband is also instructed to be careful not to insult his wife with words, both in private and in public. Such an insult was seen as causing her pain.

◄86► What about the wife's rights in running the household? Traditionally, the rabbis felt that it was up to the mother to instruct the children in the daily rituals and practices of Judaism, while leaving it up to the father to set an over-all, lifetime model. The Talmud evinced its profound understanding of human nature and the husband-wife relationship when it said: "In the affairs of a household, and in the feeding and clothing of his sons and daughters, the man should follow the advice of his wife. Peace and harmony will dwell in his house as a result."

◄87► Is there a special attitude that leads to a successful Jewish family? While the Bible spoke of "a woman of valor," whose "price is far above rubies," the Talmud said: "Who is rich? He who has a wife whose ways are pleasant." Husbands are further cautioned to "be kindly and not demanding" in the house.

◄88► What of the woman's obligations? Wives are warned not to postpone being available to their husbands (for the conjugal act) in order to annoy or irritate their spouses. Use of the sex act as a weapon—either by the husband or the wife—in an argument or as a method of punishment is also forbidden.

◄ **89** ► What are the fundamental duties of a Jewish wife? Citing the biblical passage about a woman of valor, one can summarize this as follows: A good wife is one who is ready to change her father's way for her husband's, who is prepared to stand by him in times of adversity as well as in periods of plenty, who is happy when her husband is happy, who does not idle away her time even if she is wealthy enough to have servants, whose appearance is pleasing to the eye, who is attentive to everyone who speaks to her, and who is generous with help for the needy. These of course are by no means the only criteria for a successful Jewish wife, but it is assumed that a woman who nurtures these basic traits will develop the other necessary characteristics that will make for a happy family.

◄ **90** ► How many days are involved in the separation of husband and wife, sexually, in the prohibition against coitus during the wife's menstrual period? About twelve: seven days, counting from the start of the menstrual cycle (decreed in the Bible) and an additional five, by talmudic edict, so that there is no risk of sexual relations during or immediately after the woman's period.

◄ **91** ► Doesn't this lead to the husband's sense of sexual frustration? Actually, despite the period of abstinence, those who observe this religious law attest to the fact that resumption of the marital relations is tantamount to a sense of renewal and great joy, a feeling that observant Jews state they would not have possessed if there were no restrictions.

◄ **92** ► Do most Jewish women today practice the laws of family purity? Most Orthodox Jewish wives do, and probably the majority of Conservative Jewish women enter a *mikvah* for the ritual immersion at least once—just prior to their marriage.

◄ 93 ► If a gentile child is adopted by a Jewish family, does that child become Jewish automatically? No. The child would have to undergo formal conversion to Judaism in order to become officially a member of the Jewish community. In virtually every other religious ruling, an adopted child is considered in the same way as a natural child. Legally, it is permissible for such a child to marry the natural-born child of his parents, since there is no question of consanguinity, but the practice is discouraged. A child legally is not required to recite the mourner's prayer (*kaddish*) for his adoptive parents, but here, too, the law is ignored and in most instances the adopted child behaves exactly as would a natural child. If an adopted child is known to be Jewish, he is called to the Torah as the "son of ———" and uses the name of his natural father.

◄ 94 ► Does Judaism have special rules with regard to the aged? Beginning with the biblical verse about rising "before the hoary head" and honoring the "face of an old man," Jewish tradition has laid great store on the importance of showing respect and consideration for the aged. The moving lines of the Psalmist "Cast me not off in the time of old age; when my strength faileth, forsake me not" are incorporated into the High Holy Days liturgy. The fifth of the Ten Commandments, on honoring one's father and mother, is interpreted to mean that although caring for aged parents may be burdensome, it is rewarded by long life for those who fulfill this command. Virtually every Jewish community maintains some kind of special home for the aged, seeing these institutions as a communal responsibility for those who can no longer cope with their daily needs.

43

◄ **95** ► Is there a Jewish view of reincarnation? There is no biblical or postbiblical reference to reincarnation, and in the eighth century the great sage Saadyah Gaon wrote a treatise ridiculing the whole concept as "nonsense and stupidities." Jewish mystics did, however, assert a belief in the transmigration of souls, claiming that a sinful person could be punished by having his soul enter the body of an insect. Some of the less-educated Jews in seventeenth- and eighteenth-century Eastern Europe also believed in a *dibbuk:* a sinful person's soul enters the body of an innocent person, which called for exorcism. Practically no Jews today believe in reincarnation, even among those who claim to be followers of Kabbalah, or Jewish mysticism.

◄ **96** ► Warding off the evil eye—is this a widespread Jewish superstition? Not today, although there are probably still large numbers of Jews, even among the educated, who will laud a child and then add softly, *"kein ein ha-ra"* (may the evil eye not befall him). Belief in the efficacy of an evil eye, i.e., a source of malevolence generally out of envy or spite, continued through the Middle Ages to a lesser or greater degree up until the twentieth century. Charms, amulets, and other devices were used through the centuries to negate the effect of the alleged influence of the evil spirit. Nearly every rabbi looks upon this and similar phenomena as silly superstition which deserves to be dismissed out of hand.

◄ **97** ► Does Judaism permit euthanasia? Jewish law expressly and sharply condemns any effort to cut off the life of a person by even minutes, considering all such efforts acts of murder. Nevertheless, citing talmudic precedents, modern rabbis take the view that a patient who is suffering an unquestionably terminal illness may not be injected with a drug that would speed up the end but such a patient suffering great agony could be given pain-deadening drugs, even if it was known that a corollary effect would be shortening his life. The same view is held of artificial life-sustaining devices: if the patient is incurably ill and there is no hope whatsoever for recovery, most rabbis today agree that nature should be allowed to take its inexorable course and allow the suffering patient to expire in dignity.

◄98► Is there a Jewish view of sterilization? Talmudic law stipulates that no man, woman, or animal may be sterilized, a view that is not accepted by Conservative and Reform rabbis unanimously but is in the Orthodox sector. If a woman has suffered in childbirth and wishes to be sterilized, the Orthodox view today is that she may use the contraceptive pill, on the theory that it is most like the "cup of roots" described in talmudic days but whose precise meaning is lost today. The exception is permissible for a woman, since the talmudic sages ruled that the obligation to have children was intended for men but not for women.

◄99► Does Judaism have anything to say about organ transplants? Although this is relatively a new phenomenon in modern life, Jewish thinkers, by and large, take the view that there is nothing wrong with such operations, since the duty of a physician is to save lives and it is under this heading that transplants fall. Mutilation of a corpse is forbidden, but use of organs to save a life is acceptable. Taking such discussions to the nth degree, there is already discussion among some rabbis as to whether transplantation of a pig's heart to that of a human being is permissible. Although the consumption of food derived from the pig is forbidden, there is no such ban on using it for life-saving purposes, the modern rabbis argue, so that in theory it is permissible.

◄ **100** ► Why don't Jews marry on Mondays and Wednesdays? No one is quite sure as to the origin, but the belief has persisted since the Middle Ages that both days are unlucky for a prospective bride and groom—despite the fact that at one time Wednesday was considered the most fortuitous day of the week to enter into marriage.

◄ **101** ► What is the *ketubah?* The Jewish marriage contract, in which the groom spells out his obligations to his future wife. It is written in Aramaic; the centuries-long, abandoned practice of preparing artistically beautiful marriage contracts in recent years has come back into vogue. The Reform wing of Judaism has dispensed with the *ketubah.*

◄ **102** ► Why do the bride and groom fast on the day of the wedding? This centuries-old custom evolved from the belief that the young couple, upon entering the matrimonial state, should purify themselves of any past transgressions and enter their new life together free of any sin. The fast is generally on the day of the wedding and concludes at the time of the ceremony.

◄ **103** ► Do Jews still employ the services of a *shadchan,* a matchmaker? To a very limited degree, the practice is still in force, notably among the Orthodox Jews and to a limited degree in Israel. The custom of parents' arranging matches for their children while they are still very young, which resulted in the couple's meeting for the first time under the wedding canopy, has all but disappeared from the contemporary Jewish scene.

◄**104**► What is a wedding canopy? A *huppah,* or wedding canopy, is a reminder of the ancient wedding chamber into which the bridal couple entered, remaining for seven days, while the marriage was consummated. It is usually a large velvet covering, held up by four men or stretched out and held aloft by four poles, under which the wedding ceremony is solemnized. It can also be a *tallit,* or prayer shawl, held aloft, a custom in vogue among traditional Jews in Israel. Other Israelis, especially members of the armed services, have their *huppah* elevated on the ends of rifles.

◄**105**► May a husband divorce his wife if she is childless? Legally, if a wife does not bear him a child after ten years of marriage, a husband has the right to divorce his wife—a law that is seldom observed today.

◄**106**► Why is a glass crushed by the groom at the conclusion of the wedding ceremony? As a reminder— never to be forgotten, even at this most joyous of moments —of the destruction of the Holy Temple in Jerusalem.

◄**107**► What is the special grace recited after the wedding meal? The *sheva b'rachot,* or seven blessings, in which God is thanked for forming man and woman in His image, ending with the words "Who makes the bridegroom rejoice with the bride." They continue all week after the wedding.

◄**108**► Is there a special song sung at weddings when the youngest child is married? Yes, it is a popular Yiddish tune that congratulates the parents on having married off the youngest of their children, thus freeing them of parental obligations in the sense that the new bride or groom will now be fully responsible for her or his own actions and life.

◄109► In Jewish weddings, is a rabbi always required? Although almost every Jewish marriage today is performed by a rabbi, it is possible to be married by a *m'sader kiddushin*—a performer of marriages—a person who is trained in the regulations of marriage and is himself an observant Jew. In the United States, he must also be licensed by the state in which he resides. At least two witnesses are required at all wedding ceremonies.

◄110► What is a levirate marriage? Where a man dies without having had children, Jewish law stipulates that one of his brothers is to marry the widow, and the eldest son of such a marriage is regarded as perpetuating his late uncle's memory. If the brother refuses to marry the widow, he is required to free the widow to marry another person, and does so in an ancient ceremony known as *halitza*.

◄111► Are there any restrictions on prospective marriage partners? Yes; among them: a man may not marry the sister of a former wife so long as the latter is living, a man may not marry his aunt (although a niece may marry her uncle), a member of the priestly tribe (a *kohen*) may not marry a divorcee or a convert, a divorced woman may not marry her paramour, and one may not marry a child born in an incestuous marriage.

◄112► What is a *zivig*? Ancient Jewish tradition holds that marriages are made in heaven, i.e., there is a preordained partner for every person in the world, and when a couple are happily married they are often referred to as a *zivig*, a heaven-blessed couple.

◀ **113** ▶ What is *tenayim?* The official betrothal contract attesting to the fact that a given man and woman are to be married. In Orthodox circles, it is generally executed immediately before the wedding ceremony.

◀ **114** ▶ What is an *aufruf?* It is customary for the groom-to-be to be called to the reading of the Torah on the Sabbath morning preceding his wedding and for the officiating rabbi to extend best wishes to him and his family during the service. Among Orthodox Jews, where the bride and groom do not see one another for at least a day prior to the wedding, the bride is generally not present, but among other Jewish groups she and her family attend the service, which is usually concluded with a festive family meal or congregational *kiddush.*

◀ **115** ▶ What is a *badchan?* Seldom seen today, the *badchan* was a professional merrymaker whose function at weddings, in Eastern Europe in particular, was to entertain the guests, often with rhymes in which he described the various wedding gifts from both sides of the family.

◀ **116** ▶ What is an *agunah?* A wife whose husband has deserted her, or one whose husband's death could not be formally established, is known as an *agunah.* The problem of the *agunah* is still very much in force today, especially among women whose husbands were believed to have perished during the Second World War but, lacking proof, they could not apply for remarriage. There are also cases of wives whose husbands abandon them for years at a time and who are thus left in limbo, unable to remarry. The Jewish community maintains special organizations that seek to aid these unfortunate women either by tracing the deserting husbands or establishing proof of death.

◄117► What is a *mamzer?* Incorrectly translated as a bastard, a *mamzer* is one born of a proscribed union, such as the child of an adulteress or of an incestuous relationship. A child, on the other hand, born to an unwed mother, although illegitimate in Jewish law, is not considered a *mamzer.* The term has also come to mean, in colloquial usage, a shrewd, conniving person.

◄118► What is *nachas?* A special term referring to the joys and satisfactions that parents derive from seeing their children grow into mature, happy adults. An old Yiddish wish is that one be blessed with good health and *nachas.*

◄119► What are *mehutanim?* The parents of the bride and of the groom, after the wedding, are now related to one another as *mehutanim,* poorly translated as in-laws; in Jewish life the connotation is stronger, implying that both sets of parents now share a common interest in one another's children. The word is derived from the Hebrew word for a wedding, *hatunah.*

Chapter 4

THE SYNAGOGUE

"If only two Jews remained in the world, one would summon
the other to the synagogue—and the latter would go there."

—YIDDISH FOLK SAYING

◄120► How long has the synagogue been a Jewish institution? Most authorities agree that the synagogue goes back at least two thousand years. Then, as now, a synagogue was considered to have a threefold purpose: to serve as a house of worship, as a house of assembly, and as a house of study.

◄121► How many synagogues are there in the United States today? The exact number varies from year to year, owing to shifting populations and changing communities, but *in toto* the number is around 3,500. Of these, approximately 750 are Reform, 850 are Conservative, a small number are Reconstructionist, and the remainder are considered Orthodox. Among the Orthodox, a synagogue can be a modest, one-room affair, sometimes referred to as a *shtibel,* although there are also many hundreds of modern Orthodox synagogues comparable in size, influence, and scope with the Conservative and Reform congregations.

◄122► Is a synagogue comparable to a Christian church? Only to a degree, i.e., since most synagogues (especially in the United States) are in use daily, serving as centers for daily religious services, educational establishments with classes ranging from nursery-age children through high school, meeting centers for a wide variety of organizations, lectures, performances, and fund-raising functions. Most modern synagogues in the United States also maintain catering facilities for the celebrations of weddings and Bar and Bat Mitzvahs, making them nearly year-round beehives of activity. During the summer months, however, most synagogues confine their activities to religious services.

◄ 123 ► What is the *mizrach?* The eastern wall in the synagogue, a place of honor where the Holy Ark (containing the Scrolls of the Law) and the pulpit are situated. The eastern wall, facing Jerusalem from the Western world, denotes the Jews' constant prayer for a restored Jerusalem and Zion.

◄ 124 ► What is a *bimah?* The raised platform in front of the pews, from which the service is conducted. A large table usually stands on one side, where the Torah is placed when it is read aloud, while a lectern (an *amud*) on the other side is maintained for the rabbi to use as a pulpit. The cantor often leads the service from the table on which the Torah rests, before and after the Scroll is replaced in the Ark. In Orthodox synagogues, the arrangement of the *bimah* and the *amud* differs somewhat.

◄ 125 ► What is the light that is always lit and usually hangs above the *bimah?* The *ner tamid,* or Eternal Light, symbolizing the Jewish people's perpetual faith in the teachings of the Bible and in the Jewish religion itself, and a reminder of the menorah in the Temple.

◄ 126 ► Are there family pews in synagogues? The custom has been introduced in recent years, notably in the non-Orthodox synagogues. However, almost everywhere, the seating arrangement is on a first-come, first-seated basis; an exception is made during the High Holy Days.

◄127► What is a *parochet*? The curtain covering the Holy Ark, usually adorned with silver or gold thread and sometimes depicting the Ten Commandments. Generally made of velvet, it is in most instances blue, red, or purple, except on the High Holy Days, when a white curtain is substituted—to symbolize the sense of purity associated with the Days of Awe: the ten days from Rosh Hashanah (New Year) to Yom Kippur (the Day of Atonement).

◄128► Just what is the Scroll of the Law? A handwritten version of the Torah, or the Five Books of Moses (the first of the three sections of the Jewish Bible), inscribed on parchment by a specially trained person known as a *sofer,* a scribe. The Scroll of the Law (in Hebrew, *Sefer Torah*) contains no vowels and no punctuation, making it necessary for the reader to bone up on the material to be read aloud ahead of time (usually a congregant stands nearby during the public reading, comparing the reading from the scroll with a printed, voweled book; if the reader errs, he is quickly corrected). The Torah is taken from the Ark for public reading on Sabbath, holidays, fast days, and on Mondays and Thursdays. A popular fear prevalent in the synagogue is that someone holding the Torah might drop it accidentally, in which case every congregant present would be required to fast. Such accidents are extremely rare.

◄129► What is the name of the crown placed on top of the Scroll of the Torah? A *keter Torah,* literally, a Torah crown, beautifully embellished, indicating the supremacy of the Bible in all facets of life.

◄130► When someone is called to the reading of the Torah, what happens? It is considered an honor to be called, to stand near the Torah while the reader chants a portion aloud. In most synagogues, the first to be called is a *kohen,* a member of the priestly tribe; the second, a *levi,* a member of the Levite tribe; and then, others known collectively as Yisrael, or ordinary Jews. Special honors are set aside for special occasions, e.g., a groom, a Bar Mitzvah, someone who has recovered from a serious illness, someone who has returned from a perilous journey, and sometimes one celebrating a birthday or anniversary. Also, when someone is reciting the *yahrzeit* or annual memorial prayer for a loved one, he is also called to the Torah.

◄131► How is one called? Is there a special designation? A worshiper is told beforehand, or his normal name is called out to come forth for the reading of *r'vee-ee,* or the fourth portion, for example. He then ascends the *bimah,* touches the Torah with the fringe of his *tallit,* kisses the fringe, makes the appropriate benediction, and waits till the conclusion of the reading, when he recites another blessing. He is then blessed, and his Hebrew name (his first name and his father's first name) are used at this time. Afterward, he returns to his seat among congratulatory greetings by his fellow worshipers.

◄132► What is a *yad?* A pointer used by the Torah reader to help him with the reading. It is usually in the form of a hand with the forefinger extended.

◄133► What is an *etz hayyim?* The wooden rollers on which the Scroll of the Law rests. Literally, a tree of life.

◄134► Sometimes men are called to the Torah merely to lift it and put it down. What is this called? *Hagbahah.* The man summoned to raise the Torah on high (when the congregation rises to show its respect) is known as the *hagbah;* he and his partner, whose job it is to roll the scroll tight, tie it with a special cord and encase it in its special mantle, known as *glilah.* These are considered secondary honors. The Torah is not replaced in the Ark during this part of the service, when the portion from the Prophets known as the *haftarah* is read. If there is a Bar Mitzvah boy, he does the chanting; if not, it is a special honor surpassing all the other Torah honors of the day and is assigned to a congregant or a guest.

◀135▶ Why are women not called to the reading of the Torah? Technically, there is no legal ban forbidding women this honor; in recent years, with the growth of feminism, women are now called to the Torah in some non-Orthodox synagogues. The policy of whether or not to do so is left entirely to the individual congregation.

◀136▶ When is a girl called to celebrate her Bat Mitzvah? The Bat Mitzvah ceremony is only a few decades old and is not known in Orthodox synagogues. The ceremony is usually reserved for Friday-night services, and the girl, who can be anywhere from twelve to fifteen years of age, chants the same haftarah portion that a Bar Mitzvah boy would on the following Sabbath morning. A very recent innovation is the special Bat Mitzvah ceremony for women who never had one. They usually take a special intensive course, and often a number of women are called together for a joint ceremony.

◀137▶ Is there any significance to the various types of skullcaps offered to guests coming to a Bar Mitzvah celebration? Not really, but in recent years there has grown up a new appreciation of Jewish religious and ceremonial art, which is translated by mothers of Bar Mitzvah boys designing and crocheting (or purchasing) *yarmulkes* (skullcaps) made of a wide variety of material in a multitude of colors, with the Bar Mitzvah's name embossed or sewn into the inside of the cap.

◄ **138** ► Most synagogues have a candelabrum as part of their décor. What is the significance? It is reminiscent of the giant seven-branched candlestick that was featured in the Holy Temple and denotes light and life itself. Known as the *menorah,* the candelabrum is the official emblem of Israel. It is a very ancient Jewish symbol, found on tombstones and in synagogues dating back many centuries.

◄ **139** ► What is a *siddur?* A prayer book. There are in use daily prayer books, and special prayer books for the Sabbath and holidays. The High Holy Days prayer book has a special designation: *mahzor.*

◄ **140** ► What is a *minyan?* A religious quorum of ten male Jews over the age of thirteen. Although many people pray at services alone, particularly the daily morning service, certain prayers require a *minyan,* including the mourners' *kaddish* service. A small but growing number of Conservative congregations have begun to count women in the minyan.

◄ **141** ► What is a *mehitza?* Found predominantly in Orthodox synagogues, it is a separation between men and women during religious services. It can be either a balcony reserved for women only or a separate section on the main floor of the sanctuary divided from the men's area by a curtain.

◄ **142** ► Are there differences in the services of Jewish communities in various parts of the world? Only minor ones. The two most prevalent standard prayer services are known as the Ashkenaz and Sepharad respectively, the former referring to customs and rites of Jews from Central and Eastern Europe and the latter to Jewish communities from the Iberian Peninsula, which have also been taken over by Jewish communities in countries bordering on the Mediterranean such as Yugoslavia, Greece, and parts of North Africa. (The Reform service is different in that it is shortened and in early versions omitted all reference to Zion and the restoration of the Temple.)

◄143► In other words, could an American Jew accustomed to an American service find the religious service of a synagogue in Norway or Israel recognizable and compatible? Definitely. The one big difference is that the prayer book in the more modern synagogue contains both the Hebrew and the translation of the language spoken in a given country. Thus, there are Hebrew-English, Hebrew-Russian, Hebrew-Spanish, etc., prayer books.

◄144► Is the organ played in the synagogue? Most Reform temples employ an organist, as do a small number of Conservative congregations. In the larger congregations, of all denominations, a choir will sometimes accompany the cantor, particularly on holidays.

◄145► How many prayer services are there daily? Basically, three: *shaharit, minha* and *ma'ariv,* the morning, afternoon and evening services (the latter two are generally combined, beginning just before sunset and ending after the sun is down). In addition, on Sabbath and holidays there is a *musaf* service, which is incorporated into the morning prayers. (The word means "additional".) One special service is recited only once a year—*n'eila,* on Yom Kippur, in the waning hours of the day just before the daylong fast is concluded.

◄ **146** ► Are the prayers regarded as communal or as individual? The entire service is seen as a public service, in which everyone participates; the exception is the special prayer, *shmoneh esray,* also known as the *amidah,* which is recited silently while standing, and which is seen more as the individual's personal prayer to the Almighty. It is included in each service of the day.

◄ **147** ► Do Jews prostrate themselves in the synagogue? By and large, no, although there are moments in the service (when saying the *barchu* and the *aleinu*) when it is customary to bow. However, on Rosh Hashanah and Yom Kippur, in Orthodox and Conservative synagogues, the rabbi and the cantor do prostrate themselves briefly before the Holy Ark, an action reminiscent of the ancient Temple service. Congregants who are invited to help them rise from the floor consider it a signal honor.

◄ **148** ► What is the Yizkor memorial service? The word means remembrance and is a memorial for loved ones who have died; the prayer is included in the service on Yom Kippur, Passover, Shavuoth, and Shmini Atzeret (the penultimate day of the Sukkoth holiday). Although it is intended for each person as a private memorial to a loved one, in recent years the Yizkor has also evolved into a community-wide memorial for the six million Jews who perished at the hands of the Nazis. Many people, fearful of being in a room where the service is recited if they have living parents, leave the service until the Yizkor is concluded, although most rabbis frown on this custom.

◄ **149** ► Is it true that the synagogue service includes a special prayer for dew and rain in Israel? Yes. The link between Jewish communities in the diaspora and the Land of Israel has always been unbroken, and at the Passover service a special prayer for dew is recited (of great importance to Israel as it approaches the dry season in the spring and summer), while at Sukkoth a prayer for rain is recited, also of vital importance to Israel, as the onset of the rainy season will guarantee a bountiful crop.

◄ 150 ► What is the weekly portion that is read from the Torah called? The *sidra;* the Torah is so divided into weekly portions, with allowances for special holiday sections, that the beginning of the cycle of reading and the conclusion of the previous year's reading fall on the joyous holiday of *Simhat Torah* (usually in October), when there is much dancing and singing in the synagogue, with each male expected to carry a Scroll of the Law around the synagogue.

◄ 151 ► Isn't the Torah carried around the synagogue at Sabbath services too? Yes, immediately after its removal from the Ark and just prior to its being returned to the Ark, the Torah is carried around the synagogue, often in a small procession that includes the rabbi, the cantor, the synagogue's president, and the Bar Mitzvah boys, if there are any on a particular Sabbath. As the Torah passes by, it is customary for the congregants to touch it with their fingertips, which they then kiss as a sign of love and respect.

◄ 152 ► What is a *mi-sheberach?* A special prayer recited for an ailing congregant or for someone who is ill and whose name has been given to the rabbi.

◄ 153 ► What is the name of the special service on Saturday night, when the Sabbath ends? *Havdalah.* The word literally means division and is intended to signify the dividing line between the holy Sabbath and the mundane remainder of the week. The ceremonious, brief service includes a blessing over a tall, braided candle and the sniffing of spices. It is also recited at the end of a holiday.

◀**154**▶ What is a rabbi? The term literally means "my master" and has been in use for about two thousand years. Long ago, the term was used to indicate respect for someone who was more learned in Jewish law than most people, a person who could be approached for counsel and guidance. In ancient times, those who were designated rabbis earned their livings in a wide variety of occupations. Rabbi Yochanan was a cobbler; the great Rashi, the foremost biblical commentator, was a vintner. The concept of a rabbi who is a paid employee of his congregation evolved in the nineteenth century; most synagogues today have a rabbi who is the spiritual leader of the congregation, leading the services, delivering sermons, officiating at weddings and Bar and Bat Mitzvah ceremonies, and—more frequently nowadays—acting as a family counselor. The rabbi of course also is called on during times of grief, delivering a eulogy at a funeral service and conducting a burial service. All modern rabbis are ordained by recognized seminaries, where they pursue both Jewish and secular studies. The sermon delivered by the rabbi is known as a *drasha*.

◀**155**▶ What is a *hazzan?* A cantor, who conducts the service, interspersing the recitations with liturgical singing. Although the cantor need not necessarily be a learned man, he is expected to be a fully observant Jew. Some Reform temples, however, engage non-Jewish cantors who have excellent voices and who in many cases sing the service from a transliteration.

◀**156**▶ Is it necessary to be a member of a synagogue to worship at services? No, everyone is welcome. In many Conservative and Reform synagogues, especially when there is a Bar or Bat Mitzvah celebration, guests will include non-Jews who can easily follow the service from the English translation of the prayer book or the Bible.

◄157► When the Torah is read at Sabbath or holiday services, does every congregant follow the reading with his own Bible? Yes. Often, the congregant's Bible includes at least one commentary so that he must move fast if he is to read silently along with the Torah reader and find time to examine some of the special comments on a particular section.

◄158► Is it permissible for a congregation to applaud the rabbi's sermon or the cantor's singing or the Bar Mitzvah or Bat Mitzvah's chanting? No, at least not at religious services. However, if there is a meeting, lecture or recital, and if it is held in the sanctuary, applause is permissible.

◄159► Is the *kiddush* (sanctification of wine) that follows Sabbath and holiday services in the synagogue the same as the *kiddush* recited at home? No. Traditionally, on Sabbath mornings and holidays, following services, the congregants gather around a table to have a sampling of *hallah* (the special Sabbath bread) or to taste some wine (and often a stronger drink), to socialize briefly before going home for the noonday meal. The *kiddush* at home, recited on Friday evenings before dinner and also on holiday eves, is a recitation and blessing over sacramental wine, with each person at the table given a taste and thus made to feel a full participant in the ceremony.

◄160► What is the *shalosh seudot?* Literally, "the three meals." Unlike today, in ancient times most people had only two meals a day; for Sabbath, it was felt that an additional meal was called for, and the third meal was instituted. Nowadays, an hour or two before the onset of sunset on Sabbath afternoons (between the afternoon and evening services), Jews meet in the synagogue for an hour of light refreshment, singing, and a brief talk by the rabbi—all just prior to the evening service and the conclusion of the Sabbath. This is now referred to as *shalosh seudot.*

◄161► When people enter or leave the synagogue, is there any special greeting or word of farewell? During the week, no. On Sabbath, it is customary to greet one another with the words *Shabbat shalom* (a peaceful Sabbath) and on holidays, *Hag same-ah,* a happy holiday. In the more traditionalist synagogues, one can still hear the greetings exchanged as *gut Shabbes* or *gut yomtov,* the Yiddish version.

◄162► Are any Sabbath services considered more important than others? Generally, the Sabbaths that coincide with the blessing for the forthcoming new month or when holidays fall are regarded as especially meritorious of an effort on the congregant's part to attend.

◄163► Do most Jews attend synagogue services regularly? No. With the exception of the High Holy Days, when attendance reaches as high as 95 per cent of the community, weekly Sabbath services in Conservative and Reform temples are attended by relatively small numbers. Orthodox services attract a higher percentage of worshipers. The daily service is usually poorly attended, often mostly by those reciting the *kaddish* memorial service, once again with the exception of the Orthodox sector.

◄164► When is the synagogue usually filled with people? In addition to the High Holy Days, such special occasions as family weddings and Bar and Bat Mitzvahs, and some of the holidays, the synagogue often attracts large numbers of people for lectures by prominent people, for adult-education classes, Sunday-morning Talmud classes, PTA meetings, and the like.

Chapter 5

HOLIDAYS AND FESTIVALS

"The Sabbaths are for rest, and the festivals for joy . . . to eat and drink on a festival in the company of your family without providing for the poor and distressed is but the joy of your stomach. It is a disgrace."

— MAIMONIDES

◄**165**► Is there a distinction between Jewish holidays and festivals? Yes, the former are religious celebrations and the latter are more historical or ethnic in nature. Some of the major religious holidays include Rosh Hashanah and Yom Kippur, Sukkoth, Passover, and Shavuoth. The festivals would include Hanukkah, Purim, Yom Ha-Atzmaut and Tu b'Shvat. Separate and apart are the fast days such as Tisha b'Av, commemorating the destruction of the Holy Temples in Jerusalem, and special anniversary days such as the recently instituted Holocaust Memorial Day, marking the massacre of the six million Jews in the Nazi era.

◄**166**► Since Rosh Hashanah is the first day of the Jewish year, why does the date vary from year to year? Basically, the Jewish calendar is lunar-solar; with the general (Gregorian) year solar, counting 365 days to the year, the Jewish calendar has a complicated method of adjusting itself so that the holidays and festivals fall at approximately the same time each year. If not for these adjustments, we might find Passover in mid-August and Hanukkah in June.

◄**167**► Doesn't the Bible list the first month of the year as Nissan, which falls in springtime? Yes, but the rabbis computed that the creation of the world took place in Tishri, which is now the first month of the Jewish year.

Rosh Hashanah, literally "head of the year," falls on the first and second days of Tishri.

◄168► What other names are used to describe the Jewish New Year, Rosh Hashanah? It is also called the Day of Remembrance and the Day of the Sounding of the Shofar. It marks the first of the ten Days of Awe, culminating with Yom Kippur, and is also regarded as the day of the world's birth.

◄169► What is the significance of the shofar? The shofar, or ram's horn, was sounded in ancient times for a number of purposes: to proclaim the start of the jubilee year (when slaves went free) or the anointing of a king, and to warn of the approach of an enemy. It is sounded now during the month preceding Rosh Hashanah, on the New Year itself (except on Sabbath), and at the termination of Yom Kippur. Its high-pitched, somewhat eerie tone helps worshipers to concentrate their prayers and thoughts on their hopes for the coming year and to consider the events of the year just concluded.

◄170► What is a *Baal T'kiyah?* The man who is trained to sound the shofar in accordance with set rules is called a *Baal T'kiyah,* literally "master of the sounding."

◄171► What are the special sounds called that one hears each year when the shofar is sounded? The three distinct sounds, believed to have come down from ancient times, are the *t'kiyah* (long, drawn-out), the *shevarim* (broken, plaintive) and *teruah* (sharp, staccato).

◄172► Does the shofar sound have a mystical meaning? The sound, according to Jewish tradition, is meant to convey the mood of the Israelites standing at the foot of Mount Sinai when Moses received the Torah. It is also a call to the Jews to repent, the Talmud stating: "Awake, sleepers, from your sleep, ponder your deeds, remember your Creator, and return to Him in penitence."

◄173► Why do Jews greet one another on the eve of Rosh Hashanah "May you be inscribed for a good year" (*L'shana tova tikatevu*)? Jewish tradition says that on Rosh Hashanah, God inscribes the fate of all people and seals the inscription on Yom Kippur. Hence, the wish that the recipient of good wishes be well inscribed. The correct greeting on Yom Kippur, therefore, is *L'shana tova teihatamu* (may you be sealed for a good year).

◄174► At the Rosh Hashanah dinner table, people dip a piece of *hallah* or apple into honey. Why? On the theory that the symbolism will help usher in a sweet year. A special blessing accompanies the act of dunking.

◄175► The traditional Sabbath loaf, the *hallah*, is round, rather than ovular, for Rosh Hashanah. Why? The symbolism is meant to convey the fact that life is never-ending, it goes around and around, and so the hope is expressed that the new year will also bring in its wake an unbroken chain of continuity.

◄176► Why is it traditional for people, either before the ten-day period of the Days of Awe or during that period, to visit the graves of loved ones? By no means a religious law, this custom has nevertheless held fast, since it provides an opportunity for the visitors to pay their respects annually to the departed and at the same time to hope that the souls of the departed will intercede for them in the new year. The latter hope is generally understood rather than openly voiced.

71

◄177► Some Jewish communities traditionally eat carrots during the Rosh Hashanah holiday. Why? The reason is rather quaint: the Yiddish translation for carrots is *meren,* which also translates as "to increase." Hence, the hope is that the new year will increase the good deeds that the Almighty will compute before deciding the fate of the individual.

◄178► What is the *tashlich* ceremony? Still practiced by Orthodox Jews today, the ceremony consists of proceeding on the first day of Rosh Hashanah (except on Sabbath) to a river or other body of water and reciting biblical verses regarding penitence and forgiveness of sins. Men and boys will empty their pockets into the water, allowing the crumbs or lint that may be found there to symbolize their "casting off" of sins. The word *tashlich* means casting off, as when the prophet Micah said, "Thou wilt cast all their sins into the depths of the sea." In actuality, despite the somber mood of the day, the *tashlich* ceremony and the gathering at a nearby body of water has become a semisocial occasion on which people meet in midday, between the morning and afternoon services.

◄179► What is a *kittel?* A simple white outer garment symbolizing purity and worn by the rabbi and cantor (and most Orthodox Jews) on the High Holy Days at services. (It is also donned by Orthodox Jews at the Seder table and by Orthodox grooms during the wedding service.)

◄180► What is the Sabbath that falls between Rosh Hashanah and Yom Kippur called? Shabbat Shuvah, or the Sabbath of Repentance. In many communities, especially in Eastern Europe a century ago, the great rabbis of the time seldom delivered weekly sermons as we know them today. They did, however, speak to the community on Shabbat Shuvah and also on Shabbat Hagadol, the Great Sabbath, that occurs in the Passover week. These were very special discourses, often attended by overflowing crowds.

◄181► Is there a special reason for dressing up on Rosh Hashanah? There is a talmudic reference to the fact that worshipers should approach the holiday in a mood of confidence and hope, which in turn is seen as a reason for the wearing of festive rather than somber garments. White is still preferred by many, since it combines a sense of purity with cheerfulness.

◄182► What is the late-night *selihot* service, which precedes the High Holy Days? The special service of penitential prayers that takes place at midnight on the Saturday preceding Rosh Hashanah. The concept of a midnight service originated in the Psalmist's verse "At midnight, I rise to praise Thee." Many congregations, an hour or two prior to the actual service, hold an informal meeting during which the rabbi reviews the rules and traditions of the approaching holiday season.

◄183► Can a person who has committed wrongful acts during the preceding year atone for them merely by attending High Holy Day services and praying with great fervor? Jewish tradition states unequivocally that a sinner must ask and receive the forgiveness of anyone he has sinned against during the past year before he can hope to obtain divine pardon. Further, if that person truly wishes to repent, he must chart a new course based on three concepts: *t'shuva* (penitence), *t'filah* (prayer), and *tzedakah* (the giving of charity). Mere words will not bring God's forgiveness.

◄**184**► Aren't the prayers in the *mahzor* (the Rosh Hashanah and Yom Kippur prayer book), collective, communal prayers, rather than individual, personal prayers? Yes, on the theory that although each and every person is judged separately for his or her actions, nevertheless an entire group is also judged—family, community, a nation— and each person is partly responsible for the actions of the entire larger group as well as for his own deeds.

◄**185**► Why does Rosh Hashanah never fall on a Sunday, Wednesday, or Friday? Since Yom Kippur, a day of fasting, occurs on the tenth day of Tishri, the rabbis felt it would be a great inconvenience for the community to have Sabbath the day before or the day after, making preparations extremely difficult; they calculated the holiday in such a way that this was avoided. Hence, the first day of the New Year is a Monday, Tuesday, Thursday, or Saturday.

◄**186**► What is a *shulklapper?* A wooden mallet in the form of a shofar, used in the Middle Ages mostly to knock on the doors of Jewish families an hour before the *selihot* (midnight penitential) service, reminding them to get dressed and come to synagogue. The Yiddish word literally means "synagogue knocker."

◄**187**► Is a shofar always taken from a ram? No, the horn of any clean (kosher) animal is acceptable except that of an ox or a cow. The reason for the exception is that the ox or cow reminds Jews of Israel's greatest collective transgression, the building of the Golden Calf in Sinai, which led Moses to destroy the first set of the tablets of the Law. The long, curled elk's horn is a popular shofar among Jews from the Islamic countries.

◄ 188 ► Is there a special ruling that Jewish women must hear the sounding of the shofar? Yes. In general, those religious regulations governed by the element of time do not apply to women, on the theory that they have more pressing duties in the home, such as caring for the children. The hearing of the shofar blasts, however, is an exception. Thus, if a woman is ill and confined to her home, it is customary for someone to come to her residence and sound the shofar so that she will not miss out on the commandment.

◄ 189 ► Does the cantorial part of the Rosh Hashanah service differ from that of the rest of the year? Yes, a special holiday melody is used in most Ashkenazic congregations for the reading of the Torah and for the recitation of certain parts of the service.

◄ 190 ► What is the reason for reading the story of Abraham's near sacrifice of Isaac on Rosh Hashanah? The principal moral of the biblical narrative is that Abraham withstood the supreme test of faith when ordered to sacrifice his beloved son; his reward, it is interpreted, is the eternal survival of the Jewish people.

◄ 191 ► What is the *kapparot* ceremony, which takes place on the morning of the eve of Yom Kippur? An ancient ceremony dating to Temple days, the rite consists of a person holding a live chicken, waving it three times, and reciting, "This is my exchange, this is my substitute, this is my atonement—this fowl will go to its death, and I will enter a good and long life and peace." It is reminiscent of the days when sacrifices were used as a form of worship, when the sacrificial animal paid the penalty, so to speak, for the individual's sins, and the person himself was absolved.

Many rabbis oppose the use of a chicken; nowadays the custom is usually one in which the celebrant waves some money in lieu of a chicken, and turns the funds over to charity.

◄ 192 ► Is it true that some Jewish communities practice a custom of flogging prior to Yom Kippur? Rarely observed today, this custom of lashes as a symbol of bringing on a person's confession of past sins dates back several hundred years. Token, purely symbolic blows were administered to the individual (in such places as Kurdistan, for example), who would then recite the confessional prayer *ashamnu* while the flogger consoled him with the thought, "He is merciful and forgives iniquity."

◄ 193 ► Is there a special quality to the pre-fast meal consumed on the eve of Yom Kippur? Usually eaten an hour or two before the time to go to synagogue services for the moving Kol Nidre service, the pre-fast meal is solemn and yet festive. Partakers are expected not to gorge themselves despite the period of abstinence that is to follow. The meal, of course, must be completely done with before sunset, since, like the Sabbath and all holidays, Yom Kippur is observed from sunset to sunset of the following day.

◄ 194 ► Does Judaism, particularly on so solemn a day such as Yom Kippur, regard life as a ladder? What is the significance? People are regarded in Jewish thinking as being able to attain the noblest of heights and to sink to the lowest of depths. In other words, each person can climb up or slip down the ladder of life, his passage determined by the ethical values and achievements of his life. Although Yom Kippur is seen as *Yom ha-Din,* the Day of Judgment, when each person must pray for and strive for a higher plateau of ethical behavior and by righteous living can achieve atonement, it is also in a sense an annual second chance for all to retrace their steps and start afresh a new life of goodness.

◄195► Why is Yom Kippur termed *Shabbat Shabba-ton,* the Sabbath of Sabbaths? In addition to being a day set aside for self-contemplation, fasting, and a search for atonement, it is also a day of rest, with each worshiper finding that the service leads him gradually from a feeling of guilt (for previous transgressions) to a sense of confidence and joy that the new year will be blessed and kind to him.

◄196► Did Moses come down from Mount Sinai on Yom Kippur? Yes. There is a tradition that he descended from the mountain, bearing the second set of the Ten Commandments tablets, informing the people that God had pardoned them for their sinful behavior in erecting the Golden Calf.

◄197► In Temple days, did the high priest have a special function on Yom Kippur? Only on Yom Kippur did he enter the inner sanctuary, known as the Holy of Holies, to officiate at a service in which he enunciated the tetragrammaton—the four-letter name of God that is never vocalized by traditional Jews to this day.

◄198► Besides food and drink, what else is forbidden on Yom Kippur? Everything that is forbidden on the Sabbath, primarily labor, is also prohibited on Yom Kippur. Since one is expected to "afflict" one's "soul" on this day, other bans include sexual relations, bathing for pleasure (as opposed to washing for requisite cleanliness), and among the Orthodox, the wearing of leather shoes, leather being symbolic of warfare.

◄**199►** What if someone is ill; must he observe the fast? The concept of *pikuach nefesh,* guarding of life, takes precedence over all in Jewish teaching, so that a sick person who is required to eat or drink is excused from the fast.

◄**200►** At what age does the fast become obligatory for children? Under the age of nine, children are not allowed to fast, but after that it is expected that they will be introduced to the fast at gradual stages so that girls at the age of twelve and boys at thirteen will be able to observe the fast as fully as any adult.

◄**201►** Does the donning of white on Yom Kippur, including a white skullcap for the men, have any special significance in addition to the concept of purity? Some commentators interpret the use of white as a reminder to all worshipers that all people are mortal and sooner or later will be laid to rest in traditional white shrouds. Thus, it behooves the congregants to make strenuous efforts to atone for their sins and chart a new course for their behavior.

◄**202►** What is the reason for the reading of the Book of Jonah in the synagogue on Yom Kippur? The primary theme of Jonah is that God accepts man's repentance, hence its inclusion in the service. Judaism never gives up hope on people's repenting, with the second century Rabbi Simeon bar Yochai noting that even a thoroughly evil person, who had lived an entire lifetime in sinfulness, is nonetheless forgiven as soon as he becomes fully penitent.

◄**203►** Is there any difference in the methods of achieving repentance? The talmudic sages said that there are those who repent out of suffering, those who repent out of fear, and those who do so for the love of God—this last type being considered a *mitzvah,* a good deed.

◄**204**► What happens if, on Yom Kippur eve, a person approaches someone against whom he has committed a sinful act, asks forgiveness, and is refused? The law stipulates that in such a case, the offender must apologize to the injured party in front of three witnesses three times, and if he is still refused forgiveness, he is absolved of his act.

◄**205**► Supposing the injured party is dead? Then the pardon seeker must go to the graveside and make his confession in front of ten witnesses before he can expect divine pardon.

◄**206**► Is this asking of forgiveness of one's fellow man still actually practiced? Yes. Just prior to the awesome, soul-stirring Kol Nidre service, on Yom Kippur eve, congregants may be seen in many synagogues turning to their neighbors and saying, in effect, If I have in any way offended you this past year, deliberately or accidentally, please forgive me. It is rare that under such circumstances the supplicant will be refused his request.

◄**207**► Is Yom Kippur principally a personal day of atonement, or is it regarded as the Jewish people's national soul-cleansing day? Both. Each individual must find atonement and forgiveness for himself, and at the same time it is a day on which the entire Jewish community, world-wide, stands before God and seeks forgiveness and divine guidance.

◄**208**► What is the story of the red wool in the Temple on Yom Kippur? There is a legend that during the days of the Second Temple (destroyed in the year 70 C.E.) the vast throngs of worshipers surrounding the holy edifice arranged for some red wool to be affixed to the gate of the

Temple. If, at the conclusion of the Yom Kippur service, it turned white, this was seen as a sign that the Almighty had pardoned the Jewish people for their iniquities.

◄ 209 ► Has Yom Kippur always been observed as it is today? Although, during the year that King Solomon built the Temple, observance of the day was waived (and the people celebrated the dedication of the Temple with eating, drinking, and merrymaking), a report by Philo of the observance of the day in the Second Temple period says: "The holy day is entirely devoted to prayers and supplications, and men from morning to evening employ their leisure in nothing else but offering petitions of humble entreaty for remission of their sins, voluntary and involuntary, and entertain bright hopes looking not to their own merits but to the gracious nature of Him Who sets pardon before chastisement." It would seem that the Yom Kippur observance known today dates back more than two thousand years.

◄ 210 ► What does Kol Nidre mean? This deeply moving prayer, which ushers in the Yom Kippur period at sunset on the eve of the day, is a declaration annulling all vows and oaths, taken on by a person, in which no one else is involved. Since the Bible declares that "you must be careful to keep any promise you have made," the purpose of the prayer is to absolve each person who has made such pledges and is unable to keep them. Pledges involving other people, including legal contracts, of course, are excluded from the intent of the prayer.

◄ 211 ► How old is the Kol Nidre's melody? The haunting tune that accompanies this ancient prayer, recited in Aramaic, is believed to be one thousand years old.

◀ **212** ▶ Did the Kol Nidre prayer create special problems for Jews, since it nullified existing vows? During the Middle Ages there were those who claimed that oaths by Jews had no value whatsoever, since they could be canceled annually at the Yom Kippur service. This, of course, was a cruel misinterpretation of the prayer's meaning.

◀ **213** ▶ Why is the Day of Atonement sometimes referred to in the plural, as Yom ha-Kippurim? To indicate that the living and those who have died both receive atonement.

◀ **214** ▶ The High Holy Days prayer book includes liturgical poems recalling ancient martyrs. Have there been any recent additions to reflect the suffering of the Jewish people in the Nazi period? The Conservative movement has incorporated into the prayers moving descriptions of a group of ninety-six Orthodox Jewish girl students who committed suicide en masse rather than be taken to German brothels, and a liturgy for more than 150,000 Jewish children murdered in the Nazis' Theresienstadt concentration camp.

◀ **215** ▶ What is the precise meaning of the closing service of Yom Kippur, the Ne'ilah, recited only on this one day? Literally, "locking," in the sense that the heavenly gates are sealed and locked and each person's fate is determined for the next year. At the very end of Ne'ilah, the congregation stands and repeats the final verse, "The Lord, He is God," in unison seven times—the numeral seven alluding to the seven firmaments which must be penetrated for the prayers to reach the Almighty.

◀ **216** ▶ What happens immediately after the long Yom Kippur service? People greet each other with the expressed wish "Next year in Jerusalem," which is appended to the prayers—and hurry off home to waiting meals.

◄217► What does the Sukkoth holiday celebrate? It is one of the three biblically ordained pilgrim festivals, the other two being Passover and Shavuoth. It is both commemorative of the forty years of wandering by the Israelites who fled Egypt and the time of the year's final harvest (the first harvest being marked by Shavuoth, which usually falls in May or June, while Sukkoth comes in early fall).

◄218► What is a *sukkah*? A flimsy hut erected by Jews to recall the poor living accommodations that the desert-wandering Israelites had for forty years. One sage noted that the moral taught by the holiday is that even if a man owns a pleasant home and is well-to-do, it is good to be reminded of others who are forced by circumstances to live in poverty—it will strengthen his character and possibly preclude any arrogant tendencies.

◄219► What is a *lulav* and an *etrog*? The *lulav* itself is a branch of a palm tree; for the observance of the holiday it is bound together with a *hadas* (myrtle branch) and an *aravah* (willow branch). The *etrog* is a citron with a pleasant, pungent aroma. The four together are known as *arba minim*—four species, representing the Jewish people's departure from a wilderness to a fruitful land.

◄220► What goes on in the *sukkah*? Traditionally, the family eats some or most of its meals there during the holiday period (including the last day of Simhat Torah, it is observed for nine days in the diaspora but only eight in Israel). A special blessing is recited for the privilege of sitting in a *sukkah*, which is generally festooned with fruits and vegetables typical of Israel's agriculture.

◄ **221** ► Is there a relationship between Thanksgiving Day and Sukkoth? Many people feel that the early Pilgrims, who were known for their avid reading of the Bible, established Thanksgiving Day in emulation of the ancient biblical festival, since it, too, is a time of harvest.

◄ **222** ► Are there religious restrictions on Sukkoth? The first two and last two days are full-fledged holidays, when no work is permitted. The five days in between are known as *hol ha-moed,* when work is permissible, but a holiday, festive mood is retained.

◄ **223** ► Do most Jewish families have their own individual *sukkoth?* Among the Orthodox Jews, wherever it is physically possible, yes. (Some Orthodox Jews residing in an apartment house, for example, will join together and establish a communal *sukkah* in the courtyard.) Among Conservative and Reform Jews, most people rely on the large *sukkah* erected adjacent to or on the premises of their respective synagogues.

◄ **224** ► Is there any special reason why the *lulav* and the *etrog* were chosen to symbolize Sukkoth? There are many explanations, among which are that the *etrog,* or citron, is heart-shaped, while the *lulav* is seen as a human spinal cord, while the myrtle and willow leaves resemble eyes and lips, respectively. Thus, the four species represent the ability of a person's perfect harmony to obey God's will. It is traditional, therefore, to select only the finest possible specimens of these products. The end of an *etrog* is known as a *pitom,* and if it should fall off the *etrog,* it is not considered acceptable.

◄ **225** ► What does a worshiper do with the *lulav* and the *etrog?* The *lulav* is clasped in the right hand, the *etrog* in the left (with the stem up), together, and a blessing is recited. The *etrog* is then shifted, its stem down, and the worshiper waves both the *lulav* and the *etrog* in all four directions, and also upward and downward—indicating God's presence everywhere.

◄226► What is the *hoshanot* procession? A march around the synagogue by everyone holding an *etrog* and a *lulav* (with the procession on the seventh day going around seven times), reminiscent of the processions around the sacrificial altar at the Holy Temple in Jerusalem in ancient times. The procession is generally led by the cantor, who intones a special melody and prayer for the holiday. On the seventh day of Sukkoth, known as Hoshanah Rabbah, after the processions, the willow branches are beaten on the synagogue benches until they drop off. This is taken as symbolic of life's renewal: old leaves drop off in the late autumn, to be replaced by new growths in the springtime, just as older generations pass on to be succeeded by new generations. There is also a tradition that on Hoshanah Rabbah each person's fate for the year is finally, irrevocably sealed.

◄227► Are the holidays Shmini Atzeret and Simhat Torah part of Sukkoth? Technically, no, but since both days follow immediately upon the heels of Sukkoth, they tend to be regarded together. (Both days are joined into one in Israel.)

◄228► What is behind the Shmini Atzeret holiday? What do the words mean? Translated literally as the Eighth Day of Solemn Assembly, the holiday, like Sukkoth, is referred to as "the time of our rejoicing." It is as though guests were having a good time at a celebration and were reluctant to leave, so they extended their stay yet another day.

◄ **229** ► What distinguishes this holiday? Firstly, the use of the Sukkah and the four species is ended on the preceding day. The prayer for rain, *t'filat geshem,* is offered on this day. It is also a day on which people participate in a memorial service (Yizkor) for loved ones. In the diaspora, it is more of a bridge between Sukkoth and the gay, carefree festival of Simhat Torah, but in Israel both days are celebrated as one.

◄ **230** ► What does Simhat Torah mean? Rejoicing of the Torah. It is probably, for most traditional Jews and for most youngsters, the most thoroughly jubilant day, when people are expected to rejoice with abandon. In the synagogue, the center of the celebration, it is not unusual to have congregants playing pranks on the rabbi and the cantor, or taking over the conduct of the special service with such touches as singing traditional songs to the tunes of Broadway shows or operatic arias. This is all done to create an atmosphere of abandon and total joy, in the spirit of the festival.

◄ **231** ► What does Simhat Torah commemorate? The festival is of fairly recent origin, not being listed in the Bible or the Talmud, and evolved in its present form around the sixteenth century. Basically, it notes the annual completion of the weekly portions of the Torah and the immediate launching of a new cycle of weekly readings for the new year. Thus, it enforces the Jews' faith in the unbroken chain of the Torah's supremacy and of its lifetime source of light and guidance.

◄ **232** ► How is it celebrated? At the synagogue services on Simhat Torah, two people are given the special honor of being designated *hatan Torah* and *hatan Bereshit,* or the "groom of the Torah" and the "groom of Genesis"

85

1001 Questions and Answers About Judaism

(the first book of the Bible). The former is called to the Torah for the concluding section of the Torah reading, while the latter is summoned for the opening section, when the new reading cycle is begun. Most of the fun, however, takes place in between the two.

◄233► How? After the reading of the Torah is concluded, all the scrolls that a particular congregation owns are removed from the Holy Ark, and adults are invited to participate in *hakafot,* or processions around the synagogue. There are seven processions, and an effort is made to have every adult male carry a Torah. The leader of the procession, whoever happens to be first in line, chants a special melody and prayer, which every member of the procession picks up, as do all members of the congregation. It is traditional for the synagogue to be packed with adults and children at this time, and decorum is at a minimum. Thus, the entire congregation joins in the singing, and as each Torah passes by, congregants reach out and touch it with their fingertips, which are then lightly kissed. Small children wave flags which they were handed as they entered the synagogue. It is only after the end of seven *hakafot* around the synagogue, after everyone has been singing and making merry, that the *hatan Bereshit* is called up for the reading of the first part of Genesis. As one might expect, there is a good deal of noise and disorder, but since it all takes place in the synagogue, nobody gets out of hand. Young people, after the service, often gather in the rear of the synagogue for some impromptu folk dancing, and the very small children are given apples to take with them as they head for home. A good time is had by all.

◄234► Is the festival celebrated differently in Israel? Since the establishment of Israel, the festival has become an excuse for exuberant dancing in the streets with the Scrolls of the Law. In some areas, congregants take the Scrolls of the Law out of the synagogue and meet with other fellow celebrants, and the dancing and singing continue long into the night in the streets.

◄ **235** ► Why is the festival of Hanukkah (sometimes spelled Chanukah, but the first sound always pronounced with a guttural) so visible? Simply because of its proximity to the Christmas celebration. Had any other Jewish holiday or festival fallen in late December, it, too, in all likelihood would have received the special attention that Hanukkah does. That is: cognizant of the widespread holiday atmosphere that prevails around Christmastime, and not wishing their children to be drawn into observing a holiday that is essentially Christian, Jews almost instinctively laid special emphasis on Hanukkah, giving their offspring a "Jewish alternative" in a pluralistic society.

◄ **236** ► What exactly is Hanukkah? Dating back to the second century before the common era, the festival marks the victory of the ancient Jews, led by Judah the Maccabee and his heroic brothers, against a tyrannical Syrian-Greek regime that had not only subjugated the Jews but was also intent on destroying their religious beliefs.

◄ **237** ► What does the word *hanukkah* mean? Rededication, referring to the cleansing and rededication of the Holy Temple in Jerusalem, which had been violated and defiled by the pagan soldiers of the Syrian-Greek forces.

◄ **238** ► When was the first Hanukkah celebration held? In the year 165 B.C.E., making the current (1978) observance of the festival 2,143 years old.

◄239► Are the traditional Hanukkah menorah (candelabrum) and the menorah that adorns many synagogues (and is also the official emblem of Israel) one and the same? No. The Hanukkah menorah, sometimes called a Hanukkiyah for short, has a total of nine branches, one for each of the eight days of the festival and the ninth, known as the *shamash,* for the kindling of all the others. The traditional menorah has seven branches.

◄240► How old is the Hanukkah menorah? It probably originated in the first century of the common era and was deliberately altered so that it would be a reminder of the menorah, described in the Bible, that was featured in the Holy Temple and yet, since the Temple had been destroyed, would not be an exact duplicate, the feeling being that one day the original design of the menorah would be used for the restored Temple.

◄241► Which is more appropriate, oil or candles in the Hanukkah menorah? Early usage was dominated by oil, but most people kindle small, colorful candles nowadays as a convenience. Oil-soaked material is used in Israel today for the kindling of large, public Hanukkah menorahs.

◄242► Why do some Jewish families display Hanukkah menorahs, usually electric, in the windows of their homes? This is probably because of the strong sense of Jewish identity that has developed in recent years, especially since the Holocaust in Europe and the establishment of the State of Israel. The custom has sprung up in the United States primarily and is hardly known anywhere else.

◄243► What is the religious or spiritual significance of the emphasis on lights during Hanukkah? The origin of the lights is in the story that when the Maccabees entered the Holy Temple, after defeating the enemy, they found only enough oil (specially prepared for temple use) to last one day, but miraculously it continued to burn for eight days; hence the festival continues eight days. The emphasis on lights is intended to reinforce the Jewish concept that gradually spiritual enlightenment will become the main theme in the daily life of mankind.

◄ **244** ► May work be performed during Hanukkah? Yes, except, traditionally, during the half hour or so it takes for the average Hanukkah menorah's candles to burn themselves out. The institution of games during this festival is said to have begun so that family members would enjoy themselves together while waiting for the candles to flicker out.

◄ **245** ► Why isn't the Hanukkah narrative included in the Bible? It is a postbiblical celebration, and although there is a brief summation of the events in certain prayers inserted into the prayer book, the story is told in the Book of Maccabees, part of the Apocrypha.

◄ **246** ► Spinning the *dreidel,* or top, seems to be a popular Hanukkah game. How come? Actually, the modern, Hanukkah version is an adaptation of an old German game. The four Hebrew letters *nun* (representing the word *nes,* a miracle), *gimmel* (great), *hay* (occurred), *shin* (there) now cover the *dreidel's* four sides. They read: *nes gadol hayah sham* (A great miracle occurred there), referring of course to the cruse of oil that burned eight days instead of one. When children (or adults) play the game today, each of the four sides usually is interpreted as follows: *nun* (nothing, "nichts"), *gimmel* (take all, "ganz"), *hay* (take half, "halb"), *shin* (put in, "shtell"). The *drei-*

del game is usually played with small coins, nuts, or other objects.

◄247► Is there a set formula for lighting the Hanukkah candles? On the first night, the *shamash* is kindled (with the appropriate blessing), and, facing the menorah, the candle on the far left is lit from the flame of the *shamash*. On each subsequent night, an additional candle is lit, the progression going from right to left, facing the menorah, so that on the eighth and last night, all candles of the menorah are lit.

◄248► Can anyone kindle the lights? Yes, but it is generally done by members of the family together, often with each participant getting a chance to light at least one candle. The ceremony is followed by the group's singing of traditional hymns, notably *Maoz Tzur,* the Rock of Ages.

◄249► What happens on Friday night? Isn't there a conflict between the Sabbath and the Hanukkah candles? The Hanukkah candles are lit immediately prior to the Sabbath-eve candles, since the creation of fire is forbidden on the Sabbath. This is the one night of the Hanukkah week when most families find that the father has not yet arrived home and the mother does the kindling. In Orthodox homes, of course, this does not apply, since the head of the household will be home an hour or two before sunset.

◄250► Why the Hanukkah gifts or Hanukkah *gelt* (money) for the children? As a reminder of the special coins that the Maccabees struck after their victory over the Syrian-Greek Army. Also, in the United States especially, the emphasis on gift-giving at Christmastime has influenced Jewish families to extend the original idea of Hanukkah coins for small children to present their children with somewhat more expansive gifts. Some communities now give the children a small, token gift every night of the festival's eight-day-long celebration.

◄ 251 ► Why is the eating of *latkes,* or pancakes, so popular during Hanukkah? The oil used to fry potato pancakes is a reminder of that miracle cruse of oil that lasted eight days. Among Sephardi Jews, the custom is to eat *sufganiyot,* or jelly donuts, which also require frying in oil.

◄ 252 ► Who was Mattathias? The aged father of the Hasmonean family, whose names were later changed to Maccabees—the word in Hebrew means "hammer," and they were so designated because they continued to hammer away at the enemy until victory was theirs.

◄ 253 ► What is the tradition about the soldiers and the *dreidel?* During the period of Syrian-Greek rule over the Jews, the study of Torah was forbidden. Rabbis and teachers were able to get around this ban by taking their students out into the woods, ostensibly for games and picnics, but actually so as to study in secret. If a group of soldiers would chance to come upon them, the students would grab *dreidels* and pretend they had been playing all the time.

◄ 254 ► Who were the Maccabee brothers? Judah, Jonathan, Johanan, Eleazar, and Simon.

◄ 255 ► What is the story of the elephants used in an attempt to crush the rebellious Jews? Antiochus, King of Syria, who was believed to suffer from occasional fits of madness, decided to crush the Maccabees' revolt against his regime by bringing in elephants, never before seen in that part of the world, confident that the Jews would melt away in fear when they saw the huge animals. Instead, the Maccabees called in their best archers, who used their skill with bows and arrows to bring the big, lumbering beasts down, often on top of the Syrian troops. One of the Maccabee brothers, Eleazar, killed a lead elephant by plunging a spear deep into its underside but was crushed to death by the beast.

◄256► What is the Hanukkah torch relay, observed in Israel today? The tiny village of Modin, birthplace of the Maccabees, still exists today in modern Israel. As a sign of the unbroken chain of Jewish history, a torch is kindled in Modin on the eve of the first night of Hanukkah, and it is carried aloft for about a mile by a young Israeli, who then hands it on to another runner, until it is finally brought to Jerusalem, capital of Israel, where a giant menorah is lit from the flames of the torch, symbolizing the ancient, continuing struggle of the forces of light over the forces of darkness.

◄257► In contemporary times, what have been the most dramatic and poignant celebrations of this ancient festival? The secret lighting of the makeshift menorahs and candles inside Nazi concentration camps and walled-in ghettos, recorded by survivors of that infamous era; the kindling of the small candles unobtrusively and virtually in silence behind closed doors in the homes of Soviet Jewish families; and the kindling of the giant menorah atop Masada, the historic site south of the Dead Sea where some two thousand years ago a valiant struggle against Roman domination of Judea came to an end when the outnumbered, besieged Jews committed mass suicide rather than fall into the enemies' hands.

◄ **258** ► What is Tu b'Shvat? Also known as *hamisha asar b'shvat,* literally, the fifteenth day of the month of Shvat, which falls in January or February, it is a festival dedicated to tree planting. The early buds of spring begin to appear in Israel at this time of year, and the day has been set aside specifically for tree planting but in more general terms as a tribute to the grandeur of nature.

◄ **259** ► How is it observed? In Israel, children go out into the forest areas—or areas that they hope will become afforested—and plant saplings generally under the supervision of the Jewish National Fund, the Jewish people's organization devoted to reclaiming the long-neglected soil of the Holy Land. In the diaspora, where in most instances winter still rules, children in Jewish schools participate in the festival by being given fruits typical of Israel, e.g. figs, dates, raisins, and *bokser,* which comes from the carob tree.

◄ **260** ► Do trees play a special role in Jewish tradition? The Torah is referred to as an *etz hayyim,* a tree of life. King David wrote that a good person is like a "tree planted by the streams of water." Even in times of war, the Bible cautioned, fruit trees were not permitted to be cut down.

◄ **261** ► What is the tradition of the cedar and the cypress for Israeli boys and girls? An ancient custom, still observed in modern Israel, calls for a cedar to be planted when a boy is born and a cypress for a new infant girl. When the youngsters, who are expected to care for the trees planted in their honor, are grown, branches are cut down from their respective trees and are used to decorate the bridal canopy under which they stand during the wedding ceremony.

◄262► Why is the festival also referred to as *Rosh Hashanah L'Ilanot* (the New Year for Trees)? Because of the tradition that just as God judges people on Rosh Hashanah, deciding who will live and who will die, so does He determine the future fate of the trees: which will thrive and which will be blighted and die.

◄263► What does Purim mean? The word itself means "lots" and refers to the casting of lots in the ancient Persian Empire for the day to be chosen for the massacre of the Jews, under the leadership of Persia's Prime Minister, Haman—an event that never took place, thanks to the intervention of the Jewish queen, Esther.

◄264► Where is the story recounted? In the Book of Esther, found in the third section of the Bible.

◄265► When are the events described in the story of Purim believed to have taken place? In the fifth century B.C.E., in the reign of Ahasuerus, also known as Xerxes. The casting of lots decided that the Jews in the empire were to be attacked and killed en masse on the thirteenth day of Adar, but because of the king's last-minute decision against Haman's plans, the Jews were allowed to obtain arms and defend themselves—resulting in a rout and total defeat of Haman's forces.

◄266► When is Purim observed today? On the fourteenth day of Adar, with the traditional public reading of the Scroll of Esther taking place in the synagogue on the preceding evening.

◄267► What is the Fast of Esther? A fast day of fairly recent origin that takes place on the day before Purim, as a reminder that Queen Esther fasted and prayed before approaching her husband the king to intercede for her fellow Jews. (It is not observed on the Sabbath if it falls on a Saturday, but is moved back to the preceding Thursday.)

◀ **268** ▶ Why did Haman seek to destroy the Jews in the Persian kingdom? Primarily because of a hatred that he developed toward Mordecai, a Jew and the queen's cousin (the latter fact not being known to Haman). Haman described the Jews to his king as a community that was dangerous to Persia, since the Jews were "scattered and dispersed throughout the empire, refusing to obey the king's laws." Purim itself represents the many instances in Jewish history when tyrants sought to destroy the Jewish people but failed.

◀ **269** ▶ Why are there Purim masquerades and balls? The festival is a joyous occasion, when Jews are encouraged to make merry (some people even go so far as to say that one should drink on Purim to a point where it is difficult to distinguish between Mordecai and Haman). The masquerades are believed to be a way of disguising oneself from the evil that lurks all around us.

◀ **270** ▶ Why does the Purim eve reading of Megillah, the Scroll of Esther, sound like bedlam? It is expected that each person in synagogue listening to the reading, particularly the children, will stamp their feet and wave their noisemakers, known as *groggers,* each time that Haman's name is mentioned in the reading.

◀ **271** ▶ Just what is a *grogger?* A kind of rattle, dating to Central Europe of the thirteenth century, set aside for the sole purpose of creating a din at the mention of

Haman. Among some Sephardic communities, it was more customary to knock two stones together.

◄ 272 ► What is the *mishloah manot* custom, associated with Purim? The distribution of small, token gifts of food and drink to friends and neighbors and to the poor, often carried to the recipients by children.

◄ 273 ► What is the Purim *seudah*? A festive meal that is held at the end of Purim, in fulfillment of the command that Purim is a time to "eat, drink, and be merry." A special prayer is added to the daily service on Purim, summarizing the miracle of the ancient event.

◄ 274 ► What is the Purim parade held in Israel, called the *adloyada*? A gala carnival celebration calling for the children to dress up in every conceivable costume, parading through the streets in overt celebration of the deliverance of the Jews, and in the firm belief that the life of the Jewish people is everlasting.

◄ 275 ► What is the reason for eating *Hamantaschen* during Purim? Usually filled with poppy seed, these triangular pastries are said to represent the three-cornered hat worn by Haman, the villain of the Purim story. Others interpret it differently: in memory of the three people who dined together, Esther, Haman, and Ahasuerus, during a crucial meal that helped decide the fate of the Jews.

◄ 276 ► Is it true that Queen Esther's burial place is still known today? There is a mausoleum in Iran (formerly known as Persia) which is said to be her final resting place.

◄ 277 ► If Purim falls during the month of Adar, and if during a leap year there are two Adars, I and II, when is Purim celebrated? In Adar II, so that the time span between Purim and Passover, one month, does not vary.

◄ 278 ► When the Scroll of Esther is read aloud during the Purim eve service, the names of Haman's ten sons are jumbled together in one, long breath. Why? Haman's sons were hanged for their collusion in the plot to massacre the Jews; the reader runs all the names together in one long breath to show that they were all executed together.

◄ 279 ► Why is it obligatory for a woman to hear the reading of the Book of Esther? Principally because the heroine of the narrative is herself a woman.

◄ 280 ► Why is Passover so revered among Jews? Because it stresses the supreme importance of freedom. Passover (in Hebrew, *Pesah*) is many things to different people, but its essential message is freedom versus slavery.

◄ 281 ► How old is this holiday? Close to 3,300 years, certainly the oldest-known continuously observed holiday in the Western world.

◄ 282 ► How did it happen that the Israelites were slaves in Egypt? The Bible recounts that there was famine throughout the region, the Israelites came south to Egypt, where they were warmly received (especially since one of their own, Joseph, the son of Jacob, had had the foresight to establish granaries for the "seven lean years" that he foresaw). Years later, however, the Jews began to be regarded as "different," and since slavery was a commonplace occurrence in those days, the entire community was enslaved—a condition that lasted for more than two hundred years.

◄ 283 ► Why the word "Passover"? This term refers to the struggle that ensued between Moses and the Pharaoh, the former having to launch a series of plagues against the Egyptian ruler in order to convince him to let the Jews leave. The tenth, and most telling, of the plagues was the slaying of the first-born sons of the Egyptians. When the Angel of Death struck, we are told, he "passed over" (skipped) the homes of the Israelites; hence the name.

◄284► How long is the holiday observed? In the diaspora, eight days; in Israel, seven. The first and last two days (in the diaspora) are full holidays, when work is not permitted; the rules for the intermediate days allow work, but all other holiday regulations, with regard to food, for example, apply.

◄285► Why is *matza,* the unleavened bread, eaten during Passover? When the Israelites were finally allowed to leave, they did so in a great hurry, not even having time for their bread to rise—hence, in commemoration of those ancient days, unleavened bread is eaten today, too, during the Passover holiday. (Many people eat matza during the rest of the year also, but this is not what is called "kosher for Passover" matza, which must be prepared in strict conformity with a set of rules and regulations differentiating between "Pesah" foods and "hametz," i.e., normal, everyday food, which includes leavening in the breadstuffs.)

◄286► By what other names is Passover known in Jewish teaching? It is also called *zman heruteinu,* the season of our freedom; *hag he'aviv,* the holiday of spring, when it falls; and as one of the *shalosh regalim,* one of the three pilgrim festivals, when Jews were expected to make their way to Jerusalem to worship at the Temple.

◄287► Was Moses raised as an Egyptian? Yes. At the time, a decree had been issued ordering every Jewish family in Egypt to kill every newborn infant boy. Amram and Yocheved, an Israelite slave couple, had a boy and decided to hide him rather than obey the law. After a while, however, it became impossible to keep him under covers, so they decided to place him in a small basket and deposit the basket in the waters of the Nile, apparently in the hope that someone would find and take care of him. That is exactly what happened, and the finder turned out to be the Princess Bathia, who raised him in her palace. She gave him the name "Moses," which means "taken from the waters."

◄ 288 ► How did Moses then re-emerge as a Jew, indeed as a leader of the Jews? After he was grown, Moses once came across an Egyptian guard beating an Israelite slave mercilessly. Enraged, Moses killed the Egyptian, saving the Jew's life, and then felt he had to flee for his own life. He settled in Midian, married Zipporah, a shepherdess, the daughter of Jethro, and himself became a shepherd.

◄ 289 ► What caused him to return to Egypt? The explanation is given in the famous biblical story of the burning bush. One day, Moses spotted a small bush that was aflame, but it was not consumed. Curious, he approached the bush and was told by the voice of God to return to Egypt and lead his people out of slavery.

◄ 290 ► Why was it necessary for the Israelites to wander for forty years in the desert before entering the Promised Land? The rabbis explain that the Israelites who fled Egypt were still slaves in their hearts and minds, and it was necessary for a whole new generation, born and reared in freedom, to enter the Promised Land and make it prosper.

◄ 291 ► Is the Passover Seder considered a religious service or more of a festive, family affair? Both. The reading of the Passover Haggadah, which recounts the entire Passover narrative, and the observance of the many rites and ceremonies connected with Passover have transformed the occasion into a combination service and joyous gathering.

◄292► Is the Seder observed only once in Israel? Yes, and twice outside Israel, but tourists are given an opportunity to celebrate a second Seder at public functions in Israel.

◄293► What is *maot hittim?* Literally, funds for wheat, a custom whereby funds are given to every poor person in the community so that everyone will be able to celebrate this most joyous of holidays.

◄294► Why do many modern Seders become intergenerational family affairs? Basically, of all the holidays, Passover is observed in the main at home, giving the members of the family a chance to visit one another in an atmosphere of warmth and rejoicing, with emphasis, on the one hand, on the spiritual meaning of the occasion, and on the other, the once-a-year opportunity to enjoy special holiday treats, sing songs that are heard only on Passover, and bolster the sense of family unity that the holiday invariably generates.

◄295► Are non-Jews permitted to attend a Seder? Certainly. They are not expected to participate in the religious parts of the service, e.g., recitation of the *kiddush* (the special blessing on wine), the enunciation of the famous Four Questions, the opening of the door for Elijah, but they are welcome to read the Haggadah along with the Jews at the table, and certainly to enjoy the festive meal and the over-all reconsecration to the principles of freedom.

◄ **296** ► Explain the custom of "selling" the *hametz* before Passover. Since no non-Passover foods may be kept in the home during the holiday, it is customary for Jewish families to "sell" their *hametz*—a legal device whereby, in most cases, the family "sells" it to the rabbi, who in turn "sells" all the families' *hametz* food to a non-Jew until after the holiday, when it is "bought back." As a result of this custom, families do not throw away perfectly good foodstuffs that have not been consumed by the time Passover arrives. The Israel Government "sells" its *hametz* (stored in warehouses, army depots, and the like) to an Arab for the duration of the holiday.

◄ **297** ► Why do bookbinders traditionally take a vacation throughout the Passover holiday? Because the glue they employ contains ingredients forbidden on Passover.

◄ **298** ► What is meant by "counting of the *omer*," which begins on Passover and ends at Shavuoth? The word *omer* refers to a barley sheaf; the Bible commands the ancient Hebrews to bring the first fruits of the barley harvest to Jerusalem for the use of the priests in the Temple; this is done on Passover. Nowadays, during the seven-week period between Passover and Shavuoth, services include a counting of the *omer* section, meant to determine when new agricultural offerings could be brought to the Temple. (Shavuoth is often referred to as the festival of the first harvest.)

◄ **299** ► Is it true that there are still some people who observe the ceremony of the paschal lamb, in memory of the ancient Israelites who sacrificed a lamb on the night preceding their departure from Egypt? Yes, the small community of Samaritans, who have resided for many centuries in the Samaria section of the Holy Land (near Nablus), still sacrifice a lamb on the night of the Seder in a ceremony reminiscent of Bible days. The ceremony is carried out on Mount Gerizim. Although not regarded as full-fledged Jews, the Samaritans have gradually been drawing closer to the mainstream of the Jewish community, especially since the establishment of Israel.

◄300► What is the ceremony of "burning of the *hametz"?* Since the home must be free of all non-Passover food during the holiday, the days before Passover generally become a period for spring cleaning. Every nook and cranny of the home is cleansed, and the special dishes and cooking utensils used only at Passover time are taken out of storage, washed, and gotten ready for use, while the normal dishes and cooking paraphernalia are put away. On the night before the Seder, in traditional homes, there is a ceremonious search for *hametz,* in which the head of the family, often holding a symbolic feather, brushes the last vestige of *hametz* (prepared in advance) into a paper bag, and burns it the next morning, indicating that the home is now "Passover pure."

◄301► Why does the matza always come perforated? If it were not, it would rise and expand during the baking process and no longer look like matza. (Exact rules for baking the matza are laid down in the Talmud.)

◄302► What is *shmura matza?* The term means "guarded matza"; this type of matza is eaten by very devout Jews, who arrange for the careful supervision of the flour from the time the wheat is harvested. Among some Orthodox groups, there are once-a-year bakeries that do nothing except bake this special *shmura matza* in ovens that are not used the rest of the year, usually in an atmosphere of singing and rejoicing. Tastewise, the ordinary and the *shmura matza* are practically indistinguishable.

◄ 303 ► At the Seder, there are three sheets of matza; what do they represent? The three religious groupings of Jews: the Kohen (priest), Levite, and Yisrael.

◄ 304 ► Is it true that, in ancient times, the matza perforations were often of artistic designs, rather than the straight lines of punched holes that are in use today? Yes, using a special tool that resembled a comb (i.e., having many teeth), people baking matza would first design motifs of animals, flowers, and other objects into the dough before it was placed in the oven. Until the modern, factory-produced matza, most matzas came in a round shape, as do most *shmura matzas* (produced by Hassidic Jews under superstrict conditions) today.

◄ 305 ► What does the word Seder actually mean? "An order" or "arrangement"; it refers to the fact that there are set rules and customs for the proper observance of this ancient holiday, each of which has a special significance.

◄ 306 ► The white tablecloth and the candles on the Seder table obviously add holiday cheer to the celebration of Passover. Why, however, is it obligatory to drink four cups of wine? During the reading of the Haggadah, which narrates the full story and meaning of Passover, there are four separate occasions when participants are expected to drink from their wine cups as a reminder of the fact that God promised, on four, separate occasions in the Torah, to liberate the Israelites from slavery.

◄307► What is the cup of Elijah, featured on the Seder table? The Jewish tradition believes that Elijah the prophet will herald the ushering in of a Messianic era, and the untouched cup of wine placed in the center of the table is meant for him, should he happen to visit that particular household.

◄308► The Seder plate is the centerpiece on the table and contains various items of food, all of them symbolic and rather odd. Would you explain what they stand for? There is a roasted egg (still in its shell), representing the ancient holiday sacrifice offered during Temple days; the egg is also a symbol of mourning, and thus it also serves as a reminder of the destruction of the Holy Temples. In Hebrew, the roasted egg is known as *beitza.* There is also *maror,* which means bitter herbs, usually represented by horseradish, denoting the bitterness of slavery in ancient Egypt and the bitterness of the lot of Jewish communities in countries that to this day do not permit the Jews to follow the teachings of their faith. The *carpas* (usually a little lettuce, parsley, or celery) represents the poor diet the ancient Israelite slaves suffered while they were in Egypt. A slice of *carpas,* during the Seder rite, is dipped into salt water, symbolizing the tears of the Israelites under the yoke of slavery. A *shankbone* stands for the Passover lamb sacrificed by the Israelites at Temple services in ancient times. *Haroset,* a mixture of wine with crushed apples, almonds, and cinnamon, represents the mortar that the Israelite slaves mixed in their labors for the Egyptians. Finally, the three covered matzas, in memory of the haste during which the Israelites fled from slavery, their bread not having time to rise.

◄309► What is the Afikoman? Half of the middle matza (of the three placed on the Seder table), which early in the ceremony is given to the children at the table for "safekeeping," since it is required for the closing of the Seder service. Traditionally, the children hide it, and when the head of the household asks for it, they demand a "ransom"—a promise of a gift—before they return it to the table. The custom is said to have arisen so as to keep the children's interest in the Seder at a peak level.

◄310► What is the meaning of the opening words of the Haggadah, *ha-lahma anya?* At the opening of the Seder, the head of the household, or whoever is conducting the Seder, rises, picks up the plate with the three symbolic matzas, and intones the opening lines of the service, which begin with *ha-lahma.* He says: "This is the bread of affliction that our fathers ate in the land of Egypt. Let all who are hungry come and eat. Let all who are in need come and celebrate Passover with us. Now we are here; next year, may we be in the Land of Israel. Now we are slaves; next year, may we be free men."

◄311► When does the youngest present at the Seder recite the traditional Four Questions? What are they? Immediately after the opening recitation of *ha-lahma,* the youngest child at the table (in some homes, the honor is given to all the small children) recites the Four Questions, which are answered by the reading of the Haggadah. Summarized, the questions are: Why do we eat unleavened bread on this night? Why do we eat bitter herbs on Passover? Why do we dip the *carpas* into salt water and the *maror* in *haroset?* Why do we sit in a reclining position at the Seder?

◄312► What is the Passover tradition about the Four Sons? A section in the Haggadah tells the story of four types of sons—one who is wise, one who is cruel, one who is simple, and the fourth, who does not even know how to ask questions about Passover. The wise son symbolizes a Jewish person who is dedicated to his people and heritage; a cruel son is one totally disinterested in Judaism; the simpleton is one ignorant of Jewish teaching; and the last, one who is not even aware of the fact that he is Jewish.

◄313► What foods are traditional at Passover? At the Seder table itself, egg soup, i.e., hard-boiled eggs and salt water, and *kneidlach,* also known as matza balls, are served in a broth, in addition to a full, festive meal. During the rest of the holiday, a great favorite is *matza-brei,* pieces of matza dipped in egg, and fried on a skillet.

◄314► Do all Jews around the world celebrate Passover the same way? Practically, but not entirely. Jews originating in the isolated villages of the Caucasus do not have a Seder plate, but instead use a tablecloth on which the holiday symbols are embroidered.

◄315► At the Seder table, everyone uses a Haggadah. What was done before the advent of printing made this possible? Each family in ancient times had at least one handwritten and illustrated Haggadah, which was passed down from generation to generation. Some of these very rare Haggadahs are now kept in museums and offer a view of beautiful art, including biblical scenes, portrayals of Jews in earlier times seated at a Seder table, and graphic illustrations of the Four Sons.

◄316► Why do Ashkenazic Jews refrain from the use of vegetables in the pea family, as well as rice, corn, and peanuts, during Passover? In times gone by, some of these foods were ground and baked into a kind of bread, causing confusion between them and the proscribed *hametz* grains.

◄317► What is *Lag b'Omer?* Literally, the thirty-third day of the counting of the *omer,* between Passover and Shavuoth, marked today mostly by schoolchildren with out-of-door picnics, outings, bonfires, and the like. During the seven-week period of the counting of the *omer,* weddings and other happy events are proscribed, but the ban is lifted on Lag b'Omer; hence it is today a day of wedding celebrations, particularly in Israel. The reason for the mournful nature of the seven-week period is believed to stem from the belief that thousands of students and disciples of Rabbi Akiva perished in a plague in the second century—a plague that ended on the thirty-third day of the *omer* counting. Another belief, whose basis is lost in antiquity, is that manna began to fall from heaven on this day for the starving Israelites wandering in the wilderness following their departure from Egypt. Among Hassidic and other Jewish groups, Lag b'Omer is traditionally believed to be the day on which Rabbi Shimon bar Yohai died and was buried in Meron, in the Galilee; hence it has become customary for followers of Hassidic movements and others to journey to Meron and give their young children their first haircuts.

◄318► Why is Lag b'Omer also called Scholars Day? In memory of the students, believed to number twenty-four thousand, who died in the plague.

◄319► Why do students go forth on this day to the woods, for picnics and bonfires? As a reminder of the unsuccessful attempts, after the destruction of the Holy Temple by the Romans, to wrest Jewish sovereignty from the Romans, under the military leadership of Bar Kochba and the spiritual guidance of Rabbi Shimon bar Yohai. Some students carry bows and arrows, the weapons of those days.

◄ **320** ► What is Yom Hashoah? Observed in Israel of the twenty-seventh of Nissan, and outside Israel on April 19, this is a recently innovated memorial day for the six million Jews who perished in the Nazi era. Two minutes of silence are observed throughout Israel on this date.

◄ **321** ► What is Yom ha-Atzmaut? Israel Independence Day, observed on the fifth day of Iyyar (usually in May), a joyous occasion for Jews everywhere. As a sign of thanksgiving, the special, Hallel section is added to the prayer services in many synagogues.

◄ **322** ► What is Shavuoth? Sometimes referred to as the Feast of Weeks, since it culminates the seven-week counting period of the *omer* from Passover, Shavuoth commemorates the giving of the Torah to Moses on Mount Sinai, and at the same time is an agricultural holiday marking the first harvest of wheat.

◄ **323** ► Is it mentioned in the Bible? Yes, together with Passover and Sukkoth, Shavuoth was one of the three pilgrim festivals, when the ancient Jews were expected to proceed to Jerusalem on foot to worship at the Temple.

◄ **324** ► Why is Shavuoth also known as *hag ha-bikkurim?* The term means "the festival of the first fruits," and takes note of the first-fruits harvest that takes place in Israel at this time of year (late May or early June), samples of which were brought to the Holy Temple in ancient days.

◄ **325** ► Why do Jewish families traditionally eat *blintzes* on Shavuoth? The sages explain this custom as deriving from God's promise to the Jews to bring them to a "land flowing with milk and honey," hence the emphasis on dairy foods (*blintzes* are fritters filled with cheese). Another explanation offered is that the Bible on the one hand instructs the Jews to bring the "choicest first fruits" to the Temple, and on the other admonishes against the boiling of a "kid in its mother's milk"—the basis for the laws of *kashrut,* separating meat from dairy dishes. The eating of dairy food on Shavuoth is therefore interpreted as acceptance of and abiding by the rules of both the written and the oral Torah.

◄ **326** ► Are there special Shavuoth celebrations in modern Israel? Yes, children from the agricultural communes and settlements dress up in clothes reminiscent of the ancient Israelite farmers and carry samples of first fruits through the streets amid singing and dancing. They then sell the produce, with the funds going to the Jewish National Fund, for its afforestation and land-improvement programs.

◄ **327** ► Are there agricultural aspects to the holiday observed in the diaspora? Traditional families adorn their homes with plants and flowers to indicate the nature aspect of the holiday. The synagogues are also decorated with greenery.

◄ **328** ► Why is the Book of Ruth read on Shavuoth? The story centers around the harvest season and is therefore appropriate to Shavuoth. Ruth's acceptance of the Torah and entry into the Jewish faith are also deemed suitable for this holiday.

◄ **329** ► What is the *Akdamut* service, recited only on Shavuoth? A special paean of praise to God, emphasizing gratitude to Him for the Torah. A centuries-old melody in which this special prayer is chanted is as traditional for Shavuoth as Kol Nidre's melody is for Yom Kippur eve.

◄ 330 ► Why do Reform Jews (and some Conservatives, too) conduct Confirmation ceremonies for their young people on Shavuoth? The ceremony officially welcomes the young people into the Jewish community; it is conducted on Shavuoth because this is the day on which the Torah is believed to have been given to the Jewish people by God.

◄ 331 ► Why is Shavuoth sometimes referred to as Pentecost? Because it occurs on the fiftieth day after the first day of Passover.

◄ 332 ► Is there a special synagogue reference to the Ten Commandments? On the first day of the two-day holiday of Shavuoth (one day in Israel), there is a recitation of the Decalogue, during which the entire congregation remains standing.

◄ 333 ► What are the major fast days in the Jewish year? Not counting Yom Kippur, which is in a category all by itself, there are a number of fast days which commemorate historical events and which are observed to this day by Orthodox Jews in the main. First and foremost is *Tisha b'Av,* the ninth day of the Hebrew month Av, which falls during the summer months. It is the date on which the first Holy Temple was destroyed (in 586 B.C.E.) and the date attributed to the second Temple's destruction by the Romans (in 70 C.E.). Tisha b'Av is observed by fasting and by a special service in the synagogue.

◄ 334 ► Did other tragic events in Jewish history fall on the ninth day of Av? In 1492, the same year that

Columbus discovered the Western Hemisphere, some 150,000 Spanish Jews were forced into crowded ships and expelled from Spain—the beginning of the removal of all Jewish life from Spain, some five hundred years ago. The opening incident took place on the ninth of Av.

◄ 335 ► What is the reason for the three-week period of mourning? The three weeks after the seventeenth day of Tammuz (which falls in the summer) mark the growing threat of the Roman conquest of Jerusalem and, in effect, the beginning of the exile of the Jews from their homeland. The period culminated in the day when sacrifices had to be discontinued at the Temple, the seventeenth of Tammuz, which is observed today by Orthodox Jews as a day of fasting.

◄ 336 ► What are the "nine days" of sadness? The nine days preceding the observance of Tisha b'Av, when all festive and joyful activities are traditionally forbidden, including such things as having one's hair cut, swimming, and of course attending concerts or performances. The idea is that, in every generation, Jews must remember the dark days that transpired some two thousand years ago that led to their exile from the Holy Land and the creation of the diaspora.

◄ 337 ► Is the Tisha b'Av service different from other services? In very traditionalist synagogues, prayers are recited by the light of candles only, and congregants sit on very low benches or on the floor, as is the custom of mourners. The cantor's chanting of the service is mournful.

◄ 338 ► What is the prayer book called *kinnot?* A special collection of dirges containing vivid descriptions of the destruction of Jerusalem and the Holy Temple, added to the regular services on Tisha b'Av.

◄ 339 ► Is a special biblical portion read from during the Tisha b'Av service? The Book of Lamentations is traditionally read aloud on this day, to a very doleful melody.

◄ 340 ► What are the other customs associated with this fast day? At the morning service, the men who normally put on their *tallit* (prayer shawl) and *tefillin* (phylacteries) refrain from doing so, but don them instead at the afternoon service.

◄ 341 ► What about the Western Wall, also known as the Wailing Wall? Does it play a part in the Tisha b'Av service? As might be expected, the only remaining vestige of the Temple period is today a magnet drawing thousands of worshipers to it on Tisha b'Av, where people may be seen praying fervently and emotionally, voicing their hope for a restored Temple and an era of peace.

◄ 342 ► Do all Jews observe Tisha b'Av? Reform Jews observe only Yom Kippur as a fast day.

◄ 343 ► What are the other minor fast days? The *tenth day of Tevet,* marking the beginning of the siege of Jerusalem by the Babylonians, some 2,500 years ago. The *Fast of Gedaliah,* which falls on the day after Rosh Hashanah, commemorating the assassination of the Jewish governor appointed by the Babylonians after the destruction of the first Temple, whose death shattered the Jews' hopes. The *Fast of Esther,* on the day preceding Purim, when the Jewish queen of Persia fasted before interceding with her husband, the king, to abrogate a decree imperiling the Jews.

1. Interior of Shearith Israel, the Spanish-Portuguese synagogue in New York City, housing the oldest Jewish congregation in New York.

2. The Yochanan Ben Zakai synagogue, recently reconstructed in the Jewish Quarter of the Old City of Jerusalem.

3. A Torah scribe lettering the Hebrew characters on the parchment Torah scroll.

4. A Megillah—the scroll telling the biblical story of Queen Esther—decorated in silver filigree by artist Peter Ehrenthal.

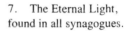

5.   Menorah (candelabrum) used during the festival of Hanukkah.

6.   Sterling silver Havdalah sct.

7.   The Eternal Light, found in all synagogues.

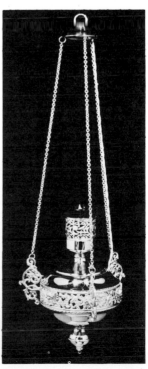

8.   A *huppah,* the traditional Jewish wedding canopy, under which the bride and groom take their vows. This one was designed by Efrem Weitzman for Congregation Rodeph Sholom, New York City.

9.   The Holy Ark, open and showing the Torah Scrolls fully dressed, from Woodsdale Temple, Wheeling, W. Va. The brass Eternal Light and bronze figures on the doors of the ark, representing traditional religious symbols, were executed by sculptor Willard Hirsch.

Chapter 6

CUSTOMS AND CEREMONIES

"What nation on earth has customs as strange as ours? Our poor *demand* alms, as if they were collecting a debt, and our bene-factors invite paupers to their table."

— MENDELE MOCHER SEFORIM

◄344► What is *Shma Yisrael?* Probably the most hallowed words in Jewish liturgy. They are the first words of the prayer that is encased in the mezuzah, found on Jewish home doorposts (and on synagogues and, in Israel, on most public buildings).

◄345► Why do Jewish families affix a mezuzah to the doorpost of their home (and sometimes additional mezuzahs to interior doorposts)? In fulfillment of the biblical command in Deuteronomy "You shall write them on the doorposts of your house and on your gates."

◄346► Is there a special way of hanging a mezuzah? It is placed on the right doorpost (as one enters), at a slant. The word *Shadai,* a name for God, must appear in the small opening of the casing.

◄347► What about the mezuzahs that people, both men and women, and children too, now wear as pendants? This is a recent innovation, which most rabbis neither encourage nor discourage. If it is worn as a good-luck charm, it runs contrary to Jewish tradition and teaching; if it is worn as a sign of pride in the Jewish heritage, it is regarded with tolerance. Actually, Maimonides wrote that those who wear amulets, including the mezuzah, are "fools who defeat the fulfillment of a great commandment."

◄ **348** ► What is the *klaf* in the mezuzah? A piece of parchment on which the Hebrew text from the Bible is inscribed; only one that is done by hand (as in the Scroll of the Torah) is considered acceptable. In Israel, purchasers of a mezuzah generally inspect the *klaf* to determine if it has the rabbinate's approval.

◄ **349** ► What is a *mizrah?* The word means "east"— the direction that most Western Jews face when they pray, i.e., toward Jerusalem. Since many people pray at home as well as in the synagogue, it is customary to adorn the eastern wall with an attractive plaque on which the word *mizrah* is spelled out in Hebrew.

◄ **350** ► Is there any etymological connection between the word *seder* (at Passover time) and the word for prayer book, *siddur?* Both are variations of the same root, meaning "order," i.e., the Passover-eve service follows a prescribed order, and the prayer book is really an orderly arrangement of prayers assembled over a long period of time.

◄ **351** ► What are the principal contents of the *siddur?* There are selections from the Bible (especially from Psalms) and the Talmud, and compositions by rabbis most of whom lived many centuries ago. Some new versions contain also contemporary material, by living or recently deceased authors.

◄ **352** ► Is the prayer book in Hebrew only? In the main, yes, but there are also sections in Aramaic. Conservative and Reform services also interpolate the prayers with English translations, usually found on pages facing the Hebrew. The special prayer book used only on the High Holy Days is called a *mahzor.*

◄353► What happens when a prayer book, or for that matter a Bible or some other religious, holy volume, is worn and tattered? Jewish law states that such holy but no longer useful books must be buried in a Jewish cemetery, with the same respect that is accorded a human being who is being laid to rest.

◄354► What, then, is a *genizah*? Another method of discarding holy books is to bring them to the synagogue, where they are placed in an unused storage place, or *genizah*. Ritual objects that can no longer be used may also be stored in the *genizah*. The most famous such *genizah* was discovered in a Cairo synagogue in 1896, which contained some two hundred thousand rare pages dating back many centuries, proving to be of enormous historical value. During the Nazi era, some Scrolls of the Law and other objects of religious significance, as well as rare works of Judaica, were stored in hiding places in the hope that they would be opened and their contents utilized again after the defeat of the Nazis. Some of these modern genizah places have been uncovered, but not all.

◄355► When a woman kindles the Sabbath-eve candles, why does she customarily cover her eyes while reciting the blessing? So that she will better concentrate on her prayer, and so as not to use the light of the candles for a utilitarian purpose, even if it is only for a fraction of a minute.

◄356► Does the number of candles in varying households used on Sabbath eve have any significance? No, although most housewives like to match the number of candles with the number of members of the family. Two candlesticks, however, are the minimum required by tradition, which stems from the fact that the commandment regarding the Sabbath is introduced by two different words ("remember" and "observe") in the two versions of the Ten Commandments included in the Bible.

◀357▶ What happens if the woman of the household is absent or is physically unable to kindle the Sabbath candles? Then the man of the house does so. If a man lives alone, he, too, must light the candles every Friday evening.

◀358▶ Are special candles required? No, except that they should be big enough to last at least through the Sabbath-eve meal. The candles are generally white, and the candelabrum or candlesticks are traditionally reserved for the sole purpose of the Sabbath-eve ceremony.

◀359▶ How does a woman know when to light the candles? The time is determined by rabbinic authorities and varies with the time of year in different parts of the world, but is always shortly before sunset. Most Jewish religious calendars list the precise times for various time zones.

◀360▶ After the woman of the house lights the candles and makes the appropriate blessing, what then? She generally turns to her family (the children often are close by, watching her) and wishes one and all *Shabbat shalom* —a peaceful Sabbath. This is the official inauguration of the Sabbath.

◀361▶ And the man of the house? Traditionally, he will then proceed to the synagogue, accompanied by his children if they are of age, for the Friday-night service. After his return, the family will sit down to the festive Sabbath meal, after performing a number of ceremonial acts.

◀362▶ When does the father bless the children? Nowadays, this custom is observed almost exclusively in

Orthodox families only: upon returning from the synagogue on Friday evening, the father and the children who accompanied him join with the woman of the household and the younger children who may not have been old enough to leave the house for services and—sometimes holding hands, forming a circle—they will sing the age-old hymn "Shalom Aleichem." It is a song of welcome to the angels of the Sabbath. Then, before sitting down to eat, the father places both his hands on the bowed heads of his children and blesses them.

◀363▶ When does the traditional Friday night *kiddush* take place? Now, after the children have been blessed, the family is ready for *kiddush,* which is the ceremonious sanctification of wine. The head of the household stands, holding a special cup of wine, and sings the special blessing reserved for the occasion, while those at the table may either sit or stand, depending on family custom. When the *kiddush* blessing song is concluded, the cup is passed around for all to sip and recite an abbreviated version of the blessing.

◀364▶ Now can the family finally get down to eating? Not quite. After the kiddush wine has been tasted (in many families, each person has an individual goblet of wine to drink from), and the hands have been washed ceremoniously, the traditional *ha-motzi* blessing on bread is recited (only now it is on Sabbath bread, known as *hallah*), the head of the household, after taking a small piece of the *hallah* for himself, passes a bit of it around to each person at the table. The law is for each participant then to recite the appropriate blessing before eating the *hallah.* During the course of the meal, normal slices of *hallah* are cut and handed around.

119

◄ 365 ► Can any kind of wine be used for *kiddush?* No, it must be a kosher wine made from grapes. If someone is not allowed to drink wine for health reasons (or in the case of children), unfermented grape juice may be substituted.

◄ 366 ► Why are there traditionally two *hallah* loaves on the Sabbath table? In remembrance of the biblical account of the miracle of the manna that fell from heaven to feed the wandering Israelites in the wilderness; on the Sabbath a double portion fell, hence the two loaves.

◄ 367 ► When do the diners wash their hands and recite a special blessing? Between the recitation of the *kiddush* and the blessing over the *hallah.*

◄ 368 ► What is a *Shabbat* knife? A knife adorned with the motif of the Sabbath and used only for the cutting of the *hallah.* It is generally serrated, and the handle will often contain the words *Shabbat kodesh* ("holy Sabbath" in Hebrew).

◄ 369 ► Can others join in the *kiddush* ceremony? This is usually optional, and follows family or community tradition. Sometimes each adult male present will sing the *kiddush* separately, and sometimes the young boys will be invited to do so, too.

◄ 370 ► With the candles glowing, the wine and *hallah* having been blessed and tasted, the family's best china and cutlery on the table, and everyone attired in his or her best Sabbath clothes, is there anything else that distinguishes the Sabbath meal from the weekday dinners? In addition to the fact that there are traditional foods served only on Sabbath (and holidays), the meal is made especially festive by the singing of *zemirot*—poetry from the

Middle Ages, sung to distinct melodies, which laud the day of rest for its bestowal of tranquillity on the family. Depending on the particular family's preferences, other appropriate songs may also be appended to the repertoire.

◄ **371** ► What is meant by *bentshen?* The recitation of grace after the meal; it is also known by its Hebrew designation *birkat ha-mazon.* The grace is usually sung on the Sabbath; during the normal work week, grace after meals is recited softly.

◄ **372** ► Is there a relationship between the words *kiddush,* the blessing for wine, and *kaddish,* the special prayer for mourners? Both words stem from the root meaning holy. The wine is hallowed and the Sabbath observance is, too, by the singing of *kiddush;* a mourner recites *kaddish,* sanctifying the name of God in the moment of his grief, attesting to the never-ending cycle of life and death.

◄ **373** ► What is a *simchat bat?* A very new custom that has developed in recent years, which is dedicated to celebrating the birth of a daughter in a religious spirit. The words mean "joy of a daughter," and it is likely that the feminist movement generated it in view of the emphasis given to a boy and his circumcision ceremony. It is usually a celebration at the parents' home on the Friday eve following the child's birth, complete with singing, a selection of prayers, and a brief discourse on a religious subject.

◄ **374** ► Why is it customary to have guests at the Sabbath table? Hospitality is a hallmark of Jewish tradition, with the biblical narrative of Abraham and the three angels serving as a constant reminder of the importance of this duty. In the small towns of Eastern Europe a century or two ago, any Jew visiting a synagogue on the Sabbath who did not have a home-cooked Sabbath meal waiting for him could be sure that at least one congregant would invite him home so that the stranger could celebrate the Sabbath day properly.

◄375► What is *havdalah?* The special, brief service that marks off the end of the Sabbath (or holiday) from the rest of the week. The word itself means a separation, and the *havdalah* ceremony includes a blessing over a tall, braided candle and the sniffing of a spice box—the latter a throwback to ancient days when the Temple service included the burning of incense. Most *besamim,* or spice, boxes are fashioned in the form of a tower.

◄376► What is a *hanukkat ha-bayit?* A ceremony dedicating the family's new home. In addition to the traditional affixing of the mezuzah on the doorpost, every new home that a family moves into will contain bread and salt —ancient symbols of life and happiness. (To this day, distinguished visitors to Jerusalem will be greeted at the entrance to the city with bread and salt.)

◄377► What is a *tzedakah* box? A charity box, found in many Jewish homes, into which the mother of the household customarily drops a few coins every Friday, just before she kindles the Sabbath-eve candles. The boxes are emptied at least once a year and the monies sent to a deserving institution. Years ago, there were men who went from home to home, emptying out the contents of these *pushkas,* or boxes, leaving a receipt for the contents and delivering the funds to the institution they represented. Generally they were accompanied by another person, so as to forestall any possible temptation to deduct some of the money for themselves.

◄ **378** ► What is the purpose of the Jewish dietary laws? The Bible explains that adherence to the laws regarding the consumption of kosher food will help to make the Jewish people a holy people. Many people today believe that the original laws were based on sound principles of health. There are wide differences among Jews as to the degree of observance of these laws, which have been interpreted and brought up to date. It is safe to say that most Jews, at the least, refrain from eating the products banned in the Bible, e.g., those derived from the pig and shellfish.

◄ **379** ► How does Judaism regard vegetarianism? All fruits and vegetables, according to Jewish dietary laws, may be eaten (most banned animals and fowl are those that devour one another). Traditionally, Jews believe that in the Messianic era, people will subsist solely on fruits and vegetables, and see this as an ideal state for mankind. Eating of meat and fowl is regarded as a concession to people's baser instincts.

◄ **380** ► Why do observant Jews refrain from mixing meat and dairy dishes? Because of the biblical prohibition against seething "the kid in its mother's milk." Traditional Jewish homes therefore maintain a separate set of dairy dishes, a set of meat dishes, and of course two additional sets of dishes for the Passover holiday. The same applies to cooking utensils.

◄ **381** ► What is *shehitah?* The ritual slaughter of an animal or fowl, making it kosher in accordance with the dietary laws. A ritual slaughterer is known as a *shohet.*

◄ **382** ► What are the principal laws governing Jewish ritual slaughter? The animal must be slaughtered in such a way as to prevent any undue suffering, and of course it must be inspected to be sure it is entirely devoid of any disease, before it can be labeled kosher.

◄ **383** ► What is a *halaf?* A razor-sharp knife, used by the ritual slaughterer, that is constantly checked to ascertain that it contains no nicks that might cause suffering. After the animal is slaughtered, it is drained of all blood, since the eating of blood is biblically forbidden.

◄ **384** ► What is meant by koshering meat? The additional soaking, salting, and rinsing that take place even after the meat is purchased, so as to drain away any vestiges of blood that might have remained after the animal was slaughtered.

◄ **385** ► Why do kosher meat markets not sell the hindquarters? Because of the regulation that before the hindquarters can be eaten, the sciatic nerve must be removed from the animal's hip. It is less time-consuming and costly to dispose of this part of the animal to a nonkosher butcher. The prohibition is believed to have originated in the biblical story of Jacob, who was hit on the thigh during his struggle with the angel.

◄ **386** ► What is the difference between an animal designated *trefa* and one called *nevela?* The former is unfit because it has been killed in a manner other than by ritual, kosher slaughter or it is proscribed as unfit, while the latter is carrion (an animal that died a natural death), which is also forbidden.

◄ **387** ► What is meant by *tsaar baale hayyim* (literally "sorrow for the animal kingdom")? The Jewish tradition toward animals forbids the practice of cruelty to animals; hunting is looked upon as an activity that is not consonant with Jewish teaching, and the only time an animal may be killed (other than when it is meant to be used as food) is when it is intended for research that will aid humanity. A farmer who is responsible for feeding his livestock is commanded to feed the animals before he sits down to his own meal. The benevolent attitude of Judaism toward animals is reflected in the fact that owning pets has not been, until very recently, a Jewish trait, largely because it was felt that confining an animal in a home or a cage was contrary to the natural order.

◀ **388** ▶ Why are children often named for deceased relatives? It is considered a sign of respect and esteem for the departed. The custom is now not widely observed in Israel, where many children are given biblical names, including little-known ones found only once in the Bible.

◀ **389** ▶ Are there memorials for the departed found in the synagogue? Many synagogues have a special plaque containing the names of congregants, or their relatives or friends, who have died. There is a small electric bulb adjoining each name. These are all lit on Yom Kippur, and individually on the *yahrzeit* of their passing.

◀ **390** ▶ How else are people memorialized in Jewish life? Donations to a wide variety of religious, educational, and charitable institutions are made on a one-time or a perpetual basis in the name of the deceased. The recipient institutions are found both in the United States and in Israel.

◀ **391** ▶ Are there special memorials for the six million Jews who perished at the hands of the Nazis? Many synagogues have a special memorial, either in the form of a perpetual light or fashioned as a sculptured tribute to the martyrs of Nazism. Yom Kippur *yahrzeit* services also include a special prayer for them, since most of those who were killed left no heirs to recite the traditional *kaddish* prayer.

◄ 392 ► Is there a special Jewish view of death? Judaism stresses life, and looks upon death as an event that comes to all people but one that is devoid of any virtue. The traditional toast, *le-hayyim* (To life!) indicates the Jewish view that life is precious and is meant to be lived and enjoyed. As the Psalmist put it, "The dead cannot praise the Lord."

◄ 393 ► Why are all deceased Jews dressed in a simple white garment when they are prepared for burial? To emphasize the fact that all people, rich and poor, become equal at the time of their passing.

◄ 394 ► Aren't Jewish males also buried in their prayer shawl (the *tallit*)? Yes, and the fringes of the *tallit* are deliberately spoiled, symbolizing the fact that the decedent no longer is required to observe the various Jewish laws.

◄ 395 ► Do Jews have the equivalent of a wake? Traditionally, no, but the custom has developed to a limited extent in recent years, notably in the United States. Jewish teaching requires that the deceased be placed in a casket made of simple wood, constructed without metal, and that the coffin is not to be opened before or during the funeral service.

◄ 396 ► Are autopsies permissible in Jewish law? Because post-mortem examinations were considered to be a desecration of the corpse, Jewish teaching has always opposed autopsies. The exception is made, however, when it is concluded that an autopsy will contribute to the future saving of lives.

◄ **397** ► Are burials ever held on Sabbath? Never, nor on holidays. Although Jewish tradition calls for interring the dead as soon as possible, generally within twenty-four or forty-eight hours, delay is permitted to enable close relatives to arrive for the funeral from distant locations.

◄ **398** ► What is a *hevra kadisha?* A group of pious Jews who take it upon themselves, as a religious duty, to see to it that the various laws and customs of Jewish burial are observed. This includes preparing the dead for the burial and standing watch from the time of death until the actual funeral service. Customarily, the *hevra kadisha* accepts donations from the family for the use of various charities.

◄ **399** ► What is the custom of *kriah?* The word means rending and refers to the cut that is made in the clothes of the immediate family of a deceased as an ancient sign of mourning. The mourners who observe a week of *shiva* in honor of their deceased wear the same cut garment all week, except on the Sabbath, as well as throughout the thirty-day mourning period.

◄ **400** ► What are the principal customs associated with the *shiva* mourning period? The members of the family sit on low stools, shod in slippers; the men do not shave and the women refrain from the use of cosmetics. The period is one during which sexual relations are prohibited, as is all pleasureful activity, including the wearing of new garments. The only books that may be studied during this period are the biblical volumes dealing with grief, e.g. Job,

Lamentations, and sections of Jeremiah. Normal work routines are skipped, and often friends and neighbors will prepare the meals for the mourners.

◀**401**▶ Is it customary to visit the bereaved while they observe the *shiva* period? It is regarded as an important command to visit and comfort the mourners after the burial has taken place. Visitors leaving a mourner's home traditionally repeat the expression of condolence "May the Lord comfort you together with all the mourners of Zion and Jerusalem."

◀**402**▶ When entering a mourner's home, during the week of *shiva,* why do visitors usually refrain from the usual greetings? Jewish teaching felt that, under the circumstances, it was wiser to say nothing, since words could not console the mourner, but the visitor's physical presence during the bereaved's grief expressed a sense of sympathy and consolation.

◀**403**▶ What is the meaning of *shloshim?* The term means thirty and refers to the period of thirty days from the date of burial during which the mourners, following the *shiva* period, may go about their ordinary activities but must refrain from attending functions where music will be played. The custom of men not shaving or having their hair cut during the *shloshim* period is observed largely among Orthodox Jews.

◀**404**▶ For a period of eleven months after the date of death, in other words for nearly a full year after the burial, isn't *kaddish* required to be recited daily? Yes, but only for a parent. During this period, the mourner refrains from all enjoyable activities, such as attending concerts, the theatre, films, parties with music, and the like.

◄**405**► May a daughter recite *kaddish* for a parent? A son is required to do so, and daughters may do so if they are so inclined. Some Orthodox rabbinical leaders, however, are opposed to women reciting the mourner's *kaddish* under any circumstances.

◄**406**► Can another recite the mourner's *kaddish* if the deceased left no sons? Yes, but not if the individual himself has both his parents living.

◄**407**► Are there special rules concerning the erection of a tombstone? A tombstone at the head of the grave is an ancient Jewish tradition. It is usually set up sometime during the year following burial (in Israel, it is generally done soon after the end of the thirty-day mourning period). The custom of "unveiling" the tombstone is quite recent and although widely practiced in the United States is not actually based on Jewish law. The ceremony includes a rabbi's recitation of appropriate prayers and the next of kin's removing a piece of cloth covering the memorial. Most tombstones in the United States include both Hebrew and English inscriptions.

◄**408**► How does Judaism regard cremation? Both the Orthodox and Conservative wings of Judaism oppose the practice of cremation severely; Reform Judaism encourages traditional burial but is not strongly opposed to cremation. Antagonism to cremation (which was known in ancient times) stems from its practice by pagans and idol worshipers and from the traditional Jewish prohibition against mutilation of the corpse. The Talmud also interprets the act of burial of the dead as a *mitzvah,* or religious commandment; cremation is thus an avoidance of the *mitzvah.*

Chapter 7

THE SABBATH

"The Sabbath is a mirror of the world to come."

—ZOHAR

◄409► Why do Jews place such great stress on the Sabbath? Not only because it is one of the Ten Commandments and thus deeply ingrained into the Jewish people's heritage, literally a way of life that dates back thousands of years, but also because, as has been noted, the Sabbath observance has been credited with strengthening and shoring up the Jewish way of life more than any other institution in Judaism. Although today the concept of a day of rest—or two, in most Western countries—is widely accepted, its origin lies in the Decalogue, for which the Jews may rightly be given full credit. Jews see the Sabbath not only as a day of physical rest but, more important, as a day when they can recharge their spiritual, mental, and psychological batteries, as it were. During the twenty-four-hour period beginning on Friday sunset and ending after the completion of the Sabbath, a Jew is expected to desist from labor and to devote his mind and body to prayer, study, song, festive meals surrounded by family, and conversation that aims at better understanding of what life is all about—in short, a complete surcease from the mundane daily tasks that each person is required to pursue in order to earn a livelihood. Properly observed, the Sabbath can be a beautiful respite from the week's chores, at the end of which one feels oneself again ready to face the work of the coming week.

◄410► Do many, perhaps even most, Jews think the Sabbath laws and regulations restrict their freedom of ac-

133

tion? Probably, which will explain why the number of Jews who observe the Sabbath religiously is far less than the total membership of the Jewish community. There are, of course, restrictions—one may not work, one may not strike a match, one may not transact business, go shopping, handle money, do gardening, play golf or tennis—but these are seen as limitations only to the uninitiated, who do not understand the significance of these Sabbath laws and customs and who certainly have not had the benefit of having experienced a traditional Sabbath.

◄411► Why do rabbis consider Sabbath observance the very core of Judaism? Simply because they know, from history and from recent experience, that the ancient adage *averah goreret averah,* one transgression leads to another, applies to the Sabbath—that once a Jew discards Sabbath observance, chances are he will soon ignore synagogue attendance, Jewish study, and participation in Jewish communal life; and his link to the Jewish tradition will be tenuous.

◄412► Aside from the committed Orthodox Jews, including the Hassidim, has there been an increase in Sabbath observance on the part of Jews in recent years? Yes. One must first understand that when most Jews arrived in this country as poor immigrants, they had to struggle hard to eke out a livelihood. In their rush to integrate into American life, most abandoned many Jewish traditions, including the Sabbath, and found instead satisfaction in a higher material standard of living. However, a strange phenomenon took place in the next generations: children raised in affluent surroundings found a missing element in their lives, and a search for the source of serenity of their still-observant grandparents began. Often this resulted in a decision to emulate the grandparents' commitment to Jewish traditions, including of course the Sabbath. Thus, in the suburbs today, where large numbers of Jews reside, one can see more and more young people (as well as on college campuses) wending their way to religious services as part of the Sabbath day, while their parents may be off to a golf course or a department store. This is not to say that Sabbath observance has become a widespread activity among young Jews, but a trend has been developed and is likely to continue among younger Jews.

◄413► What about Sabbath in Israel? In most cases, Israeli Jews follow the same patterns as do American Jews, i.e., the Orthodox mark the day in the prescribed manner while the secular Jews tend to spend the day at the beach, on picnics, at the local sports stadiums and the like. But in Israel, too, there has been a growing interest on the part of young people in adopting the Sabbath as their own, largely because they, too, have noted that the truly spiritual restfulness of the day can be achieved only through full adherence to the ancient traditional manner of the Sabbath observance.

◄414► Is the Sabbath solely a day of rest? No, it is conceived in Judaism as a sacred day, when we not only enjoy total physical leisure, but more importantly as a day when we make every attempt possible to refresh our very souls.

◄415► Is there a rationale for the Sabbath? There are two fundamental explanations for the Jews' strong feeling about the Sabbath: first, it commemorates the creation of the world, when God rested on the seventh day after creating the world in six days, and, second, it is also a reminder that Jews are free to rest on the Sabbath, after having been slaves in Egypt.

◄416► How is the Sabbath interpreted as a day of homage to God? By desisting from labor such as cutting the grass, or catching fish, or manufacturing various goods, we demonstrate our belief in God, saying in effect that if God could rest on the Sabbath, it behooves us to do the same and thus pay tribute to Him.

◄417► How else did the rabbis explain the significance of the Sabbath? When one rests on the Sabbath and refrains from all worldly pursuits, it is tantamount to stating that this is our way of saying that the goods of the world are not ours, but God's, and that we are only using them on His authority; on the Sabbath we forfeit this responsibility and thus proclaim that we recognize our human shortcomings and Providence's omnipresence.

◄418► What about the Sabbath and the concept of freedom? The rabbis taught that observing the day of rest is a demonstration on our part of liberation from human masters, that we are free people, able to set aside one day of the week entirely for ourselves, not bound to do the labors of mind and body ordained by others.

◄419► But why can't playing ball or taking a drive in the country be considered restful activity suitable for the Sabbath? Simply because, in our tense age, the vast majority of people pursue their hobbies and relaxation activities with the same tempo that they do their work. Even if those activities do not carry any financial reward, they fail completely to transfer to the individual the tranquillity and serenity that a true Sabbath day provides.

◄**420**► What did the great essayist and philosopher Ahad Haam, mean when he said that "more than Israel has kept the Sabbath, the Sabbath has kept Israel"? Simply that the drudgery and hard toil of the work week would have ground the Jews down during their two millennia of exile had they not had the Sabbath to look forward to every week. It transformed them into a holy community, able to rise above the exigencies of their often harsh circumstances.

◄**421**► What is meant by the expression an "island in time" when referring to Sabbath? That the day of rest of the Jewish people is seen in the same light as so many people daydream of running off to some faraway island where they will achieve peacefulness and serenity, so can Jews attain this same spiritual nirvana, each and every week, simply by observing fully the laws and customs of the Sabbath.

◄**422**► What did Erich Fromm say about the Sabbath that is often quoted today? The famed psychiatrist wrote that on the Sabbath "man is fully man, with no task other than to be human." Man ceases to "be an animal whose main occupation is to fight for survival and to sustain biological life," he said, adding, "Sabbath is a day of peace between man and nature."

◄**423**► When may the Sabbath laws be violated? For *pikuah nefesh*—the saving of life. Judaism is life-oriented, and thus the saving of life transcends all other obligations and rulings. Maimonides wrote that desecration of the Sabbath in an emergency should not be relegated to women and children but should be carried out by leading Jews and sages.

◄ **424** ► Where did the line "Jerusalem was destroyed because it had destroyed the Sabbath" appear? In the talmudic tractate *Sabbath.*

◄ **425** ► When does one prepare for the proper observance of Sabbath? Preparations in the traditional Jewish home begin a day or two before Sabbath. Since the day actually begins on Friday evening, the bulk of the physical preparations are carried out generally on Friday morning and early afternoon.

◄ **426** ► How does one usher in the Sabbath? To provide the proper ambience for the day, it is customary to clean the house and cook the food, preparing the stove so that it can be used to warm but not to cook on the Sabbath. Special foods such as the traditional Sabbath loaf, the *hallah,* must be ordered (or baked).

◄ **427** ► What else must be done? To get into the spirit of the day, it is customary to bathe before the Sabbath, don fresh and suitable clothing, polish the Sabbath candlesticks, and get ready to shuck all workday cares and worries, and literally be prepared to immerse oneself for the next twenty-four hours in total physical and mental leisure.

◄ **428** ► All right, the hour has arrived, a few minutes before sunset on Friday. What now? Traditionally, the mother of the household will put some coins into a charity canister, approach the candles already placed in the candelabrum, put a kerchief over her head, light the candles, cover her eyes, and recite the blessing on kindling of the lights.

◄ **429** ► And the father-husband? By rights, he should already be in synagogue for the evening service.

Chances are that the very small children will be watching mother light the candles and will hurry to proclaim *Shabbat shalom* (peaceful Sabbath) when she finishes, while the older children will be with their father in the synagogue.

◄ **430** ► What happens when the father returns from synagogue? There will be an exchange of *Shabbat shalom* greetings, made especially meaningful in the flickering of the Sabbath candles. Often, the father will bless the children at this point.

◄ **431** ► What about the Sabbath dinner? The table will be gleaming: a white tablecloth, the best dishes and cutlery in place, and the traditional Sabbath loaves (there are customarily two) will be bedecked by a special, usually decorative covering. A decanter of sacramental wine for the *kiddush* ceremony will also be in place.

◄ **432** ► What is the prescribed *kiddush* rite? The head of the household will begin the Sabbath-eve dinner by standing at his accustomed place, holding a goblet of wine. In some families, everyone else will rise too, although in many others, only the father does so. He recites the *kiddush* —the special blessing on wine—in a traditional chant, sips a little, and passes it around the table. Then he uncovers the *hallah*, tears or cuts off a piece, often salts it, and recites the customary *motzi* blessing for breadstuffs, and passes pieces around to all. At this point, the family is usually ready to eat the meal, which comprises a number of courses, often with all or some of the traditional ingredients: gefilte fish, chicken soup, chicken, dessert, and tea.

◄ **433** ► Is there conversation during the meal? It takes skill, but the head of the house tries to involve every family member in conversation that is suitable to the occasion. Also interspersed in the evening meal are *zemirot,* songs especially sung at the Sabbath table, between courses, that are also meant to create a mood of festivity and gentility.

◄ **434** ► How is the remainder of the Sabbath evening spent? In Orthodox families, most people will read for a while and go to bed relatively early. Some families will have timers attached to their TV sets, turning them on and shutting them off at set hours, permitting them to watch without having directly tuned in themselves. Many rabbis oppose the practice. Among Conservative and Reform families, especially during the non-summer months, there will be a late-Friday-evening service, usually beginning at eight-thirty, following dinner, to which many will go for an abbreviated service, often followed by a social hour. (Friday-evening services are also utilized by most Conservative and Reform congregations for Bat Mitzvah celebrations, though this does not generally occur in Orthodox circles.)

◄ **435** ► How is the Sabbath day itself spent? Services generally begin at 9 A.M. so that people can probably sleep a little later than usual. Breakfast is usually a rather sparse affair. The morning service lasts until noon, true, but this will be followed by a traditionally full Sabbath meal.

◄ **436** ► Are the Sabbath services different from the weekday service? Definitely. Men are not required on the Sabbath to don phylacteries (*tefillin*); one puts on one's best attire, knowing that the synagogue, too, has been freshened up to greet the Sabbath day. In addition to the regular morning service, there are selections recited only on Sabbath, and there is also a whole new section called *musaf* recited only on Sabbath (and holidays). The rabbi and the cantor are wearing robes (not usually in Orthodox synagogues) and extra-high *yarmulkes* (skullcaps). It is a day when the Torah is ceremoniously taken from the Holy Ark, to be read aloud to the congregation in a melody that dates back many centuries. It is a day when a Bar Mitzvah boy is called to the Torah, and when a young couple about to be married are also honored; others are also honored by being called to the Torah on Sabbath. The whole aura of the Sabbath service thus creates a festive, joyous mood.

◄437► Does the rabbi always preach on the Sabbath? Generally speaking, yes. It is customary nowadays to expect the rabbi to have prepared a sermon based on the weekly Scripture reading, often expanded to touch on contemporary events as reflected through the ancient prism of the Torah. Many people, if probed deeply, would probably admit that the high point of the service for them is to hear the rabbi deliver a sermon, which can often be stimulating intellectually and rewarding psychologically.

◄438► What about the conclusion of the service? On Sabbath, it is customary for the congregants to gather around a table in the rear of the synagogue after services to join the rabbi in a *kiddush* (which can be merely a sampling of *hallah*, wine, liquor, or cake) and for the members and guests of the congregation to exchange news and pleasantries before proceeding to their respective homes.

◄439► After the Sabbath meal, what is the usual procedure? It depends a little on the time of year and on the individual family. In good weather, after the meal on the Sabbath, most people will take a nap or read or both. The radio, newspaper, and TV are ignored. Reading is generally confined to a suitable subject matter. Later in the afternoon, around four, people will visit one another for tea and conversation, still attired in Sabbath clothes, still feeling festive. As the sun prepares to set, the men and boys will often excuse themselves from these socials and proceed to the synagogue for the concluding services.

◄ **440** ► How is the Sabbath ended? First, there is the late-afternoon, or *mincha,* service, which during the week is virtually combined with the evening, *maariv* service, but on the Sabbath *mincha* is followed by a *shalosh seudot,* a light snack, in the synagogue, during which the rabbi will offer a brief talk on a choice intellectual morsel from the vast Jewish storehouse and those in attendance will respond with communal singing and participating in the snack. This is then followed by the evening service, capped by the beautiful *havdalah* service, in which the Sabbath is bade farewell till the following week. At this point, congregants are presumably rested and refreshed in the fullest possible sense and can turn back to their daily lives and responsibilities.

◄ **441** ► People greet one another on the Sabbath by saying *Shabbat shalom,* or peaceful Sabbath. How do they exchange greetings on Saturday evening, following conclusion of the Sabbath? By wishing one another *shavua tov*—a good week.

◄ **442** ► Reference is often made to the Sabbath as being a bride. Why? Because Moses in ancient times rejoiced in the gift of the Sabbath as a groom rejoices with his bride. Thus, celebration of the Sabbath in the prescribed manner is seen as the consummation of a happy marriage.

◄ **443** ► Is it true that there is a tradition that Friday nights are an especially suitable time for marital relations?

Yes, especially among Hassidic groups. The grandeur and beauty of the Sabbath, the sense of oneness with God, and the shedding of workday cares for the twenty-four-hour period of the Sabbath all seem to bring about the right kind of ambience for a married couple to have intercourse on Friday nights.

◄ 444 ► If a family travels and finds itself away from home on the Sabbath, how can the woman kindle the lights on Friday evening? Not only can a woman borrow a pair of candlesticks, but there are even now in use portable, collapsible candlesticks for this very purpose. In Jewish resorts, one can see scores of candles lit by women standing together in a special section of the kitchen, to attest to the fact that no matter where they are, they still wish to obey the Sabbath laws.

◄ 445 ► What is an oneg Shabbat? Literally, a rejoicing of the Sabbath; it is a fairly recent innovation during which people gather late on Sabbath afternoons to study and sing together in order to enhance and expand the enjoyment of the Sabbath. Jewish organizational conventions and conferences usually now set aside a few hours on Sabbath afternoon for such a program, in the midst of deliberations of their otherwise daily work agendas. In the newly formed *havurot*—groups of Jewish families who have banded together to celebrate religious observances with an extra dimension of companionship—the oneg Shabbat has also become a high point of the Sabbath observance.

◄ 446 ► Is riding on the Sabbath ever permitted? Not among Orthodox Jews, who tend to reside in close proximity to their synagogues, but it is permissible among Conservative Jews to drive to the synagogue. Driving is not permitted, however, for any other purpose. The rationale is quite simple: since a majority of families no longer live within walking distance of the synagogue, it is felt that it is better to allow driving to services than to have the congregants either absent themselves from services on the Sabbath or be made to feel guilty about driving. (Reform Jews are not affected, since driving is not banned.)

◄ **447** ► Do some people begin the Sabbath even earlier than required? Yes; for reasons of convenience some Jews will begin the Sabbath an hour or two beforehand, thus in effect extending the day of rest to a twenty-six-hour period. This is done largely among Orthodox Jews in the long summer days.

◄ **448** ► What is meant by the term *muktzeh* as applied to Sabbath? This refers to objects that should not be handled or touched on the Sabbath, since doing so is not consonant with the spirit of the day. Examples would be tools, machinery, money, the handling of which is seen as reducing the spiritual beauty of the day.

◄ **449** ► How do Orthodox (and Conservative) Jews get around the prohibition of switching on and off electric lights on the Sabbath? By installing timers that do it for them.

◄ **450** ► Is there a special Sabbath food in addition to the *hallah?* Yes, but consuming it nowadays is much rarer than it used to be. It is called *cholent,* a meat-and-bean dish that takes many hours to prepare and was a staple in the old country, when it could be left to warm on the stove throughout Friday night for use on the Sabbath day.

◄ **451** ► What is the weekly Sabbath portion of the Torah (the Five Books of Moses) called that is read aloud at morning services? It is known as the *sidra* of the week, and it is followed by a suitable selection from the Prophets. The Torah is so divided that it takes a full year to read and study, and on Simhat Torah the cycle of weekly readings is begun again. What is a source of constant amazement to worshipers is that no matter how many years they read the weekly portions, each year they find something new and provocative to ponder.

Chapter 8

ISRAEL

"The air of the Land of Israel makes one wise."

— TALMUD

◄452► Why does Israel play such a prominent role in Jewish life? The concept of the Land of Israel's being part and parcel of the Jewish people is ordained in the Bible. In Genesis, God said to Abraham that "unto thy seed will I give this land." Nahmanides, a great Jewish scholar and commentator, wrote: "The Torah cannot assume perfection except in Israel." Throughout the nearly two thousand years of exile, from 70 C.E. to the creation of the modern State of Israel, in 1948, Jews wherever they lived prayed daily for the restoration of the sovereignty of their ancient homeland and remained in constant contact with the country through the celebration of its holidays, recited special prayers for dew and rain for its well-being, and dreamt of a Messianic return to their ancient glory.

◄453► How do Jews regard Israel today, even those who are citizens of countries in which they enjoy full freedom and to which they give their undivided allegiance? The best answer can probably be found in the Israel Declaration of Independence, proclaimed on May 14, 1948: "The Land of Israel was the birthplace of the Jewish people. Here their spiritual, religious, and national identity was formed. Here they achieved independence and created a culture of national and universal significance." Hence one can say that Jews throughout the world see Israel as a spiritual homeland, from which will again come forth the word of the Law.

◄454► Aren't there more pragmatic views about Israel? Yes. One has to recall that the persecution of the Jews has remained a phenomenon of the past two millennia, often culminating in mass murders, forced conversions, and complete expulsions (from Spain, England, Portugal, and elsewhere). In more recent history, the anti-Jewish pogroms of Czarist Russia (and anti-Semitic attacks of Soviet Russia) beginning at the turn of the century and culminating in the unprecedented Nazi era, when six million Jews were put to death, have all left an ineradicable mark on the Jewish people. Early settlement of Palestine followed on the heels of the Russian pogroms, while the principal stimulus for the creation of the State of Israel was the Holocaust in Europe, which ended only in 1945, when World War II saw the defeat of the German armies. Quite simply, Jews today feel that if it is in their power, they will never again permit an attack against the Jews qua Jews, and see in Israel therefore a country that offers a haven for the oppressed and threatened Jews of the world.

◄455► What about the Zionist position? Zionism seeks to restore the Jewish people to their ancient homeland, because it believes that a people without a solid piece of land of its own is doomed to extinction. In that sense, one can say that the great majority of Jews are Zionists. However, the fine line that once existed between avowed Zionists and non-Zionists is now almost invisible: most Jews sense that Israel represents the future welfare of the Jewish people world wide; i.e., if Israel were to be destroyed, their own future as Jews would no longer be viable. This will explain the intense response that took place

in the Jewish communities of the world when a real threat
to her existence took place, in May of 1967, and the spon-
taneous outpouring of joy and relief that followed the Six
Day War, when the threat to Israel's survival was removed.

◄ **456** ► Do Jews feel more secure, more self-
confident now that Israel has been created? Yes. Jews can
now look to one country in the world where Jews are
wanted, where there is no anti-Semitism, and which affords
them a great sense of pride by its adherence to the democratic way of life side by side with its stress on traditional
Jewish values. In the Nazi period, when Jews were singled
out for murder and humiliation, virtually no country lifted
a finger to aid distressed Jewish communities; Jews felt de-
pressed, shamed, sometimes hopeless. All that has changed
with the creation of Israel: they now walk taller, knowing
that there is a haven for their fellow Jews, to which have already come, in the course of slightly more than two decades, two million Jews from countries of oppression.

◄ **457** ► What about those Jewish groups who oppose
Israel on theological grounds? There are a few tiny groups,
notably among the Hassidic sects, who believe that Israel
should not have been created as a political state and should
have waited for the Messiah, when a theocratic state would
have been proclaimed. They are strongly opposed, and usually ignored, by the overwhelming majority of the Jews.

◄ **458** ► Aren't there some Jews critical of Israel on
religious grounds? There are some Jews who feel the people of Israel are not religious enough (even though they
themselves may not be at all observant) and would like to
see more religious observance practiced in Israel. The usual
answer offered to them is the comment once made by the
late Chief Rabbi of Palestine (prior to the establishment of

Israel), Rabbi Kook, who was told that kibbutz workers were totally irreligious and did not even fast on Yom Kippur. He responded that when the Holy Temple was being built, the workers were also not necessarily religious but their work was creating a holy edifice. So the people of modern Israel are building a sacred community, and in the course of time the work itself will transform them into a holy, religious people.

◄459► What is the religious situation in Israel today? The percentages of Israeli Jews who observe religious laws and traditions are comparable to those of Jews in the United States, England, and other Western countries. In recent years, a growing trend has been noted toward a more religious way of life. Even the early Socialist-minded pioneering settlers now concede that they erred when they deprecated religion, an attitude they adopted as part of their desire to rid themselves of all vestiges of the diaspora.

◄460► Do Jews outside Israel owe political allegiance to Israel? Definitely not. The late David Ben-Gurion, first prime minister and the veritable architect of the old-new nation, said clearly in Jerusalem in 1950: "The State of Israel represents and speaks only on behalf of its own citizens, and in no way presumes to represent or speak in the name of the Jews who are citizens of any other country."

◄461► Does this mean that Israel cannot protest anti-Jewish persecution wherever it may occur? Of course not. If there is persecution of Jews in the Soviet Union, not only Israel but also the United States and other free countries feel themselves duty-bound to protest. Because a particular situation involves Jews, Israel feels even more deeply involved than other countries.

◄462► Is Israel considered a "Jewish state"? Yes, but this does not mean that only Jews live there or that non-Jews are denied citizenship. The population of Israel today is about 3,500,000, of whom 500,000 are non-Jewish Israeli citizens (mostly Moslems, with Christians and others making up the balance).

◄463► Were there Jews living in Israel during the past two thousand years? Yes. While the vast majority of Jews lived outside Israel, in exile, small clusters of Jewish residents continued to eke out a livelihood in out-of-the-way corners of the country, awaiting the return of their fellow Jews.

◄464► What kind of government does Israel have? A parliamentary democracy, in which there is a President, elected by the Knesset (parliament) for a five-year term, who has the power to commute prison terms, appoint judges and ambassadors, and sign all laws (except those dealing with his office). Power rests in the Cabinet, which is responsible to the Knesset. The Cabinet selects the Prime Minister.

◄465► Does Israel elect its Knesset members the same way Americans choose members of Congress? No. The system used is proportional representation, in which voters cast their ballots for a particular party, and the numbers of seats in the 120-member unicameral Knesset is determined by the numbers of votes cast for individual parties.

◄466► Who can vote in Israel's elections? Any citizen, man or woman. The Knesset membership runs a wide spectrum from a few Communist members to a few extreme rightist members, with the vast majority of the members being affiliated either with the Social Democratic, Liberal, Nationalist, or Religious groupings.

◄467► Why does Israel continue universal conscription, when many countries have abandoned this form of military service? A small country, Israel has felt threatened by the bellicosity of its Arab neighbors from the moment of its inception. Therefore, every able-bodied man and woman is regarded as important to the state's defense and receives military training. Exceptions are made for ultra-Orthodox yeshiva students and girls from ultra-Orthodox homes, where military service would be regarded as inimical to their way of life. Married women are also not conscripted. Israelis are expected to remain in the reserves for many years, and many men experience the annual hardship of having to leave their homes and jobs for a period of a few weeks to a month for reserve service.

◄468► Do Arabs serve in the Israel armed forces? Arabs, by and large, are exempted from military service, on the theory if war did break out between Israel and any of her neighbors—all of them Arab—it would be too much to expect Israeli Arabs to fight against coreligionists and kinsmen. However, the Druse (an Arab sect) in Israel insisted on being conscripted and are now part of the Israel military, and a handful of Israeli Arabs have also volunteered their services.

◄469► Do non-Jews enjoy the same rights as Jews in Israel? All Israelis have equal rights before the law, without regard to race or religion. Schools in predominantly Moslem areas are helped to foster their own culture, and classes are taught in Arabic. All houses of worship—Christian churches, Moslem mosques, Bahai temples, synagogues—are aided financially by the Ministry of Religions.

◄ 470 ► What is the official language of Israel? There are three: Hebrew, Arabic, and English. Hebrew of course predominates. Arab members of the Knesset may address the parliament in Arabic, and simultaneous translation is offered to the non-Arabic-speaking members. Newspapers and magazines are published in Israel in all three languages, plus a host of European languages. Israel, after all, is a nation of recent immigrants.

◄ 471 ► Are non-Israeli Arabs allowed to visit their families in Israel? Since the Six Day War, hundreds of thousands of Arabs have crossed into Israel as visitors, mostly across the Jordan River, coming from Jordan. They are given free entry and are not restricted to any particular parts of the country. Thus, one may see sitting at a Tel Aviv café table an Arab family, from one of the neighboring countries, that reached Israel via Jordan and is enjoying the sights in the same way that any other tourist group does.

◄ 472 ► How big is Israel? The boundaries that existed just prior to the Six Day War contained an area of about eight thousand square miles, roughly the size of New Jersey. Since then, the cease-fire lines encompassing most of the Sinai Peninsula, the West Bank, Gaza, and the Golan Heights comprise a territory of some thirty-two thousand square miles. Israel has stated repeatedly it will return the major part of these administered territories within the framework of a peace treaty.

◄ 473 ► Does Israel have a warm, Middle East climate? Yes and no. In many ways the climate is comparable to that of Florida, but there are also mountains and deserts, deep valleys, and lush terrains, giving Israel a wide variety of climatic conditions. Distances are also short, so that a trip from Tel Aviv, the largest city, to Jerusalem takes only an hour, driving. A one-day drive through Israel affords a wide variety of climatic and scenic experiences.

◄474► Why does the Israel economy seem to require constant massive doses of financial support from abroad, from governmental sources and from organized Jewish communities? In a word—because of security. Although Israel is not entirely a poor country in terms of natural resources (its chemical and mineral resources are excellent), it is required to spend a huge percentage—often 40 per cent—of its budget for defense purposes. At the same time, the country continues to provide large sums for housing, education, employment, and other services for its citizens, a great many of whom arrived only in the course of the past two decades or so. The Israelis look upon defense needs as their own guarantee of survival and look to Jews abroad (as well as to friendly governments) to join in the large-scale program of fully absorbing hundreds of thousands of newcomers. Israelis themselves have been the highest-taxed people in the world for a number of years.

◄475► Can a small country like Israel ever support itself without outside assistance? Most economists answer this with a resounding yes, pointing to the fact that while back in the early 1950s there was a serious shortage of food, forcing the government to ration all foodstuffs for a number of years, the situation has now been reversed, thanks to modern scientific agriculture and careful planning, so Israel today enjoys bountiful crops and exports large quantities of food products—especially citrus—to many overseas customers.

◄**476**► What about manufactured goods? Here, too, the dramatic change from what was to what is today the norm for Israel is quite remarkable: the GNP of Israel in 1952 was half that of Egypt, while today, despite Egypt's much larger population, the figure is equal. Exports from Israel, including highly sophisticated electronic products and machinery requiring great technological skills, have risen year after year to astounding proportions, but all these gains have continued to be offset by Israel's need to budget heavily for defense and to expend hard currency for vital imports. Thus, a peaceful settlement of the Middle East conflict and a concomitant reduction in arms expenditures would in all likelihood help Israel to develop a more balanced budget and a healthier economy.

◄**477**► Does this mean that Jews abroad will eventually cut off their financial support? Not necessarily, since Jewish communities that help to establish schools, hospitals, old-age homes, and similar institutions in Israel derive enormous satisfaction from the knowledge that they are in a very real sense partners with Israel in helping to rebuild the Jewish community—a third of whom were murdered a scant two generations ago.

◄**478**► Are there many Americans living in Israel? Relative to the size of the American Jewish community, no. A growing number of American Orthodox Jews are emigrating to Israel, where they feel they can live more intensely religious lives, but the numbers remain small. There are small groups of idealistic American Jews who have chosen to live in Israel, and another group of retired Jews who find that their pensions and Social Security checks go a longer way in Israel than they do here, but, *in toto*, the numbers are relatively small.

◄479► Does an American who decides to settle in Israel lose his citizenship? No. Dual citizenship is now available to American Jews living in Israel (this is also the case for British Jews and for those from a few other Western countries).

◄480► How many Jews were in Israel in 1948, when the State of Israel was proclaimed? About 650,000.

◄481► What was the Arab reaction to the proclamation of Israel independence? Despite the United Nations partition decision of November 1947, calling for the setting up of both an independent Jewish and an independent Arab (Palestinian) state, the surrounding Arab countries launched a massive military attack against the fledgling Jewish state. The Arab armies were repulsed, and the territory originally set aside for Israel was somewhat enlarged.

◄482► What is meant by the expression "two Israels"? About half of the Jewish population in Israel stems from the Moslem world, largely poor Jews who for centuries had had no opportunity to acquire an education, so that when they arrived en masse in Israel they could not readily take other than the menial and unskilled jobs. The Israel Government has been struggling to correct this imbalance through special educational programs, but it is a long, drawn-out process. Many of these so-called Oriental Jews—most of whom were not personally involved in the Holocaust, which touched the Ashkenazic, or Western, Jews—remained resentful when they saw the Israeli authorities provide what they felt were luxurious opportunities for newcomers from the Soviet Union and from the West—a resentment that sometimes erupted into physical violence and demonstrations. The basic problem has not been resolved; hence the expression "two Israels."

◄483► Why does Jerusalem loom so large in Israel's future plans? Basically, the ancient city is seen as a link to the past, when it was the capital of various Jewish commonwealths. In addition, recent history showed that when the city was divided—as it was prior to the Six Day War—Jewish holy places (the Western Wall, the Mount Olives cemetery, many synagogues in the Old City) were not only desecrated but Jews had no access to them. Since 1967, Jerusalem has been a unified city, with free access to all. There has been practically no conflict between Jerusalem's Arab and Jewish communities. The Moslem and Christian holy places, as well as the Jewish, are guarded and open to all, and Israel insists that this is the way it should be.

◄484► To what American city can Jerusalem be compared? Washington, D.C. Jerusalem abounds in government offices (it is Israel's official capital), and famous landmarks, in addition to the many holy places, include the Hebrew University (with fifteen thousand students), the Israel Museum, and scores of yeshivas and schools. There is some industry in and around the city but not much.

◄485► How long does it take to fly from New York to Israel? El-Al, the Israel national airline, regularly makes New York-Tel Aviv non-stop flights in about ten hours.

◄486► Are there civil marriages in Israel? Not among Jews. Only rabbis marry Jewish couples. However, if a married couple enters the country from abroad, the form of their marriage is not questioned. Non-Jewish couples may be married by their respective religious officials. Some Israelis who refuse marriage by a rabbi get around the law by flying to nearby Cyprus, where a civil ceremony is performed.

◄ 487 ► What is meant by the term *aliyah* in reference to Israel? The word literally means ascent, and is used to describe those Jews who leave their countries of residence and opt to settle in Israel. (Jews living in Israel who decide to emigrate, usually because of economic or social problems, are said to be participating in *yerida,* or descent.)

◄ 488 ► What was the Youth Aliyah movement of the 1930s, which helped rescue thousands of Jewish children, mostly from Germany and Austria, prior to the outbreak of World War II? A movement set up by the Zionist movement through which thousands of youngsters were brought to Palestine, in the hope and expectation that their parents would eventually be able to join them, a hope that proved to be vain in most cases. The children were cared for in special youth villages, and became among the most devoted and committed Israelis. A leader of the organization was Henrietta Szold, founder of Hadassah.

◄ 489 ► What does Hadassah concentrate on in its work in Israel? Medical and hospital services to the ill, irrespective of race or religion. The organization's principal facility is in Jerusalem and is considered one of the finest medical installations in the world. A number of prominent foreigners have been treated there, including some Arabs, although secretly.

◄ 490 ► What do other organizations do in Israel? Such groups as the Mizrachi Women, Pioneer Women, Women's League for Israel, and others provide full or partial support for a network of social and educational facilities, including day-care centers, nursery schools, vocational training programs, immigrant absorption aid, legal counsel to working women, special villages for young people from underprivileged families, and the like.

◄ **491** ► What about some of the major Jewish educational establishments in the United States? There are now branches in Israel of the (Reform) Hebrew Union College and the (Conservative) Jewish Theological Seminary. The (Orthodox) Yeshiva University sends its students for study periods of at least a year in rabbinical centers in Israel.

◄ **492** ► Which American Jewish organizations provide the largest sums for Israel? Two: the United Jewish Appeal, whose funds are used to help new immigrants in a wide variety of ways as well as provide care for the aged, and Israel Bonds, which invests in basic industries such as chemicals and minerals, shipping, and other productive enterprises, as well as in power stations, housing, road construction, and the like.

◄ **493** ► Are there other forms of support for Israel emanating from the United States? Many, including groups that support the various universities (Hebrew University, Technion, Tel Aviv University, Weizmann Institute, Bar-Ilan University, and more), an organization that aids the Magen David Adom (Israel's equivalent of the Red Cross), Jewish National Fund, which has been afforesting the country for some eighty years, and others that furnish aid to smaller educational and social-service agencies in Israel.

◄ **494** ► What is the difference between a *kibbutz* and a *moshav*? A *kibbutz* is a collective settlement in which members work and pool their resources, taking only what they need. Begun as agricultural colonies, most *kibbutzim* (plural) are also producers of industrial products. All property is communally owned, and all decisions as to work assignments, school curriculum courses, films to be rented for entertainment, are arrived at by majority vote. A *moshav* is a settlement in which every family owns its own home and farm but co-operates in marketing, use of heavy equipment, and the like.

◄**495**► How are children raised on a *kibbutz?* Many *kibbutzim* are characterized by "children's houses," where the youngsters live apart from their parents, who spend the day at assigned work functions. Generally, the children and parents spend the late-afternoon hours together, when all work is finished. In most *kibbutzim,* a communal dining hall serves all adults, while the children eat their meals in a separate dining room. In recent years, some *kibbutzim* have permitted the children to sleep at home, i.e., with their parents.

◄**496**► Is it true that not too many newcomers choose the *kibbutz* way of life today? Yes. Many of the newcomers coming from behind the Iron Curtain seem to be disenchanted with anything that smacks of collectivism and shy away from the *kibbutz.* Generally, Israel's economy is capitalist-oriented but with a heavy socialist influence. An outstanding example of this is the situation that prevails vis-à-vis discharging an employee; unless it is for malfeasance, it is extremely hard to do, which has produced an unhealthy situation in Israel, where sometimes unfit employees remain on their jobs long after their productivity has dropped sharply. Although members of the *kibbutzim* are highly respected, their numbers are relatively small.

◄**497**► Is alcoholism a problem in Israel? Up until about a generation ago, the answer would have been negative, but in recent years it has begun to surface. The same is true of drug addiction. While neither is anywhere near as serious as in the United States or other Western countries, they have nonetheless begun to worry the Israel authorities.

◄**498**► How about crime? Israel prides itself on its low crime rate. Muggings are almost unknown. However, there is a growing amount of burglary, with the thieves looking for money from affluent families but usually being careful not to harm their victims.

◄**499**► What about cultural life? Israel has one of the highest-per-capita reading publics in the world and probably the highest (until the advent of television a few years ago) movie-going public. Despite exhortations from cultural and educational leaders to devote their reading time to Hebrew classics and the new works of Hebrew-writing authors, most Israelis appear to be reading the same best sellers that appeal to other readers in the free world, both in translation and in the original.

◄**500**► Why do tourists report that many Israeli workers carry briefcases to their jobs? Most workers begin work very early and often end work in midafternoon. They usually take along a small snack, and it is not unusual to see even post-office clerks munching on a sandwich while doling out stamps. Another reason is the weather; workers who leave home before the sun rises need a warm sweater or jacket, but by the time they go home the sun is strong, and they prefer to carry their excess clothes in a briefcase.

◄**501**► The Israel flag consists of a blue Star of David on a white background, with two stripes of blue running parallel to each other, top and bottom. What is the significance? The flag's design is based on the traditional design of the *tallit,* the prayer shawl, which also has parallel stripes.

◄502► Is it true that the Israel Army is entirely kosher? Yes. All meals provided by the military are strictly kosher in deference to the requirements of perhaps 20 per cent of the soldiers. On Passover, visitors to an Israel Army base will see all soldiers substituting *matza* for bread.

◄503► Is there any public transportation on the Sabbath in Israel? Not in Jerusalem, Tel Aviv, or most of the smaller communities. It is available in Haifa, however, a city with a strong labor-oriented population that insists on public transport.

◄504► Is it true that Israelis customarily work a six-day week? Yes, from Sunday through Friday. However, since the country is small and the distances short, most workers work from seven in the morning to about two in the afternoon (this is not true in offices) and are home by two-thirty. This gives them a relatively long period for rest or a chance to moonlight on a second job.

◄505► Is it true that Israel has an abundance of physicians? Yes, largely because so many of the refugees from Nazi Europe were doctors (as well as many of the more recently arrived Soviet Jews). However, there are shortages of dentists, nurses, teachers, and social workers.

◄506► Why do so many trained Israelis (as well as unskilled people) leave Israel to seek opportunity in the United States and other Western countries? Primarily for economic reasons. Acquiring a home in Israel is very expensive (there is very little renting; even apartments are purchased). Also, some families with young children fear renewed fighting and feel they will be safer elsewhere. A great many of those who leave say they will return after getting a nest egg with which to buy housing and other amenities, but this has not worked out in practice.

◄ 507 ► In Jerusalem, where Arabs and Jews live virtually side by side, what are relations like between them? By and large, they are correct and outwardly friendly. There are, however, few close ties between the Arab and Jewish communities. This is true also on the university campuses where Arab and Jewish students study.

◄ 508 ► What's it like in Jerusalem on a weekend? Different—since Friday is the Moslem Sabbath, Saturday the Jewish Sabbath, and Sunday the Christian Sabbath, one must remember what day it is in terms of shopping, working, visiting, and the like. Irreligious Israeli Jews will, for example, go shopping in the Arab cities of Hebron or Bethlehem on the Jewish Sabbath, since all shops are closed in Israel proper.

◄ 509 ► How does Israel care for the elderly? The growing problem of the elderly affects Israel in the same way it affects the United States and other Western countries. There are homes for the aged and what are known as *batei horim* (parents' houses), really apartment houses with some services such as laundry, cleaning, co-operative cooking, and the like, where the aged care for themselves as much as they can amid surroundings where they are gently looked after. The Israel facilities have usually been lauded for their compassionate understanding of the needs of the aged while at the same time continuing to try to give the oldsters a sense of worth and dignity.

◄ 510 ► Are there extended families living together in Israel, as they once used to in immigrant sections of the

United States? By and large, only among the poorer and less educated, so-called Oriental Jews, who hail from the Moslem countries. (Also among the Soviet Jews, possibly because they were already used to crowded conditions before they came to Israel, three or more generations of a family will be found living together.)

◄ 511 ► Is there prostitution in Israel? Unfortunately, yes. Most of those who practice this calling are young girls who come from impoverished families and who think that this is the best way they can bring home needed money quickly. After a period, most of these girls are disowned and drift into shady and even criminal circles. Israeli authorities continue to press a campaign to turn these unfortunate girls back into productive society, and maintain special prisons and rehabilitation centers for them.

Chapter 9

JEWISH HISTORY

"A nation which has witnessed the rise and decay of the most ancient empires, and which still continues to hold its place in the present day, deserves the closest attention."

— HEINRICH GRAETZ

◄512► Who is considered the first Jew? Abraham. Even though he lived long before Moses and the era that followed the giving of the Torah to the Jews, he is regarded as the first Jew, the father of the Jewish people, because of his espousal of monotheism.

◄513► What is the biblical basis for the Jews' claim to Israel, the Holy Land? Early in Genesis, the first book of the Bible, God appears to Abraham and promises him and his descendants the land of Canaan. Jewish history is usually recorded from this time—about four thousand years ago.

◄514► Abraham in the Bible is usually referred to as a Hebrew. What does the word mean? Most scholars believe the word (in Hebrew: *ha-Ivri*) means "he who crossed over," referring to Abraham's crossing of the great Euphrates River to reach the land promised him by God.

◄515► Why are Jews included among the Semitic peoples, which also takes in the Arabs? The biblical account tells of Shem, Ham, and Japhet, sons of Noah; the descendants of Shem, or Semites, are believed to have settled in and inhabited the fertile lands stretching from the Euphrates to the Nile.

◄516► When the early Israelites, seeking relief from famine, proceeded to Egypt, where Joseph was prime minister, did any settlements of Israelites remain behind? Yes, most historians agree that some remnants of the Israelites chose to stay home rather than move to Egypt. Those who did go to Egypt, of course, eventually were enslaved.

◄517► Moses arose in Egypt to lead the Israelites out of bondage and to return them to their homeland. From which of Jacob's twelve sons was he descended? Moses was a Levite, a member of the tribe that was to be charged with supervising the religious life of the Jewish people.

◄518► By what other names is Mount Sinai known? Horeb; also, as the Mountain of God.

◄519► Jews speak of having a covenant with God. What does this refer to? At the time of the giving of the Ten Commandments—the Decalogue—to the Israelites, God and the Jewish people bound themselves to one another, renewing God's earlier covenant with Abraham, with the explicit understanding that He would always watch over them, while they in turn would take the Ten Commandments and expand them to become a code of life for all time and for all Jews. This initial expansion of the Decalogue is known as the Torah (the Five Books of Moses in the Bible). Torah can best be translated literally as "instruction." Many centuries and generations later, the Torah would be supplemented by what is known as the Oral Law (in Hebrew, *Torah She'b'al Peh,* i.e., the commentaries, interpretations, explanations, and additions found in the Talmud, the last volume of which was not completed until the fifth century c.e.). Since that time, numerous rabbinical responsa have continued to be issued, so that it would be correct to say that the Torah is still being interpreted and reinterpreted to this very day.

◄520► Moses' brother, Aaron, became the first *kohen,* or priest. What was his and his sons' chief responsibility during the forty years of wandering in the wilderness before the Israelites entered the Promised Land? They were in charge of the *mishkan,* which held the ark in which was contained the Ten Commandments. It was really a large tent that housed the sacred tablets and a golden seven-branched candlestick.

◄521► What is meant by the phrase *Moshe Rabbenu?* Literally, Moses our teacher. It is used exclusively to refer to Moses and stresses the great leader's lifelong role as a master teacher of the Torah and as a giant personality against whom future generations of leaders and teachers would be measured.

◄522► What was the name of the mountain on which Moses viewed the Promised Land, which he was not to enter? Nebo. He was able to see that Canaan was a fertile land, and he was happy that his task of leading the Israelites to that point had been completed. He died at the age of 120 and was buried east of the Jordan River. (Nowadays, in memory of Moses' ripe old age, people wish one another 120 years of life.)

◄523► Joshua took the mantle of leadership from Moses after the great lawgiver's death, and prepared to lead the Israelites across the Jordan River into Canaan. What famous phrase did God speak to Joshua on the eve of the journey to the Promised Land? God said to Joshua, "Be strong and of good courage"—a phrase that is still used today in Israel, on suitable occasions.

171

◄**524**► The division of the land among the twelve tribes descended from Jacob took place even before the crossing of the Jordan River. How many tribes were given territory east of the Jordan River? Two and a half, the remainder being parceled out west of the river, among nine and a half tribes.

◄**525**► How do modern scholars explain the miraculous story of Joshua's conquest of the city of Jericho? The walls of the city "came tumbling down" as a result of a series of marches around Jericho, during which the rams' horns—the *shofars*—were sounded by the priests. Most agree that at the propitious moment an earthquake rocked the city, causing the walls to collapse and the Israelites to enter virtually at will.

◄**526**► How long did it take for Joshua and his troops to conquer Canaan? Seven years. Not all the inhabitants of Canaan fought against the Israelites, and these people were permitted to live peacefully alongside the Israelites.

◄**527**► After peace was established, where did Aaron's son Eleazar, now the high priest, bring the tabernacle containing the Ten Commandments? To a place called Shiloh, which from that moment on became the religious center of the Jewish people—until much later, when the role was assumed by Jerusalem.

◄**528**► Which tribe did not receive an allocation of land? The Levites, since they were given the responsibility of serving the people as priests and teachers. (Twelve allocations were made, however, because Joseph's sons, Manasseh and Ephraim, each received a territory, but Joseph himself did not have an area that bore his name.)

◀ **529** ▶ After the death of Joshua, who ruled the Israelites? Eleazar, the high priest, and his son Phineas. They ruled over the holy area of Shiloh and taught the Israelites to offer sacrifices and to pray to God. Whenever the Israelites came to Shiloh, young girls would lead them in dancing, especially on the holidays of Passover, Shavuoth, and Sukkoth, as well as on the New Year, Rosh Hashanah.

◀ **530** ▶ After the death of Eleazar and Phineas, who assumed command? A woman named Deborah, who was regarded as a great judge. She was said to sit under a palm tree not far from Shiloh, where she would hear the complaints and accusations of her fellow Israelites and issue decisions that were considered fair and just.

◀ **531** ▶ Which son of which famous judge had a strong ambition to become the king of the Jews, an office that had never existed? Abimelech. His father, Gideon, ruled as a judge over Israel for some forty years but never wished to become a royal personage.

◀ **532** ▶ Did Abimelech succeed in his hunger for power? Yes, he ruled for three years, creating a reign of terror and cruelty, and was finally fatally wounded by a woman rebel throwing a rock at him. Wounded, he begged his armor bearer to run him through lest it be said that he had been slain by a woman. His aide complied, and Abimelech and his brief reign came to an ignominious end.

◀ **533** ▶ An entire book in the Bible is called Ruth and recounts the lovely story of her early widowhood and her remarriage to the landowner Boaz. What is especially remarkable about Ruth? Although not born into the Jewish faith, Ruth became a devout Jewess and fate decreed that she was to become the great-grandmother of one of the greatest figures in Jewish history, King David. (Her grandson Jesse was David's father.)

◄**534**► In addition to being one of the strongest men who ever lived, how else is Samson different from many of the biblical figures? He was raised by his parents to become a Nazirite, i.e., one who would devote his life to God, would not consume strong drink or wine, and would not cut his hair. He was trained to join a select group of those who voluntarily gave up the material pleasures of life in order to dedicate themselves to God. Of course, as the story of Samson and Delilah shows, he strayed far from the path chosen for him.

◄**535**► Who, then, was really the last honorable judge to rule in Israel, before the onset of the era of kings? Samuel. Although he named his two sons judges, both disappointed him and were known to be corrupt judges. When Samuel was quite advanced in years, the people of Israel begged him to name a king who would rule when he was gone, pointing out that his sons were not worthy of assuming the mantle of leadership.

◄**536**► Was Samuel amenable to the idea? Not at all. He told the people they did not need a king, that God was the only king and His rule was ample. But the Israelites persisted, and eventually he relented.

◄**537**► Whom, then, did Samuel choose to be the first king in what was to become a long line of royal rulers? Saul, of the tribe of Benjamin, who was known to be a man of courage and very tall and imposing. When Samuel told Saul that God had told him that he, Saul, was to be anointed king of Israel, he could not believe his ears. He told Samuel his family was not noble and Benjamin was the smallest of the tribes of Israel. Almost reluctantly, and bashfully, Saul agreed to shoulder the responsibility of becoming the king, and listened attentively when Samuel urged him to rule wisely and justly. The people of Israel, who wanted a strong ruler, for they feared the potential aggression of their neighbors, were happy.

◄538► What action of Saul angered Samuel, even after Saul and his son Jonathan proved themselves to be great heroes in battle? Contrary to Samuel's expressed wish, Saul at first spared the life of the king of the cruel Amalekites. Later, he also treated the Gibeonites—with whom Joshua had sworn a treaty of lasting peace—very harshly.

◄539► When and under what circumstances did Samuel realize that King Saul had to be replaced? At first, Saul began to seem strange and moody, and at times he would, in fits of madness, do insane things. Soon after, God spoke to Samuel and told him to proceed to Bethlehem, and in the house of Jesse he would find a suitable successor for Saul.

◄540► Which of Jesse's sons did Samuel at first think would make a worthy king in lieu of Saul? The eldest son, Eliav, who, like Saul, was tall, strong, and imposing. But God indicated that he was not His choice, and one by one (Jesse had eight sons), Samuel examined all the sons in the house but did not receive a sign from God that any of these would fill the bill. After Jesse sent for David, his youngest, who was in the field with his flocks, Samuel knew that David was the one who would be anointed king of Israel. Secretly, Samuel turned to David, who was still quite young, and whispered to him that, after Saul's death, he would become the royal successor. Amazed, young David returned to his grazing sheep, to think and wonder on the fate that awaited him.

◄ **541** ► David entered the court of Saul as a harpist, assigned to playing soft music to ease the mad moods that seized Saul. When did he become elevated to a higher role? Soon after David defeated Goliath in the miraculous encounter with the Philistine giant, Saul appointed David commander of the entire Jewish army.

◄ **542** ► Did Saul give his daughter Michal in marriage to David willingly? No, David had to pressure him and score a number of victories over the Philistine enemy before the king agreed to the match. Even while he agreed to the marriage, Saul simultaneously plotted to have David killed. He was consumed with uncontrollable jealousy, since the people of Israel openly exhibited their preference for David, who was saved by the warnings and help of his wife, Michal, and the prince, Jonathan, who had become his best friend.

◄ **543** ► What finally made Saul relent in his mad pursuit after David? An incident occurred in which David could easily have killed the king while he slept, but he made off with his spear to show he had had the opportunity but demurred. After that, Saul's hatred disappeared and he gave up his plan to kill David.

◄ **544** ► After the death of Saul and Jonathan in battle, David was crowned king of Israel. In what city did the ceremony take place? In Hebron, where Abraham had lived.

10. Actor Lorne Greene and Israeli guide are shown at the model of the Temple area in Herod's day, which is in Jerusalem.

11. View of the Knesset, Israel's parliament, in Jerusalem, and the giant menorah that was a gift to the State of Israel by the government of Great Britain.

12. The Western Wall, in Jerusalem, the only portion of the Temple still standing, is Judaism's holiest place.

13. A sculpture of the Ten Commandments, by Itzhak Amit, of Kibbutz Tzora, Israel.

14. The *mezuzah*, in several designs.

קדש
ורחץ כרפס יחץ מגיד
רחצה מוציא מצה
מרור כורך שלחן עורך
צפון ברך הלל
נרצה

15. Sterling silver Seder
plate.

16. The *shofar*, a ram's
horn which is sounded
during Rosh Hashanah
(New Year) services and
at the conclusion of Yom
Kippur, the Day of
Atonement.

17. The traditional *tallit* (prayer shawl) and *tefillin* (phylacteries) are worn by Rabbi Dr. Aharon Shear-Yashuv, Chaplain of the Technion-Israel Institute of Technology. A former German Christian, Dr. Shear-Yashuv converted to Judaism and became an Orthodox rabbi.

18. A Rosh Hashanah greeting card, c. 1917.

לְשָׁנָה טוֹבָה תִּכָּתֵבוּ
A happy
New-Year

וְתַשְׁלִיךְ בִּמְצֻלוֹת יָם כָּל חַטֹּאתָם

◄**545**► Did peace reign immediately after David's succession to the throne? No, Abner, commander of the army under Saul, had crowned Saul's son Ish-Bosheth king, and for seven years David's forces and Abner's fought to achieve supremacy. Ish-Bosheth was finally murdered by two of his servants, who hoped by their deed to win David's favor, but instead he had them killed for their act.

◄**546**► Why did David decide to make Jerusalem, rather than Hebron, the capital? Hebron, he felt, was too isolated and too far south. Jerusalem was then in Canaanite hands and acted as a dividing line between Israel's northern and southern tribes, something that David would not tolerate.

◄**547**► After David's soldiers attacked Jerusalem, which spot was the last to fall? Mount Zion, and that is where David chose to build his permanent home. The city was not only a stronghold but also a vital junction on the road from the south to Damascus and the north, and from the Jordan River to the mighty Mediterranean.

◄**548**► Who tried to destroy David soon after Jerusalem was captured? The Philistines, who had been harassing and battling against the Israelites for nearly a century. David's victory over them was the final, crushing blow that put an end to their incessant warfare. At that time, the Jewish kingdom was safe and secure and stretched from the Euphrates, near where Abraham had been born, to the Mediterranean.

◄**549**► An era of peace was now to begin. What did David compose that has come down to us as some of the most beautiful literature of mankind? The Psalms, which tradition says he wrote while he watched over his flocks, an activity that he enjoyed between his royal duties.

◄**550**► Whom did David look to for spiritual guidance in the early years of his reign? Nathan the prophet, who taught the king the inner meaning of the Torah.

◄**551**► How long did the ark containing the Ten Commandments remain in the care of a Levite family before it was brought to Jerusalem in a procession filled with dancing and shofar blowing? Twenty years, during which it was secreted in a small village, its hiding place known only to a trusted few.

◄**552**► What motivated David to aspire to build a splendid edifice to house the ark? He told Nathan, his religious mentor, that it troubled him to see that while he lived in a comfortable palace, the ark was kept in a tent on Mount Zion. Nathan advised him to proceed with his plans to acquire the beautiful cedars from Lebanon and to build a temple.

◄**553**► Did David then construct the first Holy Temple? No. Nathan had a vision from God, who said it would not be David, a man of war who had shed blood, but his son who would succeed him who would be privileged to build the temple.

◄**554**► Who accused David of committing a terrible crime in sending Uriah, husband of the beautiful Bathsheba, to his death so that he could marry her? Nathan, who then, seeing David's confession of guilt and remorse, helped him to pray for repentance and forgiveness.

◄**555**► Who was David's favorite son, and why was he exiled? Absalom; he was banished after it was established that he killed his half brother, Amnon, in a quarrel. Later, Absalom sought to wrest the kingdom from his father in battle but failed and was killed, causing the king to grieve bitterly.

◄556► How long did David reign? For forty years, thirty-three of them in Jerusalem. At the age of seventy, he became ill, and knowing that death was near, promised to appoint his son Solomon (son of Bathsheba) his successor.

◄557► Who helped put Solomon on the throne, which was coveted by David's other sons, notably Adoniah? Nathan and Bathsheba. David, still alive, ordered Solomon anointed and proclaimed king. The people rejoiced in his choice, and from his deathbed David instructed his son to keep the commandments laid down by Moses and to walk in God's ways. David was then buried on Mount Zion, where to this day there is a tomb believed to be that of the great king.

◄558► What was the first thing Solomon did upon assuming the throne? He offered a sacrifice and pleaded with God for divine guidance and help in knowing the difference between good and evil.

◄559► Solomon set about building a Holy Temple in Jerusalem, using the cedars of Lebanon. How did the Jews succeed in transporting those huge trees to Jerusalem? They were floated along the coast strapped together like rafts to ancient Joppa (Jaffa of today), and then carried overland up into the city of Jerusalem, and finally to Mount Zion.

◄560► How many people were involved in construction of the Temple? Many thousands—thousands to cut down the cedars in Lebanon and thousands more to shape the stones needed for the temple foundation.

◄561► Copper was used in the Temple's construction. Where did it come from? Until recently, no one knew, but then it was discovered that there are extensive copper mines in Timna, just north of the Red Sea port of Elath, where the copper was actually refined. (The Timna mines are back in operation today.)

◄562► How long did it take to build the Temple? More than seven years. The Holy of Holies, a room at one end of the Temple, entered by the High Priest only on Yom Kippur, contained a golden altar surrounded by five large candelabra, also made partially of gold. The ark containing the Ten Commandments was also placed in this chamber.

◄563► How long did the Holy Temple of Solomon serve as the people's principal place of worship? For nearly four hundred years, attracting tens of thousands on Passover, Shavuoth, and Sukkoth, when the Jews brought fruits and vegetables from their harvests, and on Rosh Hashanah and Yom Kippur, when special services were conducted.

◄564► Was the Temple not in use the rest of the year? The priests supervised the sacrifices that were offered there every day, and conducted the prayers. The Levites helped by playing on harps, lyres, cymbals, and timbrels, often chanting the Psalms composed by David.

◄565► Is it true that among the many wives Solomon married one was the daughter of the Pharaoh of Egypt? Yes. He even built her a beautiful palace in Jerusalem. (Thus, King Solomon's father-in-law was the Pharaoh.)

◄566► What was one of the principal sources of wealth in Solomon's kingdom? The merchant navy, which sailed to faraway places in the Mediterranean and, through the Gulf of Aqaba, to the Red Sea and then the Indian Ocean to places still unidentified to this day. One of these was a fabled land known as Ophir. The ships returned laden with gold, silver, precious stones, and animals unknown to the Jews, such as apes and peacocks.

◄ 567 ► What did the Israelites (and the Phoenicians, who often sailed with them) bring to the rest of the world? Many things, but one of the most important was the alphabet, already in use in Israel in those days but the concept of which was still unknown in the rest of the then known world. This explains why in Hebrew the first letters are known as Aleph and Bet, which the Greeks of the time transformed into alpha, beta, and so on. (The Romans adapted their own alphabet from the Greeks, but the early Hebraic influence is still visible—just think of the word "alphabet" itself.)

◄ 568 ► Solomon was famed for his wisdom. How does the Bible reflect that? By inclusion of his book of Proverbs, whose lines still help people lead better lives today. Some of the proverbs attributed to Solomon and included in the biblical book are "A merry heart is a good medicine," "He that spares his rod hates his son," "A soft answer turns away wrath," "He that tills his ground will have plenty to eat."

◄ 569 ► Were the people entirely happy about construction of the Holy Temple? No, many felt that Solomon exploited the Israelites by using too many thousands of workers for the heavy construction required and by imposing heavy taxes. There might not have been too many complaints if it were only the Temple that he built, but Solomon also constructed many palaces for his wives, and one for himself that took thirteen years to complete. The people also objected to what they deemed foreign influences introduced by Solomon, such as widespread use of Egyptian horses and chariots. As a last straw, the people turned angry when it was learned that Solomon did not object to many of his wives' pagan customs of worshiping idols.

◄ **570** ► What was the punishment that God decided to inflict on Solomon for having strayed far from the Mosaic code? To divide the kingdom in two: with ten tribes to come under the rule of Jeroboam, and only two—Judah and Benjamin—to remain under Solomon's (and his son's) hegemony.

◄ **571** ► How long did Solomon rule, and who succeeded him? Forty years; his son Rehoboam assumed the throne at his death—which was also the signal for Jeroboam to proclaim the kingdom of Israel, an act he carried out in ancient Shechem (Nablus of today). Thus were born two kingdoms, Israel and Judah, with Rehoboam reigning over two tribes in the south and Jeroboam over ten tribes in the north.

◄ **572** ► Who was king of the northern kingdom (called Israel, where the ten tribes lived) when the pagan worship of Baal, sometimes including human sacrifice, was introduced? Ahab, who had married Jezebel, daughter of a Phoenician king, who built a temple for idol worship in Samaria.

◄ **573** ► Who cried out against Ahab and Queen Jezebel for the new turn of events? Elijah, a prophet, who warned that the kingdom would be destroyed because of the flagrant violation of the Jewish laws. Jezebel tried to kill Elijah, but he escaped into the wilderness.

◄**574**► Where did Elijah hide out? In a cave on Mount Sinai, where the Ten Commandments had been received by Moses. God spoke to Elijah, telling him to prepare Elisha to continue his prophetic teaching.

◄**575**► After Elisha and Elijah succeeded in destroying the worship of idols, what happened to Elijah? Legend has it that the aged prophet ascended to heaven in a chariot of fire pulled by horses made of fire. Thus, Elijah never really died but remains to this day ready to help those in trouble. On Passover, every Seder table has an Elijah cup set aside for the prophet, which is never touched, should he enter the house. At a circumcision, similarly, a chair is set aside for Elijah, to bless the new-born boy.

◄**576**► Which prophet warned the people that worship of pagan idols, which continued both in Israel and in Judah, would lead to exile? Isaiah, who preached that prayer and sacrifice without ethical living in the spirit of the Torah were empty gestures.

◄**577**► Did Israel ever attempt to attack its sister kingdom, Judah? Yes, Israel joined with Syria and sought but failed to capture Jerusalem. Assyria then attacked both Israel and Syria, and they withdrew. At that time, Isaiah prophesied that for its attack on Judah, and for the sinfulness of its people, the kingdom of Israel would fall.

◄**578**► How long did the Assyrians wage war against Israel? For three years; despite a brave series of battles, Samaria, capital of Israel, was taken, and the kingdom of the ten tribes of Israel was seized. Most of the Israelites were enslaved and brought back to Assyria in captivity, although small numbers found refuge in Judah. The legend of the ten lost tribes stems from this time, since the Israelites were apparently thoroughly absorbed by the Assyrians, never to be heard from again. Legends persisted for centuries that the descendants of the ten tribes were various European nations or the American Indians, but most historians discount these stories.

◄579► Which prophet foretold the fall of Jerusalem and Judah? Jeremiah. He told the people this would happen because they had abandoned the teachings of the Torah. On the ninth day of Av, after a year and a half of siege, Jerusalem fell to the armies of the Babylonians, led by King Nebuchadnezzar. The Holy Temple, which had been standing and in use for four hundred years, was destroyed. Huge numbers of Judean citizens were exiled to Babylonia, with only the very poor allowed to remain in their homes.

◄580► Who finally allowed the Judean exiles in Babylonia to return to their homes? Cyrus, whose armies had conquered Babylonia. Jeremiah, who had prophesied both the exile and return of the Judean captives, lived to see their return. He spent the latter part of his life in Egypt, where he had found refuge together with other Judeans.

◄581► Which nations in the ensuing centuries fought for hegemony over the area of Palestine, i.e., what had been Israel and the restored kingdom of Judah? Egypt, Babylonia, Persia, Greece, and then the Seleucids, a Macedonian people who had seized Syria and then turned their attention to the land held by the Jews. The chief influence in Palestine for several centuries was Hellenistic.

◄582► Who were the Hasmoneans, and what was their chief accomplishment? A family of devout Jews who led a revolt against the Greco-Syrians who were attempting to forcibly destroy the religion of the Jews. The victory of the revolt is still celebrated today as the festival of Hanukkah, which literally means "dedication" and refers to the cleansing and reconsecration of the Holy Temple.

◄583► Who were the leading spiritual leaders of this era—prior to the conquest of Judah by Rome in the year 70 C.E.—who helped formulate for Jews a religious way of life centered around the Torah and synagogue worship and study? Ezra, Nehemiah, Hillel, Shamai, and others.

◄584► Which are some of the religious laws still practiced today that trace back to the teachings of Ezra? The washing of hands and recitation of an appropriate blessing before each meal, and the reading of the Torah on Mondays and Thursdays.

◄585► Who was Simon the Just? One of the last members of the Great Assembly, a body of scribes, teachers, and learned elders who sought to bolster the observance of Jewish law. They chose to remain anonymous, since they felt they were not worthy of being recorded in the same line as the great prophets. Simon said: "The world exists upon three things: Torah, worship, and the practice of charity."

◄586► What did the members of the Great Assembly accomplish? They assembled and edited prayers, edited the sacred writings of the time, decided which Torah and prophetic portions were to be read aloud each week at religious services, and issued new commentaries on the basic biblical laws that were consonant with the era. The assembly members believed it was necessary to "build a fence around the Torah."

◄587► Which group of Jews were most adamant in resisting the inroads of Hellenistic culture? The Hassidim, or the pious ones, who preached that Greek studies and the Greek way of life were inimical to Judaism and led to evil. Despite the glamorous aspects of Greek life at the time, the Hassidim pointed to the existence of mass cruelty, large-scale poverty and ignorance, idol worship, and drunkenness. Although the ordinary Jews of the time sided with the Hassidim, many of the upper-class Jews were attracted to Hellenism, leading to a serious breach of unity among the people.

◄588► How long after the Maccabee revolt succeeded in ousting the Greco-Syrian forces did the Jewish state remain independent? Less than a century, from the year 142 B.C.E. until 70 C.E., when the Roman attack finally caused the collapse of Jewish sovereignty and the beginning of an exile that was to last nearly two millennia.

◄589► Who was Hillel? One of the great figures of this period, a rabbi of the Pharisee school who taught the Torah in a liberal, lenient manner, shunning the Sadducee interpretations, which were harsh and literal. For example, a Sadducee would say that the biblical law of an "eye for an eye" meant just that, while a Pharisee would explain the line to mean that anyone who caused a person to suffer the loss of an eye should be punished by paying adequate compensation.

◄590► What are some of the famous teachings attributed to Hillel that are still in force today? Hillel taught: "If I am not for myself, who will be for me? But if I am only for myself, what am I? And if not now, when?" "Do not separate yourself from the community. Do not judge your fellow man until you put yourself in his place." "An empty-headed man cannot be fearful of sin. An ignorant person cannot be pious. A bashful man cannot learn, and an impatient man cannot teach. Someone who is too busy with business cannot grow wise." "In a place where there are no men, strive to be a man."

◄ **591** ► What happened to the Jews after the final Roman conquest, in the year 70 C.E.? Jerusalem and the Holy Temple were destroyed (the only remaining trace of the ancient structure is the Western Wall, today the holiest place for Jews, which has remained intact for more than two thousand years and is a magnet drawing thousands of worshipers and visitors daily). Huge numbers of Jews were sold into slavery and were banished to many different parts of the then known world. A tiny number remained on the land, and their descendants stayed on for nearly two millennia. The royal family and the priests and nobles of the Jews disappeared. The only thing the Jews were left with was their faith in Judaism and their optimism that one day they would be restored to their ancient homeland.

◄ **592** ► What did the rabbis of the period do to strengthen the Jews spiritually? They arranged the prayer book (the word *Siddur,* or prayer book, really translates an "order of prayers"); they decided finally which of the sacred writings should be included in the Jewish Bible, in effect closing off any possible additions; they assembled and transcribed the Oral Law, i.e., the teachings and commentaries handed down by generations of rabbis and teachers, and called this work the Mishna. With these "weapons," the rabbis felt, the Jews were ready to face exile and oppression until such time as their banishment from their homeland came to an end.

◄ **593** ► Who was the great rabbi, a disciple of Hillel, who set up a religious academy where Torah was taught even during the darkest days of Roman persecution? Yohanan ben Zakai, whose academy was established at Yavneh, not far from Jerusalem, which became an assembly point for scholars and religious leaders.

◄ **594** ► What body did he organize which sought to supervise the people's religious life? The Sanhedrin, which devoted itself to all spiritual, cultural, and social affairs, while the Romans exercised full political control. The Sanhedrin was composed of scholars, rather than priests and nobles, and the emphasis was transformed from Temple worship to synagogue, school, and home life. Each person was taught the importance of his own responsibility in religious matters, and the essential role of continuing study was emphasized.

◄ **595** ► What were the criteria of the time in selecting rabbis? Anyone could become a rabbi so long as he was regarded by the majority of the people as being learned, wise, pious, and sincere. The most outstanding of the rabbis were selected to sit in the Sanhedrin, where matters of law were raised, discussed, and voted on, with the majority decision being laid down as the law for all. The minority opinions, however, were included in the legal tomes assembled at the time.

◄ **596** ► What were some of the rules promulgated by the Sanhedrin? The exact time for the beginning of the Sabbath and festivals, the dietary laws (*kashrut*), and rules dealing with rental of property, business ethics, the giving of charity, legal processes, and a host more. Typical of the regulations handed down were: If a person hires workmen, he does not have the right to compel early-morning or late-evening labor if it is contrary to local custom. If someone rents a house in the rainy season, he may not evict the tenant between Sukkoth (October) and Passover (April) and must give the tenant thirty days' notice during the summer period. A shop that is rented out requires a full year's notice before the tenant must vacate, and if it is a shop occupied by a baker or a dyer, the notice time required is three years.

◄597► Which of the great rabbis of the period was best known as a speaker? Rabbi Meir, who interspersed his talks with fables that delighted his audiences. He is also known because of his wife, Bruriah, one of the few women scholars whose opinions and judgments were widely respected.

◄598► Who was Judah Ha-Nassi, or Judah the Prince? The last of the teachers of the Mishna, who were known as the *Tanaim* and wrote down and edited the Mishna, consisting of more than six hundred years of Oral Law, and organized this material into one orderly work, a monumental task in which he was aided by many rabbinical colleagues. He was also active in pressing the use of Hebrew as the language of the day which had been supplanted by Aramaic, in use for nearly a half millennium.

◄599► Who was Bar Kochba? Despite the destruction of the Temple and Jerusalem by the Romans, the Jews did not readily give up their fight for independence. Bar Kochba, aided by the famous Rabbi Akiva, was a military leader who in the year 132 c.e. led a rebellion against the Romans, in which nearly all the Jews in the country joined. For a while, the Jews, including the saintly Rabbi Akiva, thought Bar Kochba was the long-awaited Messiah, but his acts of cruelty soon disenchanted them. Bar Kochba was eventually crushed by the Romans, who for a while made the practice of Judaism an act punishable by immediate execution; later, they relented, and the Jews continued to live under the Roman yoke while continuing their spiritual and religious life as Jews.

◄ 600 ► Before the final canonization of the Jewish Bible, which of the sacred books were opposed by some rabbis, and on what grounds? The books challenged were the Song of Songs (it was considered out of place, since it was a love-oriented work), the Book of Esther (which recounts the story of Purim, because it does not once mention the name of God), Ezekiel (it contradicts some of the mores listed in other biblical works), and Koheleth (Ecclesiastes), because it was regarded as being too cynical and not in the spirit of Judaism, which maintains an affirmative, positive view of life.

◄ 601 ► What is the Apocrypha? Popular works of the time that were excluded by the rabbis because they felt that they contained an excess of non-Jewish influence. Among the works found in the Apocrypha are the two volume Books of the Maccabees, which recount the Hanukkah story. The rabbis, it is explained, opposed their inclusion in the Bible because they glorified war and the descendants of the Hasmoneans, who after their glorious cleansing of the Temple set out on a path of conquest and succumbed to non-Jewish influence.

◄ 602 ► Why did Jews living in exile begin to extend the Jewish holidays by an extra day? There were at the time no accurate ways of determining the exact dates, and they observed an extra day in order to be sure that they were not violating a sacred day. Yom Kippur, however, was a fast day, and it remained a one-day holiday, since a forty-eight-hour fast would have been unreasonable.

◄603► The synagogue as we know it today was developed largely during the period of the early years of exile. What are some of the basic components of the synagogue that date to this time? The Holy Ark, containing the Scroll of the Law, or the Torah; the ner tamid, or eternal light; the menorah, or seven-branched candelabrum; the bimah, or raised platform from which the service is conducted and the Torah is read.

◄604► Who instituted the colorful manner in which the Torah is removed from the Ark for the reading and its formalized return to the Ark? The rite was established by Ezra and Nehemiah.

◄605► What is the origin of the *minyan,* the quorum of ten males needed for a full-fledged service? It traditionally is attributed to the biblical injunction in which the Israelites were divided into ten-family units to facilitate governance and administration.

◄606► One of the principal features of the Jewish community, carefully regulated throughout centuries of exile, has been the observance of dietary laws. Were these instituted primarily for health reasons, as some maintain? No, the main objective behind the laws was to turn every meal into a mini-religious experience, i.e., the meal was to begin with a blessing, conclude with grace, and be restricted to foods that were considered biblically and talmudically pure. (The word *kosher* literally means "fit.") Some modern interpreters have tried to rationalize the laws by pointing out that the foods permitted are salutary and those banned are usually of dubious health value.

◄**607**► After the Romans destroyed Jerusalem and exiled the Jews, did Rome then become the main center of Jewish life? No. From about 200 to 500 C.E., the chief Jewish center was Babylonia. Scholars and rabbis had a free hand to teach, and important Jewish literary works were produced, the greatest of these being the Babylonian Talmud, comprising the existing Mishna and still another body of Oral Law—the Gemarah—which sought to explain and interpret the Mishna. Since the year 500, the Talmud has become, together with the Bible, the principal source of Jewish law and lore, and is of course studied avidly today in thousands of Jewish religious and educational institutions in all parts of the free world.

◄**608**► During the time the Jews lived in Babylonia, were they subject to persecution? By and large, no. They retained almost a government within a government, supervising their own religious and most civil laws, while giving political allegiance to the Babylonian authorities. The Jewish community in Babylonia actually waxed strong while the vestiges of the Jewish community in Palestine continued to wane. Indeed, after a while many Babylonian Jews came to believe that their flourishing centers of Jewish study were more important than a return to political rule over the ancient homeland.

◄**609**► Which were the most famous centers of learning in Babylonia? The academies of Sura and Pumbedeitha. Learning was so widespread in the Jewish community that many people studied in the early hours of the morning and in the late-evening hours, doing their daily tasks during the day. Twice yearly, during the months of Adar and Elul (usually March and August), thousands took a whole month off from work to attend a *kalah,* a retreat, and devote full time to Torah and Talmud study.

◄**610**► Who was the Resh Galuta, in Babylonia? A "Prince of the Captivity," recognized by the government as the leader of the Jewish community, descended from the Davidic line, who was supported by voluntary taxation by the Jews and who appointed judges and communal officers. Since the vast majority of the people of Babylonia at the time were idolatrous, subject to a tyrannical ruler, there was very little contact between them and the Jews in the country. Occasionally, there were conflicts between the religious leaders and the Resh Galuta, but these were usually settled without too much trouble. The independence of the scholars, and the emergence of a large mass of educated and devout Jews with strong intellectual inclinations, became the pattern of the Jewish communities that were to be established in other countries in succeeding centuries of exile.

◄**611**► Since the Talmud played such an important role in Jewish life, how does one distinguish between the earlier Mishna and the later Gemara? Basically, the Mishna, written in simple Hebrew, usually gave final decisions in matters of interpretation. The Gemara, on the other hand, done in a mixture of Hebrew and Aramaic, encompassed everything a commentator had to say on a given point, including often the students' comments, questions, stories, arguments, and the like. Thus, the thrust of Gemara scholarship was to delve into the reason for a specific ruling, analyzing the reasoning behind it, and thus to make the observance of laws more acceptable to thinking, logical people. On a typical Talmud page, therefore, one might see one lone sentence from the Mishna, surrounded by scores or even hundreds of lines of explication.

◄ **612** ► How many scholars were involved in the material included in the Talmud? About two thousand, whose ideas took some six hundred years to develop and crystallize, and whose works took about one hundred years to transcribe. The Talmud, in large folio and small print, contains some three thousand pages, with a few million words, and is really an encyclopedic compendium of Jewish life, as it touches on health, medicine, law, ethics, religious practice, history, biography, astronomy, biology, charity— almost the same spectrum of human knowledge that is taught in a modern university.

◄ **613** ► After completion of the Talmud in Babylonia in the sixth century, how long did that ancient Jewish community continue to be the principal Jewish center in the world? For about five hundred years, until the year 1,000. At that time, Islam was in the ascendancy, and Moslem science and culture had a marked influence on the Jews of the time, attenuating their exclusive interest in Jewish studies. By and large, Jews in Moslem countries were well treated, and Jewish communities sprang up in North Africa and Spain.

◄ **614** ► Which Jewish sect arose that threatened the unity of the Jews, and who fought them? The Karaites, a group that wanted to cancel out all laws emanating from the Talmud and to obey only those laws found in the Bible. Saadyah Gaon, one of the leading Babylonian scholars, opposed them and eventually persuaded the majority of the Jewish people that adherence to the literal interpretation of the Bible and discarding the Talmudic interpretations was wrong. (The Karaite sect, which at one time numbered in the scores of thousands, is believed to total about 10,000 today, most of whom live in Israel and many of whom are gradually learning to accept the wider interpretation of religious law of the majority of the Jews.)

◄**615**► Who were the *paitanim?* Jewish religious poets who, under the influence of the Moslems, began to write liturgical poems, many of which are still in use in the High Holy Days *mahzor,* or prayer book. The poems, extolling God, are known as *piyutim.*

◄**616**► What is the Midrash? A literature of stories, legends, fables, that seeks to interpret the Bible through poetry or axioms. For example, when Ecclesiastes says that God "made everything beautiful in its time," the Midrash explains that the world was created "in its due time—it was not fit to be created before then." The Midrash began as oral literature, in the form of sermons and stories recounted by preachers, until it, too, was finally transcribed.

◄**617**► Besides his successful battle with the Karaites, what else is Saadyah Gaon noted for? As the leader of the famous academy of Sura, in Babylonia, in the tenth century, Saadyah mastered not only the Bible and the Talmud but also the new Moslem sciences and Arabic, since he wanted to be in a position to guide the Jews and was cognizant of the strong forces tugging at the Jews' traditional beliefs. He wrote a Hebrew-Arabic dictionary, an Arabic translation of the Bible, a Hebrew grammar, an outline of a method of determining the Jewish calendar, and many responsa, or answers to questions on Jewish law. Whatever he did, he intended to help guide those Jews who, in his own words, "entertain impure beliefs and unclear ideas."

◄618► Where did the Jewish center develop after the decline of Babylonia? Spain, which in the ninth century began to emerge as a thriving seat of Jewish learning and life.

◄619► Where were the principal Jewish centers by the year 1200? In Europe, principally in Spain, Germany, France, and Italy, and also in North Africa. The European countries in which the Jews now lived were all Christian, and most Jews were restricted to ghettoes—a situation that was to prevail until the French Revolution, in 1789.

◄620► How did the Jewish centers of Spain and North Africa differ from those in Europe? Under Moslem rule, which venerated science and culture, the Jews thrived, producing important works of philosophy, science, poetry, and grammar. In the Italian, French, and German environments, the Jews were surrounded by people uninterested in any intellectual pursuits and generally hostile to any outsiders among them, including the Jews.

◄621► Who were some of the great personalities produced in Spain in that period? Judah Ha-Levi, Maimonides, Solomon Ibn Gabirol, Abraham Ibn Ezra, Moses Ibn Ezra, Judah Alharizi.

◄622► Who was called the "bridge" between Babylonia and Europe? Rabbi Gershom Ben Yehudah, who was born in France in 960, later moving to Germany, where he established an academy that attracted students from Jewish communities in France, Germany, and Italy. Instead of writing for religious advice to the waning center in Babylonia, Jews began to turn to Rabbi Gershom for guidance. One of his students became the teacher of the greatest biblical and talmudic commentator of all times, Rashi, who lived in France.

◄ **623** ► What was the background behind Gershom's ruling outlawing polygamy among Jews in Europe? Although in fact few Jews practiced polygamy, despite its being officially permissible, it was well-entrenched among Jews in the Moslem countries, where it was the norm. The Christian countries in which Jews now lived explained their opposition to the Jews on the grounds that they were "Oriental" and practiced such dated codes of behavior as polygamy. Rabbi Gershom therefore issued an edict banning polygamy, to help negate this anti-Jewish argument.

◄ **624** ► What other innovations was Gershom noted for? He issued *takkanot* or improvements in Jewish life, such as rulings that a woman could not be divorced without her consent, that opening other people's mail was a criminal offense, and that a copyist (this was before the onset of printing) was not permitted to alter the manuscript he was copying.

◄ **625** ► Why was Gershom referred to as "Meor ha-Golah"? Widely revered and loved, he was cited as the "Light of the Exile" for his understanding attitude toward the difficult lives of the Jews of the time. He pioneered the leadership of European Jewish scholarship and religious leadership.

◄ **626** ► Why was Rashi (an acronym for *Rabbi Shlomo Yithaki*) so highly regarded, his influence still being felt in our day? A leading scholar and a saintly person, he established an academy in his birthplace, Troyes, in France (where he earned a livelihood as a vintner); he is best known for his lucid, logical explanations of even the most unclear passages in the Bible and the Talmud. His commentary on the Bible, intended for the layman, remains to this day a model of clarity. He stressed the *p'shat,* or simple method of explanation, and sometimes resorted to the *drash* method, which was more symbolic or poetic.

◄ **627** ► Judah Ha-Levi is best known today as a poet of diverse talents. What other work is he best known for? His book *Kuzari,* addressed to a king in the Khazar kingdom, in southern Russia, who was said to be considering choosing one of the three monotheistic religions—Judaism, Christianity, and Islam—for his people. His book sought to show the king that selecting Judaism would be the wisest course, since, *inter alia,* it was the mother faith of the other two religions.

◄ **628** ► What was the chief thrust of his poetry—which ranged from religious to love themes, from poems of nature to verses hailing friendship, beauty, nature, and pure enjoyment—in the latter years of his life? He wrote extensively of the Jews' incessant yearning for a return to their ancestral homeland. At fifty-five, he set out for Jerusalem despite warnings by his friends of the great dangers involved. He died while in Jerusalem, kissing the hallowed soil, when an Arab horseman deliberately trampled him.

◄ **629** ► It has been said that from "Moses unto Moses none has risen like Moses," referring to Moses the lawgiver and Moses the son of Maimon, better known as Maimonides. Why was he singled out for so great an honor? Born in the twelfth century, Maimonides left Spain, spent some years in North Africa and Palestine, and finally settled in Egypt, where the Jewish community named him Nagid, literally prince, to lead them. He was a brilliant physician, philosopher, and commentator, who did not hesitate to tackle the problems confronting many Jews of the day. Among these was the conflict between Judaism and science, which he strove to resolve by writing a work called

Guide to the Perplexed, which he addressed to scholars and thinkers "whose studies may have brought them into conflict with religion." Defending Judaism as a religion that was philosophically sound and logical, he stressed that, for those who really understand religion and philosophy, there is no contradiction between the two.

◄ **630** ► What are the other works Maimonides is best known for? The *Maor,* or "Light," a commentary on the Mishna, and *Mishneh Torah,* a codification of all Jewish laws assembled from the Bible, the Talmud, and the responsa literature, enabling everyone to easily find answers to the gamut of religious questions. The closing hymn of the Sabbath-eve service, *Yigdal,* is a poetic version of his Thirteen Principles of Faith, which remain a basic set of tenets for observant Jews.

◄ **631** ► What is the background of his famous letter to the Jews of Yemen? In the twelfth century, the isolated Jewish community of that faraway country was not only suffering a new wave of oppression but was being subjected to pressure to convert to the dominant, Moslem faith. Many Jews were confused, some believing that Mohammed was a figure prophesied about in the Bible, and others half believing stories of a Messiah who would soon come to their rescue, destroying their enemies and returning them to Palestine. The Jews turned to Maimonides for guidance, and he wrote them that they should strive to retain their Jewish faith, and if they could not do so, they should abandon their homes and go elsewhere. He scoffed at the stories that Mohammed was foreseen in the Bible, as "ridiculous" and urged the Jewish community to shun false Messiahs, astrology, and superstition, and to hold strong to their ancient faith.

◄ **632** ► What was the lot of the Jews in Christian Europe at the time of the Crusades, from the twelfth to the fourteenth centuries? Persecution, massacres, humiliation, and exile hounded the Jewish communities during this period. The Jews became pawns in the great battles for power and religious supremacy that characterized the era. Were it not for a number of outstanding Jewish leaders, many doubt that they could have survived.

◄ **633** ► What other phenomenon took place in Europe in the medieval period that shook the roots of the Jewish community? There was a virtual outbreak of false Messiahs, who preyed on the hopes of the Jews and caused untold suffering and grief.

◄ **634** ► What other factors led the Jews to survive the terrible years of the Dark Ages in Europe? The fact that the Christian countries were not united but were relatively small principalities and kingdoms enabled the Jews to stay afloat in a sea of madness and cruelty. Many Jews chose to remain in their walled-in ghettoes, while others fled from one location to another, seeking safety.

◄ **635** ► Why did so many Jews in medieval Europe become moneylenders, a profession that only helped to exacerbate the anti-Semitic feelings of the masses of poor people? In addition to being forced to reside only in ghettoes, the Jews were ordered to be in their homes by certain curfew hours, and later they were not allowed to own land or engage in commerce or pursue a craft. The only way they could earn a living was through moneylending.

◄ **636** ► Was the Church involved in this policy of excluding the Jews from most vocations? Yes, the Church authorities of the time wished to single out the Jews as being members of a low caste and followers of a false faith, and since moneylending was prohibited to Christians, they were able to point to the Jews as ignoble people pursuing an ignoble course.

◄ **637** ► Did the Church authorities encourage anti-Semitism? Unfortunately, large segments did. They wanted to bolster their own strength among the people and labeled the Jews associates of the devil, and openly or covertly encouraged frequent attacks on individual Jews or organized communities.

◄ **638** ► When and where were there mass expulsions of Jews? England, 1290; Spain and Portugal, 1492; France, 1182, 1322, 1420; Germany, 1388, 1416, 1439, 1614, 1648; Italy, 1521, 1550, 1558, 1593, 1597; Lithuania, 1495.

◄ **639** ► Did Jews ever have to wear a "badge of shame"? Yes, by papal decree in 1215, Jews were required to be branded by wearing a yellow badge whenever they left the ghetto, so that Christians could shun them, or insult or humiliate them. In some localities, they were forced to don a conical cap, indicating their alliance with the devil. The yellow Star of David was reintroduced in the 1930s during the Nazi era.

◄ **640** ► How else did the Jews find themselves subject to oppressive conditions? They were accused of killing Christian children to obtain their blood for use in the baking of *matza* for Passover—the most bizarre of accusations in view of the entrenched Jewish ban on consuming animal blood, not to speak of human blood. (This blood libel has cropped up right through the centuries, including the twentieth.)

◄ **641** ► What was the purpose of Christian preachers inviting themselves to synagogue services to talk to the Jews? They came to harangue the Jews about their refusal to convert to Christianity, often ending their talks with dire warnings of what would befall them if they did not give up their Judaism.

◄ **642** ► What happened to the Jews during the period of the bubonic plague (known as the "Black Death"), in which hundreds of thousands, Jews among them, perished? Jews were accused of being responsible for the catastrophe by poisoning the water wells. Massacres erupted, killing thousands of Jews, especially in Germany, where a major part of the Jewish population was wiped out by crazed mobs.

◄ **643** ► What was the practice of *pidyon shevuyim*, which developed in this era? The term means ransom of captives. Jews always felt a strong sense of kinship and responsibility for one another. Often, a Jew or a group of Jews would be kidnaped and held for ransom by highwaymen on land or pirates at sea, and sometimes even by a local ruler. No matter how poor, Jewish communities could be counted on to help raise the ransom needed for their release. The Jews did not necessarily know each other—so long as they were imprisoned for no reason other than ransom, they were helped by their fellow Jews.

◄ **644** ► Did Jews of that period already have communal institutions to aid the ill and poor? Yes, they began as extensions of the fundamental Jewish religious laws and eventually became formalized communal bodies, the forerunners of modern social-service agencies.

◄ **645** ► Who were among the chief spiritual leaders who helped the Jews to carry on despite what often appeared to be insurmountable obstacles? Nahmanides, also known as Ramban, chief rabbi of Catalonia, in Spain, the country's greatest talmudic authority. He was a staunch traditionalist, unafraid to face Christian adversaries in public debate, and something of a mystic. At seventy, his enemies forced the king to exile him, and he spent his final years in Palestine, trying to revive the small Jewish community. Another great personality was Rabbi Meir of Rothenburg, who continued the tradition of academy teaching and wrote numerous responsa. Both died in the thirteenth century.

◄ **646** ► Were there others? Yes. Isaac Abravanel, in the fifteenth century, had to flee persecution, proceeding from Portugal to Spain, Sicily, Corfu, Naples, and Venice. He was a great scholar, at home in Jewish studies, especially the Bible, as well as in the secular world. Claiming descent from David, he acted as his people's spokesman, and among others sought out Marranos (Jews who practiced their faith in secret but outwardly pretended to be Christians). Isaac Luria, a mystic who lived in the sixteenth century, convinced people and himself that he was in touch with Elijah the prophet, and concentrated his study on the Kabbalah, or Jewish mysticism. Another sixteenth-century great was Joseph Caro, who wrote the basic code of Jewish laws, the *Shulhan Aruch,* and like his teacher, Isaac Luria, known as the Ari, was also a mystic.

◄ **647** ► Who was the most outstanding of the false Messiahs? Shabbetai Tzvi, who lived in Turkey and in 1648 proclaimed himself the Messiah. His fellow Jews expelled him from the community, but he began to wander about with a few followers. Gradually, he won over larger and larger numbers of people to his preachings, causing Jewish communities to become frenzied masses when he entered a given locality. Thousands of Jews sold their belongings, packed, and made ready for the Messiah-led return to the Holy Land. Then the Turkish sultan imprisoned him and offered him his life on condition that he convert to Islam. He accepted the offer, causing the entire Jewish community to sink into a deep depression. Although some refused to believe ill of him, most Jews sadly concluded that they had been duped by a charlatan.

◄ **648** ► What did the Jews conclude after this strange episode? That their true hopes for redemption lay not in self-proclaimed Messiahs or in excessive dependence on mysticism but, rather, in study, work, and faith. (Most Jewish communities at the time, in shock and anger, excommunicated Shabbetai Tzvi, who is said to have spent his declining years as a doorkeeper to the sultan.)

◄ **649** ► Late in the sixteenth century, where did Jews find hope of a peaceful life? First in Holland, whose people rebelled against the Spanish masters who governed them, later in Denmark, and finally in England, to which the Jews were allowed to return after a hiatus of four hundred years of exile. The Dutch and English Jewish communities thrived and simultaneously continued to remain steadfast in their religious practices and faith.

◄ **650** ► When did Jews first begin to settle in Eastern Europe, notably in Poland? In the thirteenth century, at the invitation of the Polish kings and nobles, who wanted their help in transforming their agricultural country into one that would also have a base of commerce and finance. By 1264, Jews were granted a charter to become craftsmen, mer-

chants, tradesmen, and tax collectors on the large estates
owned by the noble families.

◄ **651** ► Why, then, did troubles arise in Poland?
Some Christians had also become merchants and resented
the Jews' competition. The agricultural classes, most of
whom were virtual serfs, resented the huge taxes imposed
by their Polish-noble masters and vented their anger on the
Jewish tax collectors. Some Christian priests preached anti-
Semitic sermons, stirring up the masses. In time, riots broke
out and Jewish blood was shed on Polish soil.

◄ **652** ► How did the Jews survive? Up until the
seventeenth century, when the Polish nobility was in complete charge of the country, they accorded their Jewish subjects protection. The Jewish population increased substantially, largely because the Jews believed in early marriage
and large families. In 1551, the Jews in Poland—as in
Babylonia—had what amounted to a government within a
government: they elected communal officials, collected
taxes, supervised policing and health programs, maintained
courts and schools, and dealt with local criminals. Each
community had its own *kehilla* or Jewish community,
which in turn belonged to a council for the whole country,
which based its rules and procedures on talmudic law.

◄ **653** ► Did the traditional Jewish emphasis on learning develop in Poland too? Yes; from a tender age a child
was brought to the *heder* for initial instruction, and later he
transferred to the *yeshiva,* the equivalent of the academy.
Polish cultural influence at the time was weak, so that Jews
devoted themselves to religious studies even more than in
other countries.

◄654► How did the Jews fare in 1648, when Poland was invaded by the Cossacks and Russians from the east and the Swedes from the north? All Poles suffered grievously, but the Jews suffered worst of all: in addition to fighting off the invaders, the Poles often turned on the Jews living in their midst, conducting large-scale massacres. Hundreds of thousands of Jews were murdered, and some seven hundred communities totally decimated, in that bloody period. Inspired by the Cossack leader Chmielnicki, Polish serfs, merchants, and religious zealots carried out devastating mass murders of local Jews.

◄655► What helped pull the Jews of Poland out of their despair? Despite the bloody events, Jews—especially in the southern sections of Poland, near the Carpathian Mountains—who had not had an opportunity to study and develop academies (they were simple, poor people who just managed to eke out a living), found a measure of joy in the teachings of Israel Baal Shem Tov (Master of the Good Name), a mystic who taught that joy could be found among the rituals of their faith, and learning could therefore take second place. Preaching prayer, singing, dancing, love of nature and of fellow men, the new leader founded a whole new movement, Hassidism (pietism).

◄656► What distinguished the Hassidim from other Jews? Their reverence, almost worshipful, of their own rabbi, whom they referred to as Rebbe, and a great amount of singing, dancing, enthusiastic praying, and fellowship, with very little time left for scholarship. Thus, it became a faith of the senses rather than one of the intellect, and very soon attracted large numbers of people.

◄657► What did Hassidism then do for the oppressed Jews of the time? It gave them an emotional outlet, during which they could, through song, dance, and fervent prayer, rid themselves of some of their fears and apprehensions. They found in the movement ready-made camaraderie, and left the deep thinking to the Rebbe.

◄ **658** ► Who were the *mitnagdim* (opponents)? The Jews of northern Poland and the Baltic Sea area, who looked down on the raucous, singing mobs of Hassidim as boors and who preferred to lead lives based on reason, intellect, study, and continued learning. The Vilna Gaon, who came from the Lithuanian city of the same name, was the leading figure of the movement. A child prodigy, he was delivering scholarly talks before he was seven. He not only mastered all the Jewish religious works but taught himself also mathematics, astronomy, anatomy, and other sciences.

◄ **659** ► Why was the Vilna Gaon so opposed to Hassidism? He thought the idea of coming close to God through faith, joy, and good deeds, as opposed to study, would lead to superstition and ignorance. He himself was interested in mysticism but objected to sole dependence on it. He taught that the chief goal of life was perfection of character, which could be attained only through study.

◄ **660** ► When, can it be said, did Jews enter a new era in Europe? As of the mid-eighteenth century, when a campaign for emancipation of Jews began, which would entitle them to full citizenship and equality, and when simultaneously the dawn of enlightenment signaled a broadening of Jewish life through its exposure to European culture, science, and art.

◄ **661** ► What was the role of Moses Mendelssohn in this period? Born in a German ghetto, steeped in Jewish studies, he launched a drive, as writer and philosopher, to improve the attitudes of Jews and Christians to one another. To the Jews, he said they should study modern languages, science, history; to the Christians, he urged that they treat the Jews as fellow human beings, who, he promised, would flourish if given equal opportunities.

◄662► How did he try to achieve this? First, he translated the Torah into German (he was anxious for the Jews to learn the language) and then had it printed in Hebrew letters to facilitate its study. He also published Hebrew magazines in an attempt to modernize the language and make it an everyday, spoken language. He made many Christian friends and influenced them to understand that a more liberal attitude toward Jews would be beneficial to the whole country.

◄663► Did the Jews at first welcome these efforts to bring them into closer contact with the general community? No, many feared the Enlightenment would lead to diminution of Jewish studies and practices and eventual conversion to Christianity (three of Mendelssohn's children opted to become Christians, as did large numbers of other Jews at the time).

◄664► Did the 1789 French Revolution actually give the Jews full rights? No, it took two years for the granting of full civil rights to the Jews to pass, and many more years before these laws began to be carried out in daily life. Germany, Austria, and other countries eventually followed the French precedent, but here, too, implementation of the laws took many years to be achieved. (Across the seas, in the fledgling new democracy of the United States, it was not till 1877 that all Jews in the country were given the right to hold public office.)

◄ **665** ► What was the reason for Napoleon convening a Sanhedrin in 1806–7, years after the Jews had ostensibly been granted equal rights? He wanted to know if the Jews would declare publicly their unqualified loyalty to France. The Sanhedrin co-operated with him, assuring Napoleon of the Jews' absolute loyalty as French citizens, but Napoleon showed that he was not as enlightened as he led people to believe: a Jewish merchant, he ordered, would have to prove his honesty by having two Christian merchants (his competitors) attest to his honesty. It was only in 1850 that these anti-Jewish rules were abandoned in France.

◄ **666** ► Did assimilation grow during this period? Yes, many Jews thought that the Enlightenment and emancipation did not go hand in hand with Judaism, and simply converted to the dominant faith.

◄ **667** ► When and where was the first Reform-type service held? In 1810 in Germany, organized by Israel Jacobson, who arranged for a service with a choir consisting of both men and women (a complete innovation at the time), which included some prayers recited in German as well as in Hebrew. The teachers in the affiliated school conducted the children's service and taught religious classes in German, too. Soon afterward, the Reform synagogues called themselves temples, abolished head coverings for men, permitted men and women to sit together, and did away with prayer shawls for the men.

◄ **668** ► Who was the principal leader of the Reform movement in this period? Abraham Geiger, who said that rituals and ceremonies were far less important than the prophetic teachings of social justice. He also interpreted Judaism to be an ever-changing religion influenced by the needs of human beings rather than a set of divine ordinances.

◄**669**► Who was the leader of Orthodox Jewry at the time? Samuel Raphael Hirsch, who had had a thorough secular education but insisted on retaining all the laws and traditions of Orthodox Judaism. He taught that instead of abolishing the numerous Jewish religious laws, Jews should attempt to understand them better. He urged his followers to have no contact with Reform Jews, whose innovations he termed tantamount to conversion.

◄**670**► When did the so-called middle way, known in the United States as Conservative Judaism, begin? Also in the nineteenth century, under the leadership of Zechariah Frankel, who insisted that both Reform and Orthodox approaches were wrong. He agreed that there should be changes in religious practices, but in order to ensure the continuity of the Jewish heritage, they should be gradual and minimal. He said that historical Judaism, as he chose to call his approach, was always changing and yet never actually changed. Thus, for example, he agreed that men and women could worship together but men had to continue to wear a head covering. Unlike the Reform movement, which in its early stages dissociated itself from the concept of a Jewish return to the ancient homeland, Conservative Jews, along with the Orthodox, always retained a strong bond with the idea of an eventual restoration of the Jewish people to the Holy Land. (In recent years, Reform Jews have also accepted the notion of Israel as the Jewish people's homeland.)

◄**671**► When did Jews first begin to live in Russia? In the eighteenth and nineteenth centuries, Russia (and some other countries) conquered and divided Poland; without a say in the matter, about one million Polish Jews became subjects of the czar. Russia was still a medieval country, resisting any Western influence. The Russians saw themselves as heirs of the Holy Roman Empire, and proclaimed (in official documents) that Jews in their domain were enemies of Christianity.

◄672► What was the "Pale of Settlement" in Russia? A restricted area from which Jews were not permitted to move, and even a traveler on business required a special permit. It was really a large territorial ghetto, which every few years kept shrinking, forcing the inhabitants to shift into more densely crowded communities.

◄673► How did the Jews fare, especially after the Russians freed their serfs in the nineteenth century? The Russians liberated the landless peasants, but instead of allocating land for them to work, the government turned over abandoned Jewish businesses and shops to them—which became "available" since the Jews had just recently been driven into a more restricted area of the Pale.

◄674► Why was the conscription of boys into the czarist army so feared? Every community was given a draft quota to meet, and if there were not enough eighteen-year-olds, boys as young as twelve could be taken. Sometimes, Russian officials kidnaped young Jewish boys and forcibly drafted them; at times, this was done with the co-operation of the Jewish communal authorities, who feared that if the town quota was not met, the entire community would be punished.

◄675► Once in the army, were the Jewish conscripts treated fairly? No, there was a deliberate policy of breaking their spirit as Jews. The Jewish draftees were compelled to eat forbidden foods, make the sign of the cross, and urged to convert to Christianity. Refusal to do so meant corporal punishment. Military service lasted twenty-five years, so that anyone who could evade the czarist draft did so.

◀ **676** ▶ While drafting Jews into the army, did the Russians hold back on anti-Jewish propaganda? No, they informed the masses of Russians—many of them impoverished peasants, who were often illiterate—that the Jews were "revolutionaries," "superstitious," and "refused to accept Russian culture," building up a solid wall of hatred for Jews by the Russians and deep fear of the authorities by the Jews.

◀ **677** ▶ Were the Russian schools open to Jews? For a while, there were free public schools at which Russian was supposed to be taught, but they collapsed when Jews learned their children were being proselytized. Small numbers of Jewish students were admitted to the universities, but here, too, it was soon realized that this was done so as to win new converts to Christianity.

◀ **678** ▶ How long did this harassment of its Jewish population go on, and what was behind it? For more than a century. Behind it lay Russia's fear that the Jews might be a conduit through which ideas of the French and American revolutions might enter their domain and give their people the stimulus to revolt. Jews from foreign countries were not allowed to enter Russia, even on a visit.

◀ **679** ▶ What was the infamous formula promulgated in Russia as a "solution to the Jewish problem"? In 1880, Russia let it be known that one third of all Jews in Russia were to convert to Christianity, one third were to be exiled, and the remainder killed. Government-inspired pogroms ensued, and thousands of Jews perished in horrible massacres, in which criminals joined with illiterate peasants to kill, rape, and plunder the Jews.

◄ 680 ► What notorious event took place in Moscow in 1891? All the city's Jews, some twenty thousand people, were arrested, chained, and herded into railroad cars to be shipped to the towns in the Pale to join their coreligionists. The only hope for the Jews lay in emigration, which began in earnest in 1892.

◄ 681 ► Where did the first waves of Jewish emigrants from Russia go? To the United States, Palestine, and some of the liberal Western European countries. (Later, many were also to go to Latin America, especially Argentina, which encouraged immigration.)

◄ 682 ► Was the world entirely silent during this period of overt anti-Semitic activity in Russia? No, such people as Tolstoy and Gorky spoke up against the actions of their government, and a number of countries, including the United States, and a small number of Christian leaders in the West also protested, but to no avail.

◄ 683 ► Because of the horrible conditions that prevailed in Russia for so long, is it correct to believe the Jews turned to their ancient faith for comfort and guidance? Yes, they lived a life entirely apart from the harsh reality that surrounded them, eking out bare livelihoods and finding some solace in intense study and total adherence to the minutiae of religious observance. On one level, they lived on a lifelong dream and hope that redemption was at hand and the nightmare of their brutal existence would soon end.

◄ **684** ► What movements were in ferment during this time? *Haskalah* ("enlightenment"), with a special Jewish thrust, sought to encourage the Jews to study the modern, Western culture, which, it was felt, would lead to better times. Revolutionary currents also swirled, and many Jews were caught up in the national struggle to overthrow the government and replace it with a more progressive, socialist-minded regime. Hassidism found its followers growing as it preached a deeper devotion to basic Jewish values and a complete separation from the rest of the world. Zionism developed swiftly, and the first groups of pioneering Jewish groups began to leave for settlement in the ancestral homeland.

◄ **685** ► Who were some of the great literary figures whose works helped the Jews in Russia to survive their ordeal? The three most famous in Yiddish literature were Mendele Mocher Seforim, Sholom Aleichem, and I. L. Peretz. In Hebrew letters (modern Hebrew had begun to be written and spoken) the outstanding figure was Hayyim Nahman Bialik, the leading modern Hebrew poet. Another was the essayist Ahad Haam.

◄ **686** ► What was the Jewish population in the world around 1914? Sixteen million, of whom ten million were in Eastern Europe.

◄ **687** ► How many Jews were there in the United States at the time of the Revolutionary War? About 2,500, concentrated mainly in six port cities. (A handful of Jews reached the city of New Amsterdam in 1654, where they were reluctantly given refuge by Peter Stuyvesant.)

◄ **688** ► Is it correct that the early Jewish settlers, prior to the 1850s, were mostly Sephardic Jews (originally from the Iberian Peninsula), who remained observant in their religious life in their new home? Yes. There were some four thousand Jews in the United States in 1820, and a number were singled out for praise for their help to the new government (Haym Salomon, for example). Jews took part in the American Revolution in numbers greater than their population warranted, and two Jewish officers served on George Washington's staff.

◄ **689** ► How did those early Jewish settlers see America? As a dream come true after centuries of longing for a home that afforded them freedom of religion and many political rights.

◄ **690** ► Were the synagogues of the day similar to those of today? No, they were in effect small Jewish communal organizations, providing succor to the needy as well as being centers of worship, basic study, and assembly.

◄ **691** ► What was the next major wave of Jewish immigration to reach the United States? Between 1825 and the 1880s, large numbers of German Jews and others from Central Europe arrived in America, fleeing from renewed oppression in their homelands. The Jewish population in the United States soared to 250,000 by the 1880s.

◄ **692** ► Did these Jews settle in the port cities on the Atlantic, where there were already established Jewish communities? Some did, but many were seized by the pioneering spirit of the country and the time and headed for the Midwest and Far West. Starting as backpacking peddlers, many Jews founded shops and businesses that eventually developed into major enterprises. The German Jews introduced Reform Judaism to America and also laid the foundations for various Jewish organizations (B'nai B'rith, the

American Jewish Committee, YM-YWHAs, and the like). A Reform rabbinical seminary, Hebrew Union College, was established in Cincinnati in 1875.

◄ 693 ► What about schooling for the children? Jews immediately perceived that the schools in the United States were purely educational and not centers for propagating conversion, and sent their children to the public schools; for Jewish education, a system of afternoon and Sunday schools was developed.

◄ 694 ► What was the position of the Jews during the Civil War? Those who lived in the North and those in the South fought alongside their respective compatriots. (A Baltimore rabbi, David Einhorn, had to flee to the North because of his pro-Abolition sermons. Judah Benjamin, a Jew, was named to the Cabinet of the Confederacy.)

◄ 695 ► Was there much mixing between the older, established, Sephardic community and the newcomers from Central Europe? No. Their respective rituals of observance varied, prayer books were not uniform, and the more established residents tended to stick to themselves.

◄ 696 ► Were there no manifestations of anti-Semitism in America in the nineteenth century? There were, emanating mainly from some political quarters which were not anxious to see Jews enjoying full civil rights and from some church authorities who thought that efforts to convert the Jews were the most important goals to pursue.

◄ 697 ► What finally made the disparate Jewish communities in America unite? There were a number of factors: the pogroms in Russia, a blood libel in 1840 in Damascus, the confusion that reigned in Jewish communal life over such issues as *kashrut* observance, and the lack of home-grown religious and educational leaders and materials. The need for a strong, central organization was made acute by the arrival on American shores—between 1880 and 1914—of more than three million Jews, mainly from Eastern Europe, fleeing czarist persecution.

◄ **698** ► Most Eastern European Jews in this period settled in the big cities: New York, Philadelphia, Baltimore, Chicago. How did they earn a livelihood? Mainly, they entered the needle trades, working at first in notorious sweatshops and later helping to organize labor unions that fought for decent working conditions.

◄ **699** ► Was there a great boom in the launching of Jewish communal institutions as a result of this new immigration wave from Eastern Europe? Yes. Synagogues, modest one-room classrooms, and full fledged *yeshivas* were established by the hundreds. Yiddish newspapers were launched, rabbinical seminaries were started, agencies to help the needy and the newcomers were established, and a genuine effort was made to regulate *kashrut* on a communal basis.

◄ **700** ► Did the newcomers bring over with them their loyalties to socialism, Zionism, Hebrew, *Haskalah*? Yes, there was a great ferment of activity, as numerous Jewish groups were organized, each striving to implement their respective ideals. In 1897, a Zionist organization was established. In 1901, HIAS (Hebrew Immigrant Aid Society), to help newcomers, was set up. In 1917, the first Jewish-sponsored English translation of the Bible was published.

◄ **701** ► Was this also a period of a flourishing Yiddish-language cultural life? Yes, in addition to numerous newspapers and magazines in Yiddish, the Jews of the time quickly developed an active cultural life consisting of frequent visits to Yiddish-language stage plays, some of them on a high literary level.

◄702► When was the Conservative movement started in America? Although the Jewish Theological Seminary, to train Conservative rabbis, was launched in 1897, the United Synagogue of America, comprising Conservative congregations, was established in 1913, under the leadership of Solomon Schechter.

◄703► Was there any Jewish immigration to speak of after World War I? Yes, but nowhere like the vast numbers who came before 1914. In the 1920s, new restrictive immigration laws were passed, limiting the arrival of Jews and non-Jews substantially.

◄704► When was Yeshiva University, the fountainhead of the Orthodox Jews, launched? It began as a *yeshiva* in 1915 and was expanded tremendously after the conclusion of World War II.

◄705► Have the differences among the Orthodox, Conservative, and Reform Jews tended to increase or decrease in recent years? The pattern indicates that the differences are gradually eroding, although there are still very major differences in attitude and observance between the Orthodox and the Reform. Nevertheless, during World War II, when the Jewish members of the armed forces needed a single prayer book that would bridge the gaps between them, such a volume was produced without too much difficulty.

◄706► Why did the United States not do very much to help the Jews in Germany and Austria at the time of the rise of Nazism? Hitler came to power in 1933, while America was still in the midst of a severe economic depression. Relatively small numbers of Jews were allowed to enter the United States in the 1930s, but large-scale immigration was opposed, mainly on economic grounds. The Jewish community in America, in that period, was also not as well organized or as vociferous as it is today. The true situation in Europe, i.e., the Holocaust, did not become known in America until about three years after the outbreak of the Second World War, when many felt little could be done to rescue the doomed Jews. One of the reasons for the present strong movement to aid Soviet Jews who seek to emigrate is the memory of the inadequate efforts that were made for European Jewry before and during World War II.

◄707► What effect did the Holocaust, in which six million Jews perished, representing one third of the world's Jewish population, have on American Jews? When World War II ended, in 1945, and American (and other) Jews finally learned the extent of the catastrophe that had overtaken their coreligionists in Europe, they were determined that a reconstituted Jewish homeland was urgently needed which would, at the very least, become a haven for all oppressed Jews.

◄708► In the 1930s and early 1940s especially there were organized anti-Semitic movements in the United States, including the German-American Bund, Father Coughlin's Social Justice group, and other right-wing, fanatical organizations that blatantly preached anti-Semitism. Do such groups still exist? To a far lesser extent, yes. Many of these groups have disappeared, but a number of others have surfaced, largely small, devoted to right-wing philosophies. The Ku Klux Klan, for example, continues to exist, although its influence seems to have declined.

◄ 709 ► Are most Jews fearful of these anti-Semitic movements? Mostly, Jews feel that American democracy is so strong and deeply ingrained that it is unlikely any such extremist groups could ever succeed in their goals. Nonetheless, Jews are deeply sensitive about any public displays of open anti-Semitism, and maintain a watchful eye on any such development. Jews are also especially sensitive when the media publicize the activities of a criminal whose identification is obviously Jewish. Conversely, they take great pride in the positive achievements of any Jew on the American scene, no matter how tenuous his affiliation with the Jewish community may be.

◄ 710 ► What is the present political situation of the world Jewish community? It is believed to be stable and secure in the United States, Canada, and a number of Western European countries. In Latin America, where the number of totalitarian states has proliferated, and where about eight hundred thousand Jews live, the situation is considered poor. The same is true of the Jews in South Africa, where forces beyond the Jews' control may eventually lead to large-scale emigration. Despite its Jewish population of three million, Israel is still not secure, in view of the ongoing opposition by the surrounding Arab states. The Jews in Russia, long thought to have been lost because of the suppression of religion in the Soviet Union, are now seeking to emigrate in order to join their coreligionists in Israel, the United States, and other free countries.

◄ 711 ► What other perils do Jews see on the horizon? One of the great dangers confronting the continuity of the Jewish community in the United States and other free countries is the high rate of intermarriage, which more often than not results in a loss to the Jewish community. The rate of intermarriage in the United States is about 35 per cent, and although a percentage of the partners in such marriages convert to Judaism, mostly they become disaffiliated and are gradually lost to the main body of Jewry. Jews also have a very low birth rate.

◄ **712** ► What development has taken place in American Jewry that could not have been foreseen a generation ago? The resurgence of a strong Orthodox movement, with a concomitant growth in intensive Jewish education and religious life. Fully 25 per cent of all Jewish youngsters now receiving a Jewish religious education do so in an all-day school, compared to a scant 2 or 3 per cent about twenty-five years ago. Such groups as the Association of Orthodox Jewish Scientists have evolved, producing a situation in which American Jews opt to lead traditional Orthodox religious lives while at the same time pursuing careers in advanced scientific fields.

◄ **713** ► What about the problem of young Jews, mainly from irreligious homes, who have become members of Eastern cults or followers of esoteric quasi-religious groups? This development has led to much breast-beating on the part of Jews, most of whom blame themselves for not having given their young people a solid Jewish religious base. Most console themselves, however, by pointing to the relatively small numbers of Jews involved with such groups.

◄ **714** ► Is there much immigration of American Jews to Israel? Not really. Although the American Jewish community has continued to furnish massive amounts of financial support to Israel, the number of U. S. Jews who have chosen to settle in Israel is still relatively small. Interestingly, many of the more recent American Jewish settlers in Israel have come from the ranks of the Orthodox, who see in Israel an opportunity to lead fully religious lives with little danger of their children or grandchildren succumbing to the dangers of intermarriage and subsequent assimilation.

◄715► What is the current Jewish population of the United States? About five and three quarter million Jews, divided roughly as follows among the major denominations: one million Reform Jews, one and a quarter million Conservative, and an estimated one or one and a half million Orthodox. The others are not affiliated with a religious institution, although many belong to secular Jewish organizations.

Chapter 10

WHO? WHAT? WHERE?
WHEN? WHY?

"Inquiry is man's finest quality."

—SOLOMON IBN GABIROL

◀716▶ Where and when was the first Jewish community established in the Western Hemisphere? In Bahia, Brazil, in 1624.

◀717▶ What percentage of American Jews reside in the large metropolitan centers? 95 per cent.

◀718▶ What is the meaning of the word *knesset,* the name of the Israel parliament? Literally, "assembly," similar to the term for a synagogue, *bet knesset,* or "house of assembly."

◀719▶ What is the Yad va Shem? The memorial building, erected in Jerusalem, for the Six Million, i.e., the Jews in Europe who were murdered during the Nazi regime.

◀720▶ Who was Francis Salvador? The first Jew in the United States to hold elective office. He was a member of the Provincial Assembly of South Carolina.

◀721▶ Who was Louis D. Brandeis? The first Jewish justice of the Supreme Court. He was an outstanding lawyer, defender of the early labor movement, and one of the founders of the Zionist movement in America.

◀722▶ Who was the first Jew ever appointed to the U. S. Cabinet? Oscar Straus; in 1906 he was named Secretary of Commerce and Labor (then a joint office) by President Theodore Roosevelt.

◀**723**▶ What is a *mahzor?* A prayer book for the High Holy Days, i.e., Rosh Hashanah and Yom Kippur. There are also special festival prayer books, in use especially among the Orthodox Jews, that are also called *mahzorim.*

◀**724**▶ What is the custom of inserting slips of paper into the crevices of the Western Wall? People traditionally write down a hope or wish, and add the inscribed note to the tens of thousands of similar slips placed into the wall in past centuries.

◀**725**▶ When did the Hebrew University first open its doors? In 1925. Construction had begun in 1918. (The oldest university in Israel, however, is the Technion—Israel Institute of Technology, in Haifa, opened in 1924.)

◀**726**▶ What is an *Am ha-Aretz?* Literally, "a person of the soil" (ignoramus). The term is a pejorative applied to Jews who not only do not have access to learning but who adamantly refuse to study Jewish law and lore.

◀**727**▶ What is a *bet midrash?* Literally, a house of study. It is applied to the synagogue, since study is one of the three principal functions of the synagogue: *bet midrash,* house of study; *bet tefilah,* house of prayer; and *bet knesset,* house of assembly. In the European *shtetl,* husbands would often spend long hours poring over a talmudic tractate in the *bet midrash* while the wives eked out a living.

◀**728**▶ What were the *Bet Hillel* and *Bet Shamai?* Two schools of thought, named respectively for Hillel and

Shamai, who lived in the first century C.E. and held diametrically opposite views on some three hundred legal interpretations. Mostly, Shamai and his disciples interpreted the laws and the rabbinic decisions rather harshly, while Hillel and his followers were known for their lenient attitude; on the other hand, sometimes Hillel's views were far more stringent than Shamai's.

◄ **729** ► What is a *keter Torah?* Literally, a crown of the Torah. A crown, often made of silver, that is placed on top of the Scroll of the Torah, especially when the rabbi, cantor, and others carry the Scrolls through the synagogue, prior to and immediately following the traditional Sabbath or holiday reading of the prescribed scriptural passage. The *keter* is generally a work of artistic craftsmanship.

◄ **730** ► What's a *nedavah?* A donation, usually intended for a synagogue, a charitable or religious institution, or for the poor. Customarily, at daily services in the synagogue an alms pitcher is placed at the exit door, into which worshipers drop some coins. It is also traditional for the mother of the household, just before kindling the Sabbath-eve candles, to deposit a few coins into a *pushka,* or charity canister.

◄ **731** ► What is a *mezuzah?* A cylindrical housing, about one half inch or less wide and three to four inches high, containing the first two paragraphs from the *Shma Yisrael* prayer, inscribed on parchment. On the back of the tightly rolled parchment the word *Shadai,* or God, appears (in Hebrew letters) and shows through a small opening in the case. The mezuzah is traditionally affixed to the right doorpost (upon entering), is positioned at an angle, and is in keeping with the biblical command to "write them [God's words] on the doorpost" of the Jewish home.

Many Orthodox Jews will touch the mezuzah with their fingertips upon entering and leaving, and then lightly kiss their fingers.

◄ 732 ► What is the concept of reciting the *gomel* prayer, sometimes referred to as *"bentshing gomel"?* When a person has survived a perilous journey or has been restored to good health after a serious illness or has escaped safely from an accident, it is traditional for him to be called to the Torah on the next Sabbath to offer a special prayer of thanksgiving. This is called the *gomel*.

◄ 733 ► What is a *golem?* In the Bible, the term meant an embryo or shapeless mass. Later, it took on the meaning of a robot or mechanical creature controlled by an outside force. During the medieval period in Europe especially, superstitious Jews believed that such a creation could, with divine guidance, rescue them from oppressors. The legend of the Golem of Prague is the best known of these stories. The word *golem* today, however, indicates a boor.

◄ 734 ► What is a *sandak?* A godfather, the designation usually given to the man upon whose knees an infant boy rests while the rite of circumcision is performed. The honor is normally accorded to a grandfather.

◄ 735 ► What is the *motzi* blessing? The traditional blessing on bread (or *hallah* on Sabbath or holidays), recited at the beginning of a meal, and usually included in most communal meals, both private (wedding receptions and the like) and public, when the honor is given to an individual known to be observant.

◄ 736 ► What is *kaddish?* The mourner's prayer, recited by a son for a departed parent (among some Conservative and Reform congregations, daughters also recite the prayer) during the year following the individual's death. (There is also a non-mourner's *kaddish* prayer, intoned by the cantor, which is part of the service.)

◄**737**► What is *yahrzeit?* The anniversary of the death of an immediate member of the family is observed by reciting *kaddish* on that day at the evening, morning, and afternoon services. On Yom Kippur, and on Passover, Shavuoth, and Shemini Atzeret (the eighth day of the Sukkoth holiday), there are special *yizkor,* or memorial, sections added to the service when everyone who has ever suffered a personal loss is expected to participate in a public, communal prayer for the departed.

◄**738**► What's a *yahrzeit* lamp? A wax-filled glass with a wick that burns for a little over twenty-four hours; it is traditionally lit during the day of a private *yahrzeit* memorial, and it is also lit just prior to Yom Kippur eve.

◄**739**► What is *kiddush?* The special blessing on wine recited on Sabbath and holiday evenings. Depending on the holiday, there are slight variations in the wording and also in the melody. *Kiddush* is also recited in the *havdalah* ceremony, ushering out the Sabbath, on Saturday evening.

◄**740**► What is the Kabbalah? The term today is used to refer to Jewish mysticism, dating from the twelfth century and still fiercely believed in by some Hassidic groups. It has long been a subject of scholarly study. The city of Safed, in Israel, has through the centuries come to be known as a center of Jewish mysticism, where the movement's principal work, the *Zohar,* was studied avidly for many centuries.

◄ **741** ► What is a *nusah?* A particular form (of synagogue worship or prayer-book contents). There are, thus, an Ashkenazi and a Sephardi (and other) rites. The word is also used to refer to cantorial styles.

◄ **742** ► What does the term *hefker* mean? Property that seems not to have a lawful owner and thus can sometimes be exempted from certain religious commands. The popular usage of the term today connotes anarchy.

◄ **743** ► Which is the oldest remaining synagogue in Europe? The Altneuschul in Prague, which dates at the least to the twelfth century.

◄ **744** ► Why is the town of Metz, France, especially remembered? It was the scene of the first attacks on Jews in the First Crusade, in 1096. A Jewish community was re-established there in the sixteenth century but was annihilated during the Nazi era. Some 3,500 Jews reside there today.

◄ **745** ► What's a *mitzvah?* A religious precept, usually translated as a good deed.

◄ **746** ► What is *gemilut hesed?* The term is usually translated to mean charity or the performance of good deeds, but Jewish law and tradition stipulate that these acts must be personal deeds, such as visiting the sick, comforting the bereaved, and the like. There is no limit, the Talmud teaches, on the amount of *gemilut hesed* that a person may perform.

◄ **747** ► What is the *modeh ani* prayer? The first words of a short prayer (the words mean "I give thanks") said upon awakening and usually taught to very small children.

◄ **748** ► What was the *musar* movement? A late-nineteenth-century ethical-behavior movement (*musar* means ethics) aimed at indoctrinating every individual in living as highly moral a life as possible.

◄ **749** ► What is the Reconstructionist movement? An American Jewish religious movement, launched by Dr. Mordecai Kaplan, which stresses that Judaism must concentrate on the needs of this world rather than on the hereafter. Founded in 1922, the movement now has its own rabbinical seminary and a network of affiliated congregations. Although the services are very similar to those in Conservative synagogues, the Reconstructionists avow their disbelief in anything supernatural.

◄ **750** ► What's a *gabbai?* An usher in a synagogue (usually a voluntary, honorary position), who helps maintain decorum during the service.

◄ **751** ► When did the first Jews settle in what is today Libya? In the second century B.C.E. Like many Jewish communities in Moslem countries, they were usually confined to a separate quarter known as a *hara* or *mellah*.

◄ **752** ► What is a *parnas?* A leader of the Jewish community. The term is also used to designate the head of a congregation or community group and is usually an elected position.

◄ **753** ► What was a *shtadlan?* A Jewish community spokesman whose task was to intercede with high political officers to avert possible anti-Jewish legislation or decrees. The practice remained in vogue until Jews won full political rights in most countries, in the eighteenth and nineteenth centuries.

◄ 754 ► What is the OSE organization? A world-wide Jewish organization, begun in 1912 in Russia, whose chief aim was to intensify hygiene, child care, and modern health practices among backward Jewish groups. The name is an acronym (in Russian) for Jewish health society: *Obshtchestvo Zdravookhranyenie Evreyev.*

◄ 755 ► What is the ORT organization? A world-wide Jewish group founded in Europe for the primary task of providing vocational training to impoverished Jewish youths so that they would be able to earn a livelihood. The name is an acronym for Organization for Rehabilitation through Training. Programs are now concentrated in Israel, France, Iran, and North Africa.

◄ 756 ► What is *halitza?* A ceremony in which the brother of a deceased husband grants permission to the widow to marry someone other than himself.

◄ 757 ► What is a *shtetl?* An Eastern European rural Jewish village especially of the eighteenth and nineteenth centuries.

◄ 758 ► What is an *etrog?* Sometimes pronounced *esrog,* it is a citron; it is used in the observance of the Sukkoth holiday. It is one of the four species associated with the holiday.

◄ 759 ► Who are the Falashas? A community of black people living in Ethiopia who observe a literal interpretation of biblical law and claim to be of Jewish origin. Once a very populous community, their numbers have dwindled to about twenty-five thousand. Educational, vocational, and other assistance is given them by some American Jewish and Israeli groups.

◄**760**► What's a *latke?* A potato pancake traditionally eaten at Hanukkah time. Among Jews from the Moslem world, the Hanukkah dish is usually a *sufganiyah,* similar to a jelly doughnut.

◄**761**► What is meant by the Law of Return? One of the earliest pieces of legislation passed by the Israel Government, stipulating that every Jew has the right to immigrate to and settle in Israel.

◄**762**► What is *hachnasat kallah?* Literally, ushering in the bride. A strongly entrenched tradition in Jewish life is that the community must do everything possible to help its young women to marry. Special societies existed in European communities to implement this program.

◄**763**► What is *s'micha?* Rabbinic ordination. Although most modern rabbis receive their *s'micha* from recognized seminaries, it is possible for a group of rabbis to ordain a rabbi without benefit of formal study and testing.

◄**764**► What is the Hagiographa? The third section of the Jewish Bible, known in Hebrew as *Ketuvim,* or Holy Writings. The first third is the Torah, also known as the Pentateuch, or Five Books, of Moses. The second section consists of the major prophets and is known in Hebrew as *Nevi'im,* which means Prophets.

◄**765**► When did the first Jews settle in Pennsylvania? In the second half of the seventeenth century. A Jewish cemetery in Lancaster dates to 1747.

◄**766**► What are *tzitzith?* The fringes of a prayer shawl. Orthodox Jews wear a four-cornered garment, under their outer clothing, to which *tzitzith* are attached.

◄ 767 ► What are *zemirot?* Literally, songs. Ashkenazi Jews sing special *zemirot* during the course of the Sabbath meal, while Sephardi Jews sing the verses just prior to the morning service.

◄ 768 ► What is "Ha-Tikvah"? The Israel national anthem and the Zionist movement's rallying call since it was introduced, at the turn of the century. The lyrics of "Ha-Tikvah" (the word means "hope") were composed by the poet Naftali Herz Imber, and the melody, based on a Romanian folk song, was set to music by an early settler in Palestine, Samuel Cohen.

◄ 769 ► What is the Mount of Olives? A sacred cemetery overlooking Jerusalem, whose tallest peak is Mount Scopus, site of the first campus of the Hebrew University.

◄ 770 ► What is a *mikvah?* A ritual bath, used by observant Jewish women following their menstrual periods. Converts to Judaism also undergo immersion in a mikvah. It is also used by Orthodox brides prior to the wedding.

◄ 771 ► What is a *ketubah?* A Jewish marriage contract, in which the husband agrees to provide his wife with her personal and financial needs during the marriage. Written in Aramaic, it is part of the modern Orthodox and Conservative wedding ceremonies. Hand-painted, illuminated forms of the ketubah are an original Jewish art form dating back many centuries.

◄ 772 ► What is the Anti-Defamation League? An organization established in the United States by B'nai B'rith for the primary task of defending the civil and political rights of American Jewry. Thus, the ADL monitors the activities of hate groups that seek to arouse anti-Semitic passions, and keeps an eye on local legislative efforts to ascertain that there are no violations of civil-rights law that might affect Jews and other minorities.

◄773► Who are the Bukharan Jews? A group from the Uzbek region of the Soviet Union, dating their settlement in the area to the thirteenth century, many of whose members were forcibly converted to Islam. Settlers began to arrive in Jerusalem in the mid-nineteenth century. They speak a language known as Tajiki-Jewish and are renowned for their colorful dress.

◄774► What was the Ararat plan to settle Jews in the Buffalo, New York, area? Early in the nineteenth century, Mordecai Manuel Noah conceived the idea of establishing near the upstate New York city a modern, Western Hemisphere Zion, to be called Ararat. A foundation stone for the projected community dates to 1825, but that is all that remains of the plan.

◄775► What does the phrase *Ha-Makom yenahem,* spoken to a mourner, mean? It is the first part of a verse that says, "May God comfort you, together with all mourners of Zion and Jerusalem."

◄776► Why is there a recent custom of having a Bar Mitzvah at the Western Wall? This has developed since the city of Jerusalem was reunited in 1967, permitting Jews to worship again at the ancient shrine. It demonstrates the deep emotional feeling Jews hold toward the Temple of old and all that the Jewish past represents.

◄777► What is meant by *trup?* The special cantillation notes that indicate how a particular scriptural passage is to be chanted during the reading of the Torah.

◄778► What is the *adloyada?* The Purim carnival, celebrating the deliverance of the ancient Jews from the diabolical plans of Haman, is so designated because of a tradition that one should revel in the celebration until it is not possible to distinguish between Mordecai and Haman.

◄779► What is meant by the term *hasidei umot haolam?* Literally, "righteous gentiles." The Talmud says that righteous gentiles are to be considered on an equal plane with Jews, in having "a share in the world to come." A special garden in Jerusalem has been planted bearing the names of all gentiles who risked their lives to help Jews during the Nazi era, all of whom have been designated "righteous gentiles."

◄780► What is a *bentsher?* A small book containing the appropriate graces after meals.

◄781► Is the wearing of a small *mezuzah* as a pendant a law or tradition of old? No, it's a fairly recent innovation for women, and extremely recent for men. (Some rabbis object to the practice, but most ignore it.)

◄782► What does the word *shalom* mean? Literally, peace, as in *shalom aleichem* (peace be unto you). The word is used in modern Hebrew as a greeting, for both hello and good-by.

◄783► What is meant by *frum?* A person so designated is fully observant of all Jewish religious laws. In some Hassidic circles, non-religious Jews are referred to as people who are "not yet *frum*."

◄784► What is the Halachah? Jewish religious law, encompassing all of the biblical and postbiblical enactments, decisions, and rabbinic decrees.

◄**785**► Is the organ played during a synagogue service? Only in Reform temples and in some Conservative synagogues. (Music is played in all synagogues during receptions, parties, and weddings.)

◄**786**► What is *shehitah?* Ritual slaughter of animals, designed to be carried out in such a way that the animal feels a minimum of pain and to ensure that the consumer will eventually receive meat or fowl that is unblemished, i.e., kosher. The ritual slaughterer is known as a *shohet,* and the special, razor-sharp knife he uses in his calling is a *halaf.*

◄**787**► What are the three principal designations of kosher food? Food that is *milchig* (dairy), *fleishig* (meat dishes), or *pareve* (neutral, i.e., fruits, vegetables, eggs, and the like, which may be eaten with either meat or dairy meals).

◄**788**► What is the *gematriah?* The system of giving numerical equivalents to Hebrew letters. Thus, the Jewish year that begins in the fall of 1978 is the year 5739, which in Hebrew is shown as תשל"ט.

◄**789**► Which historic American synagogue has been officially designated a national shrine? The Touro Synagogue, in Newport, Rhode Island.

◄**790**► May a suicide be buried in a Jewish cemetery? Although Jewish law stipulates that anyone who takes his own life may not be buried in consecrated soil, most modern rabbis do not follow this law; they get around it by saying that the suicide was not in his right mind when the act was committed and thus is regarded as insane, entitling him to traditional burial.

◄ **791** ► What is Ladino? The language developed by Sephardic Jews and still in use to a limited extent today. Written in Hebrew characters (like Yiddish, which has a strong German base), Ladino is a mixture of Spanish, Latin, and Hebrew.

◄ **792** ► What's a *shtreimel?* A large, fur-trimmed hat worn by certain Hassidic followers, which has its origin in Poland.

◄ **793** ► What's a *shadchan?* A matchmaker, an institution that was in great vogue in the Eastern European villages, where often bride and groom did not set eyes on each other until they stood under the canopy at the marriage service. In Israel, and in some Orthodox circles, the matchmaker is still a viable factor in arranging marriages. Conservative Judaism recently instituted a modern version of the idea by setting up a computer service in which prospective brides and grooms could hope to meet—if the programmed entries to series of questions indicated that they had common interests. The word is sometimes used loosely to refer to anyone who brings two people together; for business, for example.

◄ **794** ► What's a *landsman?* Someone who originates from the same town or village as oneself. In more modern usage, it will be used to indicate that certain suburbanites came originally from the same area of an urban community.

◄ **795** ► What is a *hora?* An Israeli folk dance, performed in a circle, with the tempo reminiscent of Eastern European folk dances.

◄ **796** ► What is a *halutz?* A pioneer in the early days of Jewish settlement in Palestine, usually an idealistic young man (a young woman was known as a *halutza*) willing to surrender material comforts to undertake difficult labor (swamp drainage, for example) to help fulfill the ideals of Zionism. Thus, some modern Israeli leaders speak of the need for a return to the *halutzic* spirit.

◄ **797** ► What is *kiddush ha-Shem?* Literally, sanctification of the Name, i.e., readiness to die for the sake of not desecrating God's name. Thus, martyrs who perished in the Nazi concentration camps, and—during the period of the Spanish Inquisition—Jews who chose to go to their deaths with a Hebrew prayer on their lips, are referred to as people who died for *kiddush ha-Shem.*

◄ **798** ► What does *le-hayyim* mean? To life—the traditional Jewish toast, stressing Judaism's strong conviction that people's most precious gift is life.

◄ **799** ► What is *pikuach nefesh?* The concept that protection of life supersedes all other considerations. Thus, on Sabbath, Yom Kippur, and less religious occasions, the guarding of life in moments of danger assumes top priority. The most recent demonstration of this took place during the 1973 Yom Kippur War, when, on the most hallowed day of the Jewish year, worshipers in Israel, including aged rabbis still wearing prayer shawls, did not hesitate to interrupt the service to shoulder arms and rush to the front to help resist the invading Arab armies.

◄ **800** ► What is a handkerchief dance? Among Orthodox Jews, men and women often do not dance together, for reasons of modesty. Instead, each partner, at a wedding or other occasion, will hold the end of a handkerchief at arm's length and dance, maintaining physical distance from each other.

◄ **801** ► What does the word *shechinah* connote? Divine presence. The term is used to describe the ambience of a particularly spiritual, holy assembly, as for example a congregation of unusually devout people.

◄ **802** ► What great principle did the commentator Nahmanides teach? He expounded the view that worship can help to refine and improve people's character.

◄ **803** ► What are the Noachian laws? Also known as the Noachide laws, these were the seven laws laid down to Noah which must be obeyed by all peoples: idolatry is forbidden; bloodshed, sexual sinfulness, blasphemy, stealing, and eating limbs torn from living animals—all are forbidden; and a legal system applying to all must be set up.

◄ **804** ► What was the jubilee year? In ancient Israel, this was the fiftieth year, when all debts were canceled, slavery was terminated, land purchased since the previous jubilee year was returned to the original owners, and the land was to lie fallow. After the second Temple, this system was no longer observed.

◄ **805** ► What is the sabbatical year, known also as *shemitah?* The seventh year in a cycle of seven, during which the land was not cultivated and debts were canceled. In some Orthodox agricultural settlements in modern Israel, the practice is still observed (the Hebrew year 5740, corresponding to 1979–1980, is a Sabbatical year). Some ecologists see the law as helpful to the soil, giving it a respite from active farming every seventh year.

◄ **806** ► What is a *sabra?* Literally, a cactus fruit. The term is applied to a native Israeli, since it is "tough and prickly on the outside and sweet on the inside."

◄807► Where are there full-fledged Jewish museums in the United States? In New York, Philadelphia, Chicago, Los Angeles, and Berkeley, California.

◄808► Which state has the smallest Jewish population? Wyoming, with an estimated 345 Jews, making up only 0.1 per cent of the total population of 356,000.

◄809► Percentage-wise, which state has the largest Jewish community? New York. The Jewish population is about 2,150,000, or 11.9 per cent of the total population.

◄810► What are the Hebrew months of the year? Tishri, Heshvan, Kislev, Tevet, Shvat, Adar, Nissan, Iyar, Sivan, Tammuz, Av, Elul. (In a leap year, there arc an Adar I and an Adar II.) The Jewish year usually begins and ends in September.

◄811► What Jewish emblem did Einstein always keep in his home? The menorah, the seven-branched candelabrum that has become the official emblem of Israel.

◄812► How many years ago was the first Passover celebrated? About 3,300 years ago, making it the oldest recorded holiday still observed every year by millions of people.

◄813► Some Jewish families leave a chair empty at the Passover Seder table. Why? As a gesture of solidarity with Jews in the Soviet Union, who are discouraged from celebrating this and other Jewish observances.

◄814► What does the word Jerusalem mean? *Ir shalom,* or city of peace. (American communities named Salem adopted an Anglicized version of the Hebrew word for peace.)

◄815► Why do donations to charity often come in multiples of 18? The Hebrew word for life is *hai,* which, numerically, is 18. Donations are thus made as a "gift of *hai,*" or "twice *hai,*" etc.

◄816► What is meant by the expression of offering a *mi sheberach* prayer? A special prayer, beginning with the words *Mi sheberach* (He Who has blessed), is pronounced in the synagogue in behalf of critically ill people. The custom is for the sick person to be named as the son (or daughter) of, and then the mother's rather than the father's name is invoked.

◄817► What was the notorious *Kristallnacht?* An organized series of assaults on thousands of synagogues and Jewish-owned shops carried out on the night of November 9, 1938, by the Nazis in Germany and Austria. The German word refers to the night of broken glass.

◄818► In the Talmud, which group of people are designated "the real guardians of the state"? The teachers. Teaching and study have traditionally been hallmarks of Jewish life.

◄819► Why do Jews traditionally eat a round, rather than an oblong, *hallah* on the occasion of Rosh Hashanah? The custom includes dipping the hallah into honey, and signifies the hope that the new year will be round, smooth, and sweet.

◄820► Is it true that the chess term "checkmate" is a Hebrew word? Yes, it means the king is dead. "Check" is the equivalent of the modern "sheik." "Mate" means dead in Hebrew.

◄ **821** ► What are the *arba minim?* The four species, used in observance of the Sukkoth holiday: an *etrog* (citron), *lulav* (palm), *hadas* (myrtle), and *aravah* (willow).

◄ **822** ► What do the following terms, used fairly extensively in show-business English, mean: *gelt, mavin, chutzpah, shekel, shamus? Gelt* means money, a *mavin* is an expert, *chutzpah* denotes colossal nerve, *shekel* refers to money (usually in the context of dues), and a *shamus* is a private detective.

◄ **823** ► For which biblical figure is the great Jewish women's organization Hadassah named? For Queen Esther, heroine of the Purim story. Hadassah is the Hebrew equivalent of the Persian name Esther.

◄ **824** ► When was the first Talmud printed, and by whom? The Talmud was printed in Venice in the sixteenth century by an early Christian printer.

◄ **825** ► What was the early biblical precept of inheritance? That the *bechor,* or first-born son, was to inherit twice as much as his brothers.

◄ **826** ► Which are the Five Books of Moses, comprising the Torah? Genesis, Exodus, Leviticus, Numbers, and Deuteronomy.

◄ **827** ► What is a *sofer?* A scribe who copies the Scroll of the Law, a task that often takes a year. The work is done with a quill pen and India ink. All punctuation is omitted. The Scroll is made up of sixty-two sections sewn together by hand with a wooden needle; the thread is animal sinew.

◄ **828** ► How old is the oldest Jewish cemetery in New York? It dates to 1682 and today is wedged in between the financial district and Chinatown, in lower Manhattan.

◄ **829** ► What's a *falafel?* A Middle East dish, popular in Israel and introduced to the United States in recent years. It consists of a hollow soft bread called *pitah* crammed with ground chick-peas, sesame sauce, and salad.

◄ **830** ► Commodore Uriah P. Levy served in the fledgling U. S. Navy in the early part of the nineteenth century. What did he do to indicate his commitment to the Jewish heritage? In 1812, he nailed a *mezuzah* to the doorpost of his cabin.

◄ **831** ► Which is the smallest book in the Bible? Obadiah; it contains only one chapter.

◄ **832** ► The inscription on the Liberty Bell in Philadelphia is taken from Leviticus; what does it say? "Proclaim liberty throughout all the land, unto all the inhabitants thereof." (Chapter 25, v. 10.)

◄ **833** ► Why are jeans also known as "Levi's"? In honor of the nineteenth-century merchant-clothier who first developed them, Levi Strauss.

◄ **834** ► How long is the Jordan River? It meanders for 157 miles. In some places, however, it is shallow enough to be waded across.

◄ **835** ► Who are the *shomrim?* The first use of the word, which means watchmen, goes back more than a half century, to the early days of Jewish settlement in Palestine, when the farmers organized self-defense units, whose members were known as *shomrim.* In New York today, the association of some 2,500 Jewish policemen who work for the city is called the Shomrim Society.

◄ **836** ► What is an *eyshet chayil?* A biblical phrase referring to a woman of valor. The term is used to describe an exemplary Jewish woman.

◄ **837** ► What is a *dvar Torah?* A short, usually homiletic talk on a biblical or religious subject, most often delivered by the rabbi at *shalosh seudot* (on Sabbath, in late afternoon) and on other suitable occasions.

◄ **838** ► When someone has been honored by being called to the reading of the Torah or to hold the Scroll or to open the Holy Ark, what is the customary phrase used to wish him well? *Yasher koach,* which best translates as "May your strength be confirmed."

◄ **839** ► What does *mazal tov* mean? Good luck. It is a suitable phrase for weddings, anniversaries, Bar and Bat Mitzvah celebrations, birthdays, and the like.

◄ **840** ► What is the *amidah?* The part of the service, recited silently (aloud in the Reform service), containing eighteen blessings and hence sometimes also known as the *shemoneh esray,* or the eighteen. It is included in the three daily services and the additional Sabbath and holiday *mussaf* service, and is considered a personal devotion.

◄ **841** ► What is the *ne'ilah?* The concluding service on Yom Kippur, recited only on that day and regarded as so important that most congregants remain standing throughout the service.

◄ **842** ► What is a *metivta* (or, in the older form, *mesivta*)? The high school equivalent of a *yeshiva,* or all-day school with special emphasis on Jewish studies.

◄ 843 ► What is a *simcha?* A joyous occasion, such as weddings, Bar and Bat Mitzvah celebrations, engagements, and the like. Upon departing from such an event, it is customary for celebrants to express the hope that they all continue to meet only at *simchas.*

◄ 844 ► What is a *mezinek?* The word refers to the youngest male child in the family (a girl is known as a *mizenke*) and is used in great joy when that child is married, i.e., the parents rejoice that they have lived to attend the wedding of their youngest offspring.

◄ 845 ► What is the *she-he-che-yanu* blessing? A special blessing in which God is thanked for having enabled an individual or a family to reach a given milestone. It is recited on the major holidays as part of the *kiddush* blessing on wine, and in many synagogues it is customary for the rabbi to lead the parents of a Bar and Bat Mitzvah in pronouncing the benediction.

◄ 846 ► When someone wears something new, what is meant by the expression of *tithadesh?* Literally, "may you be renewed" but meant to convey the idea of "wear it in good health."

◄ 847 ► Jews wish one another a healthy and happy new year on the eve of Rosh Hashanah. What is said on the eve of Yom Kippur? Wishes for an "easy fast" are voiced. In England, Jews traditionally wish one another a "happy new year—and well over the fast."

◄ 848 ► What is *Shabbat ha-Gadol?* The great Sabbath, referring to the Sabbath preceding Passover.

◄ 849 ► What is *Shabbat Shuvah?* The Sabbath of repentance, which falls between Rosh Hashanah and Yom

Kippur, a ten-day period known as the Days of Awe, or *Yamim Noraim* in Hebrew.

◄**850**► What is a *baal t'shuvah?* A penitent who sincerely wishes to repent for past transgressions and return to a life of righteousness. In Judaism, the door is never closed on a potential penitent, since only God is regarded as perfect.

◄**851**► What is a *lamed vavnik?* The term stems from the alphabetic equivalent of 36 (the Hebrew letter *lamed* is 30, and *vav* is 6); it refers to an age-old belief that God permits the world to exist because of the righteousness of thirty-six saintly people in the world. Thus, if someone is described as a *lamed vavnik,* it is the highest possible accolade.

◄**852**► What is the *yetzer rah?* The "evil inclination," contrasted with the *yetzer tov,* or "good inclination." Jewish belief holds that people are born with both and that life is an unending struggle to supplant the evil inclination with the *yetzer tov.*

◄**853**► What is an *averah?* A sin or transgression, which can be a deliberate act of wrongdoing or the failure to live up to basic Jewish tenets.

◄**854**► What is an *eruv?* A symbolic act that gets around religious probibitions, such as a territorial boundary within which it is permitted to carry articles or push a baby carriage, activities that Orthodox Jews do not normally do the Sabbath and holidays. The *eruv* is observed by strictly Orthodox Jews.

◄**855**► What is the *haftarah?* The portion of Prophets that follows the chanting of the Sabbath reading of the

Torah, and that is traditionally assigned to the Bar Mitzvah.

◄**856**► What are the Rebbe's *shirayim?* Among the Hassidic Jews, the *shirayim* are the food morsels left over by their Rebbe, or rabbi, at a festive occasion; their consumption is believed to help the ordinary Jew attain some of the holiness of her or his spiritual leader.

◄**857**► Why do people, when wishing someone a long life, use the figure of 120 years of age? This was the age that Moses attained, according to the Bible.

◄**858**► What is meant by *tachrichin?* The white, unadorned shroud in which the Jewish dead are traditionally buried. The shroud is loosely sewn, with long stitches.

◄**859**► Who are some of the leading Jewish sports figures of yesterday and today? Hank Greenberg, baseball; Barney Ross, boxing; Mark Spitz, swimming; Dick Savitt, tennis; Sandy Koufax, baseball; Nat Holman, basketball; Hank Wittenberg, wrestling; Sid Luckman, football; Ike Berger, weight lifting; Angelica Roseanu, table tennis; Emanuel Lasker, chess; Walter Miller, horse racing.

◄**860**► What is a *ger tzedek?* A proselyte who chose to be converted to Judaism out of sincere conviction that this was the faith in which he or she wished to live. Although traditionally Judaism has not encouraged non-Jews to adopt the Jewish faith, throughout history there have been proselytes who insisted on becoming Jewish and were accepted. There is a much more positive attitude today toward would-be converts to Judaism than existed in the past, particularly in view of the high percentage of marriages between Jews and non-Jews.

◄ **861** ► What is a *meshumad?* A Jew who opted to renounce his faith and adopt another religion, usually for ulterior material considerations, is described pejoratively as a *meshumad.* The campaign to convert Jews—resisted by the Jewish community—is known as *shmad.*

◄ **862** ► Who are the *Marranos?* Spanish and Portuguese Jews forcibly converted to Christianity who continued to live as Jews in secret, in the hope that they would one day be able to return fully and openly to the Jewish community.

◄ **863** ► What is a *mezuman?* A quorum of three adult males, required for the recitation of the grace after meals. Grace may also be recited alone.

◄ **864** ► What are *payot,* also known as *payos?* The long side curls worn by ultra-Orthodox male Jews, in compliance with the biblical injunction against rounding the corners of the head.

◄ **865** ► What is a *yarmulke?* Also known as a *kipah* in modern Hebrew, a skullcap worn by Jewish men and boys. It is obligatory among Orthodox and Conservative Jews in the synagogue, school, and at mealtimes (when blessings have to be offered), but its origin is postbiblical and not precisely known. Some Jewish collegians, although not necessarily religious, wear them as a mark of Jewish identity.

◄ **866** ► What is meant by *trefa,* or *traif?* The opposite of kosher; forbidden food.

◄ **867** ► What is *shatnez?* A biblical injunction against the mingling of wool and linen is still observed by many Orthodox Jews, who buy clothes that have been approved in a *shatnez* laboratory, i.e., indicating there is no prohibited mixing of fibers.

◄ **868** ► How many tourists visit Israel annually? Close to a million, more than 60 per cent of whom come from European countries.

◄ **869** ► What is meant by the phrase *Baruch ha-ba?* Literally, "Blessed be the arrival." It is a phrase signifying welcome, to which the usual rejoinder is *Baruch ha-nim-tzah,* "Blessed be he who is here."

◄ **870** ► On Sabbath, people wish one another Shabbat shalom, or peaceful Sabbath. What is the proper salutation for a holiday or festival? *Hag sameah,* or *"happy holiday."* The more old-fashioned greeting is *Gut yomtov,* which is Yiddish for "Good holiday."

◄ **871** ► Who was Stephen Wise? One of the greatest Jewish figures produced in America in the twentieth century. A reform rabbi, he carried on a lifelong struggle for social reform and equal justice for all, and was in the forefront of all efforts to help establish a Jewish state. He died in 1949.

◄ **872** ► When a Jewish child is born, male or female, what are the parents wished? That the parents will be privileged to share with the child in "Torah, *huppah* and *maasim tovim.*" That is, the child will study and know the Torah, enter a suitable marriage (*huppah* is the wedding canopy), and will live a life of *maasim tovim,* i.e., good deeds.

◄ **873** ► When visiting the sick or speaking of the ill, what does the expression *refuah shlemah* mean? Literally, a "complete healing."

◄ **874** ► When someone is asked how he or she is, why do religious Jews usually respond by saying, *Baruch ha-Shem?* The phrase means "blessed be God" and indicates that the individual attributes his well-being to God's beneficence.

◄ **875** ► Similarly, if a religious Jew is asked about his future plans, he usually responds, *Im yirtze ha-Shem.* What does that mean? Literally, "If God wills it." In other words, plan as he might, the final decision about his plans is really in God's hands.

◄ **876** ► Where does this phrase first appear: "The righteous shall flourish like the palm tree, they will grow like a cedar in Lebanon. Planted in the house of the Lord, they shall flourish in the courts of our God. They shall yield fruit even in old age"? Psalms 92, 12–14

◄ **877** ► What is a *hatunah,* or, in the older version, *hasunah?* A Jewish wedding ceremony, at which a minimum or quorum of at least ten adult Jewish males, must be present. A bride is known as a *kallah* and a groom as a *hatan,* or *hassan.*

◄ **878** ► What is a *naden?* A bride's dowry for the groom, a practice that is almost unknown today, although it is customary for the parents of the bride and groom to provide the couple with wedding gifts that will enable them to set up housekeeping.

◄ **879** ► What is the *aufruf* ceremony? On the Sabbath before his wedding, the groom is ceremoniously called to the reading of the Torah, where he is blessed on the occasion of his impending marriage. Among Orthodox Jews the bride is absent, but among Conservative and Reform

Jews she joins him at the synagogue, sometimes sharing in the rabbi's blessing.

◄880► At last count, about how many trees had the Jewish National Fund planted in Israel? More than 130,000,000, a program carried out over an eighty-year period.

◄881► What is a *shalom-zachar?* A Friday evening celebration, held on the occasion of the birth of a son, preceding the circumcision ceremony.

◄882► What is *pidyon ha-ben?* A ceremony of "redemption of the first-born son," held on the thirty-first day after birth. The custom stems from the concept that the first-born belongs to God (in ancient days, through service in the Temple), so the redemption ceremony "restores" the infant to the parents. Sons of *Kohen* or *Levi* families are excluded.

◄883► What is a *simchat bat?* A very new ceremony in which a newborn girl is formally welcomed into the Jewish community. It is usually conducted at a Sabbath-eve family festive meal, during which special prayers are recited for the mother and the child and her Hebrew name is announced.

◄884► What is a *get?* A divorce carried out according to Jewish religious law. A divorced Jewish couple seeking to remarry are usually required to have a *get*, in addition to a civil divorce, if they wish to be married by an Orthodox or Conservative rabbi.

◄885► What does the phrase *goldene medinah* mean? It is a Yiddish term for the United States. Literally "the golden land," it reflects the great hopes that Jewish immigrants had for their new home. Most of them came from lands of persecution and discrimination.

◄**886**► What is "numerus clausus"? A term used to describe the artificial limitations that were placed on minority groups—especially Jews—who sought entry to educational institutions, particularly universities, in pre-1914 Europe. Hungary at the time cut off Jewish enrollment in universities at the 5 per cent figure. Restrictions were known in the United States, too, although not as formal legislation, up to the 1940s.

◄**887**► What are the three cardinal sins? Idolatry, adultery, and murder. Judaism teaches that a Jew may save his life by ignoring all other laws except these; i.e., he must accept death rather than commit any one of these three sins.

◄**888**► What is meant by the phrase *"etz hayyim"*? Literally "tree of life," the phrase is used to describe the Jewish or Torah concept of life. Also the wooden rollers to which the Scroll of the Torah is attached are each called an *etz hayyim*.

◄**889**► What is *kavanah?* The term is applied to indicate intense devotion and concentration during the prayer service. Thus, a worshiper reciting the silent *amidah* prayer who appears to be totally immersed in his devotional prayers may be said to be experiencing *kavanah*.

◄**890**► What is a *sidrah?* The weekly biblical portion read at the Sabbath service. It is sometimes also known as a *parsha*.

◄**891**► What is the *duchanen* ceremony? Now found only in Orthodox services, it is a part of the *mussaf* holiday service (except Yom Kippur), when it does not coincide with Sabbath, during which the *kohen* (priestly members of the congregation) ascend the *bimah* to bestow a blessing on the worshipers.

◄892► What is the name of the special prayer recited for dew? for rain? The former, known as a prayer for *tal,* or dew, is recited on the first day of Passover, and the latter, known as a prayer for *geshem,* or rain, is recited on the eighth day of the Sukkoth holiday. The prayers of course are intended for the special climatic conditions prevailing in the Holy Land and are indicative of the strong attachment that Jews always had for the ancestral homeland, even during the long centuries of dispersion.

◄893► What does the word *amen* mean? May it be so—it is a congregational response to blessings recited during the service.

◄894► When each of the Five Books of Moses, constituting the Torah, is concluded in the weekly Sabbath cycle of readings, what is the traditional form of celebration? The congregation rises at the closing words and proclaims together and loudly, *Hazak, hazak, v'nithazek,* i.e., "Let us be strong and strengthen ourselves" (to continue the reading of the Torah).

◄895► What are *hagba* and *gelilah?* The former is the designation given to the person to hold the Torah aloft at the conclusion of the reading, and the latter is the one who rolls it together and replaces the cover before the Torah is returned to the ark.

◄896► What is the difference between a *baal tefilah* and a *hazan,* or cantor? While the latter is usually a synagogue employee, the former is a layman who enjoys leading

the less important (usually the earlier) part of the service
and does so as a volunteer.

◄ **897** ► What is a *baal kriyah?* The person who reads
from the Torah, who must be well versed in the cantillation
and in the text, is called a *baal kriyah,* or master of reading.

◄ **898** ► What is a *kaddish zugger?* A person, usually
an elderly religious man, who recites the mourner's prayer
for another, for a modest fee, when a mourner is unable to
do so.

◄ **899** ► What is a *mohel?* A person qualified, both
religiously and medically, to perform the rite of circumcision. Like the rabbi and the cantor, the mohel, too, must
by tradition be an observant Jew.

◄ **900** ► What is a *bet din?* A Jewish religious court,
which deals in matters such as divorce. It is usually made
up of three judges, who must be thoroughly knowledgeable
in Jewish law.

◄ **901** ► What is a *mesader kidushin?* A marriage performer. The role nowadays is generally filled only by
rabbis.

◄ **902** ► What is a *meshulah?* Literally, an emissary,
but referring to someone who travels from community to
community seeking financial support for a deserving Jewish
institution, usually a *yeshiva.*

◄ **903** ► What is *rosh hodesh?* The new month, celebrated on the preceding Sabbath in the synagogue by the
addition of a special prayer in which the worshipers pray
for a month of good tidings.

◄**904**► Who were the *rishonim?* Literally the "early ones," the term applies to the early prophets as contrasted with the later ones. It is also used to distinguish between the talmudic commentators who lived before the publication of the *Shulhan Aruch* and subsequent commentators and authorities, known as the *aharonim,* or the "later ones."

◄**905**► What are *hakafot?* On Simhat Torah, when the annual conclusion of the reading of the Torah is celebrated and the new cycle of reading is commenced, all the Scrolls of the Law are removed from the ark and paraded around the synagogue in seven circuits, amid much singing and merrymaking. Small children wave flags to indicate their participation. All the congregants touch the Torahs with their fingertips as they pass by, and then kiss their fingers lightly.

◄**906**► What is a *mashgiach?* A person, often a rabbi, whose job is to supervise the adherence of a restaurant, hotel, or caterer to the Jewish dietary laws.

◄**907**► What is the *megillah?* Literally a scroll. Thus, the *megillah* of Esther, the equivalent of the Bible's Book of Esther, is read aloud on the eve of Purim.

◄**908**► What is the *Shulhan Aruch?* The code of Jewish law assembled by Joseph Caro in the sixteenth century and still recognized by Orthodox Jews as the most authoritative compilation of *Halachah.*

◄**909**► What is a *seudah?* Literally, a festive meal, it usually refers to the Purim day dinner, a time for a family gathering.

◄ **910** ► What is *shalach manot?* The pre-Purim custom of sending small gifts (usually of food) to the poor, as well as to friends and neighbors.

◄ **911** ► What is a *shabbes goy?* Literally, a "Sabbath gentile." Before the introduction of modern conveniences, religious Jewish families hired a non-Jew who would come to their home on Sabbath morning to light the stove, since they were forbidden to do so. The system has all but disappeared, but there are still some families in Israel and in Orthodox areas of the United States who keep it going.

◄ **912** ► What is *hametz?* Leavened food, which may not be eaten during the Passover holiday. It is also extended to refer to dishes and utensils; i.e., observant Jews celebrate Passover by putting away their *hametz* dishes and cutlery and using a special set of eating and cooking utensils reserved for Passover use only. These latter are usually known as *Pesachdig,* or Passover dishes and utensils.

◄ **913** ► Who was Theodor Herzl? A remarkable personality who died at the age of forty-four, in 1904, but who managed in a very brief span of time to dramatize the Jews' desire and need for a homeland and is therefore regarded as the father of political Zionism. Although an assimilated Jew and a well-regarded playwright and newspaper columnist, he was profoundly affected by the Dreyfus trial in Paris and threw himself into the task of hastening the establishment of a Jewish state.

◄ **914** ► What is the *mah nishtanah?* The four questions that open the reading of the Passover Haggadah at the Seder begin with the words *Mah nishtanah,* or "Why [is this night] different"? The reading of the Haggadah is in

257

effect a reply to the four questions, sometimes referred to in Yiddish as the *feer kashes*.

◀**915**▶ What are the "special Sabbaths"? The Sabbath of *shekalim,* read during the month of Adar to remind worshipers of the ancient shekel tax; Sabbath *zachor,* or the remembrance Sabbath, which falls before Purim, is in compliance with the biblical law to "remember what Amalek did"; the Sabbath *parah,* a reminder of the importance of ritual cleanliness, which precedes the Sabbath *ha-Hodesh,* which comes before the Passover holiday and is a reminder of the impending festival.

◀**916**▶ Why is a person's name changed during a critical illness? It is a custom derived from talmudic teaching that offers hope that a sick person's changed name will also bring with it a full cure. For a man, the name is usually changed to *chayim,* meaning life; or it is appended to his existing name.

◀**917**▶ What is meant by *vidui?* The word means confession and is recited by a person who feels he is approaching death. A rabbi is not required during such a time, but often one is present to help the confessor in his last moments of life.

◀**918**▶ When one is told of a person's death, what is the customary response? *Baruch dayan emet,* i.e., Blessed be God, the true judge. The same phrase is recited by next of kin when the rabbi cuts their outer garments in the *kriyah* ceremony, indicating a state of mourning.

◀**919**▶ What is meant by the *galus?* Sometimes pronounced *galut,* the word means exile, and refers to the fact that Jews have lived outside Israel since the destruction of the Temple in the year 70. The term Diaspora is also used to refer to the Jewish community outside Israel.

◄ **920** ► Who was Hannah Senesh? A heroic Palestinian Jewish girl who volunteered to parachute into Nazi-held Europe to aid her coreligionists but was caught and executed in her native Hungary.

◄ **921** ► What is a *matzevah?* A monument erected over a gravesite. The contemporary custom of unveiling the monument is an American innovation.

◄ **922** ► What is meant by the expression *alav ha-shalom?* In referring to a male decedent, the phrase means "peace be upon him" or "may he rest in peace." (The word *aleha* is substituted when referring to a deceased woman.)

◄ **923** ► What is a *dibbuk?* According to Eastern European folk belief, the spirit of a deceased person that has entered the body of a human being, causing all kinds of extranatural problems. Exorcism, practiced to a limited extent among some simple Jewish villagers, was believed to be the only solution.

◄ **924** ► Why do some people inscribe all their letters, diaries, even business papers, with the two Hebrew letters equivalent to в"н? The abbreviation represents the words, *B'ezrat ha-Shem,* or With the Help of God, indicating the writer's sense of the divine will.

◄ **925** ► How do Jews, in speaking of the hereafter, refer to heaven? It is called the Garden of Eden, reminiscent of the biblical account of complete bliss that prevailed until the expulsion of Adam and Eve. Whenever a rabbi or a cantor intones the poignant *El Maleh Rachamim* prayer for the dead, he strikes a responsive chord at the part when he hopes the decedent's soul will find repose in *Gan Eden,* or the Garden of Eden.

◄ **926** ► Does the word *goy* (*goyim* in the plural) have a derogative connotation? Definitely not, despite the misconception among some that it does. The literal meaning of the word is a "people" or "nation," and it is applied to non-Jews, but not pejoratively.

◄ **927** ► What is an *apikoros?* An atheist who dissociates himself from Judaism on philosophical grounds. The word is taken from the Greek for Epicurean.

◄ **928** ► What is a Bar Mitzvah? A Jewish boy, upon reaching the age of thirteen, becomes a "son of the commandment" (the literal translation); i.e., he is now able to be counted in a religious quorum and is expected to assume all other religious obligations borne by adult male Jews. Traditionally, the father's responsibility for the young man's transgressions now passes to the Bar Mitzvah; religiously, he is now on his own. A *Bat* Mitzvah ceremony has been developed in recent years for girls, who are usually ushered into Jewish womanhood at the age of twelve. Reform Judaism has a confirmation ceremony for boys and girls which takes place at Shavuoth, when the Torah was given to Moses, and which coincides with completion of a basic Jewish educational program.

◄ **929** ► What is meant by *hol ha-moed?* The intermediate days of the Passover holiday are so designated, indicating that they are only half holidays, i.e., normal work may be carried out but the proscription of leavened foods must still be observed. The Sukkoth intermediate days are also described as *hol ha-moed.*

◄ 930 ► What are some of the better-known holy places in Israel? The Western Wall, where the Temple once stood, in Jerusalem; Rachel's Tomb, in Bethlehem; and the Machpela in Hebron, where the patriarchs and matriarchs (except Rachel) are said to have been buried.

◄ 931 ► Many synagogues include a prayer for the government in the Sabbath services. Why? In compliance with the statement, found in Jeremiah, "Seek the peace of the city whither I have caused you to be carried captive, and pray for it unto the Lord" and the talmudic dictum "Pray for the welfare of the government."

◄ 932 ► What obligation does a Jewish father have toward his son? The Talmud stipulates: "A father is obliged to circumcise his son, teach him Torah, teach him a trade, and marry him off."

◄ 933 ► How did some rabbis speak of their mothers? While some said that their best teachers had been their mothers, one was quoted as saying that when he heard his mother's footsteps approaching, "I stand up before the divine presence."

◄ 934 ► What is a *moshav zekenim?* A residence for the elderly.

◄ 935 ► Which days of the week, in addition to the Sabbath, are marked by brief Torah readings? Mondays and Thursdays, which are also observed by some as partial fast days.

◄**936**► What is meant by *yihus?* Genealogical distinction, usually in reference to a background involving a great scholar or rabbi.

◄**937**► What does the phrase *Yimah shmo* mean? Literally, "May his name be erased," used in talking of a hated foe of the Jewish people, e.g., Hitler.

◄**938**► Why is the Hebrew month of *Heshvan* known as *MarHeshvan?* The addition of the "mar" makes it translate as "bitter Heshvan," because it is a month without any holidays or festivals.

◄**939**► The Lubavitch Hassidic group follows the concept of "Habad." What is this? An acronym for *hochma* (wisdom), *binah* (understanding), and *daat* (knowledge).

◄**940**► How often do leap years occur in the Jewish calendar? Seven times in a nineteen-year period.

◄**941**► What is the origin of the six-pointed Star of David? It is said to have been the form of the shield borne by King David. Known in Hebrew as Magen David, it means the Shield of David.

◄**942**► Is it true that Columbus had a number of Jews on his voyage of discovery to the Western Hemisphere? Yes. Luis de Torres, the interpreter (the first to set foot on American soil); the ship's doctor, known as Bernal; the ship's surgeon, Marco; and Rodrigo de Triana—all were Jewish. (There has also been a persistent speculation that Columbus himself was of Jewish descent, but this has never been proved conclusively.)

◄**943**► What is Biro-Bidjan? An area of millions of acres in Western Siberia, set aside soon after the Bolshevik revolution and intended as an autonomous secular Jewish republic in the U.S.S.R., with Yiddish as one of the official languages. Although it is still in existence, the number of Soviet Jews who live there today is relatively small.

◄**944**► What is the Maccabiah? A quadrennial sporting competition in which Jewish athletes from all parts of the world participate. It has been held in Palestine (later Israel) since the early 1930s (except during World War II), the most recent being in 1977.

◄**945**► What was the contribution of Judah Cresques to science, two centuries before Copernicus? Known as the "map Jew," he advanced the theory that the earth was round, a belief that was not universally accepted until after Copernicus.

◄**946**► What was the wartime (World War I) contribution of Chaim Weizmann, a noted chemist and Zionist leader, later to become Israel's first President? He succeeded in developing a new method of producing wood alcohol, needed by the British in manufacturing gunpowder.

◄**947**► Is it true that Uganda was once under serious consideration as a Jewish homeland? Yes, in the early Zionist period it was proposed that Uganda, then ruled by Britain, should be developed as a homeland and refuge for Jews. The suggestion was rejected by the majority of Zionist leaders.

◄**948**► What world religious movement other than Judaism maintains headquarters in Israel? The Bahai, whose chief temple is situated on a high point in Haifa and is marked by a gleaming golden dome.

◄**949**► Why is Moses depicted by some artists as having horns emerging from his forehead? Because of an incorrect translation of the Hebrew word *karnayim,* which means both "horns" and "rays of lights." The latter is the correct meaning of the term.

◀950▶ Which Jewish inventor devised the zeppelin? An Austrian Jew by the name of David Schwartz patented his ideas in 1894. After Schwartz's death, Count Zeppelin bought the patent rights from the widow and gave his name to the airship.

◀951▶ Prior to the destruction of the Holy Temple in Jerusalem by Rome, what was the Jewish population in the country? According to Flavius Josephus, the historian, about five to six million. A census taken in the twelfth century put the total world Jewish population at just over one million.

◀952▶ How often does it snow in Jerusalem? Generally every seven or eight years.

◀953▶ Who are the Beni Israel? A group of Indian Jews, residing mainly in the Bombay area, whose physiognomy is akin to that of most Indians but who claim descent from a group of seven men and seven women, the survivors of a shipwreck off the Indian coast about 1,800 years ago. The ship was said to have been filled with Jews fleeing persecution.

◀954▶ Who was Emma Lazarus? A nineteenth-century poet whose verse that begins, "Give me your tired, your poor" is emblazoned on the Statue of Liberty. She became profoundly aware of her Jewish background only after witnessing Russian Jews who had fled from oppression reach the shores of America. She studied Hebrew and soon began to translate the works of great Hebrew poets of the medieval period.

◄ **955** ► Who was the first Jew to serve in the U. S. Senate? David Levy Yulee, from Florida. He was also a delegate to the Confederate Congress.

◄ **956** ► After the United States, Israel, and the Soviet Union, which country has the fourth largest Jewish community in the world? France, with Britain next.

◄ **957** ► What is meant by the phrase *rachmanim bnai rachmanim?* Literally, "compassionate people, the sons of compassionate people"—it is used by Jews to describe their traditionally profound interest in the needy.

◄ **958** ► Maimonides listed eight degrees of charity. Which did he say was the highest form? The last, which he said was help that would make the recipient of charity self-supporting.

◄ **959** ► Who first described the Jews as the "people of the book"? Mohammed.

◄ **960** ► What is a *leviyah?* A funeral procession. It is considered a mark of respect to attend a funeral service and to accompany the deceased to his final resting place. The word literally means "accompanying."

◄ **961** ► What was a *moser* or a *malshin?* A Jew who willfully denounced other Jews to the civil authorities, acts which occurred in Jewish history, especially when economic conditions were at their worst. These people acted as betrayers of their own community in order to win material gains, and remain the most condemned figures in Jewish history.

◄ **962** ► Was there really a Jewish military unit that fought in the Revolutionary War? A company of militia, commanded by Richard Lushington, was composed almost exclusively of Jews from Charleston, South Carolina.

◄963► Who was Moses Montefiore? A great philanthropist and champion of Jewish rights in the nineteenth century. He rescued the threatened Jewish community of Damascus from a blood libel in 1840, purchased land in Palestine for early settlements there, built many schools and hospitals, and organized many charitable organizations.

◄964► Why is the Rosenwald family especially revered in the United States by the Blacks? Because of massive financial support to help young Blacks acquire a higher education.

◄965► Are there any Jews in mainland China? Virtually none. During World War II, however, there were large Jewish communities of German Jewish refugees who found haven in Shanghai and other cities.

◄966► What is a *tzadik?* A righteous person. The word is from the same root as *tzedek* (justice) and is related to *tzedakah* (charity).

◄967► What kind of person is meant who is described as a *basar v'dam?* Literally, "flesh and blood," the term signifies one who is content to go through life without any ambitions other than gratifying his physical needs.

◄968► What's an *akshan?* A stubborn person, usually one who has a closed mind and is unwilling to rectify or adjust an earlier view. The Jews often describe themselves in the biblical phrase as a "stiff-necked people," but the connotation here is that they are determined to fight on, despite all obstacles, for their religious or national ideals.

Who? What? Where? When? Why?

◄ **969** ► What is *lashon ha-ra?* Talebearing, which is heavily condemned in Jewish tradition, since it is harmful to three people at the least: the one who spreads the stories, the one who willingly listens, and the person affected.

◄ **970** ► What is meant by *parnasah?* Gainful employment, which is seen in Jewish thought as a sure road to self-respect. To become a recipient of alms is, in Jewish tradition, the direst of fates.

◄ **971** ► What is Yiddish? The language spoken by Jews from Central and Eastern Europe, which has produced an impressive literature. It is closely allied to German, with many Hebrew and some Slavic words added. Jews originally from Russia, Poland, Romania, Hungary, Germany, and Austria all conversed freely in Yiddish. Jews from the Iberian Peninsula, as well as those from Italy, Greece, Yugoslavia, Bulgaria, and Turkey, do not know Yiddish but have used Ladino for several centuries. This is a language derived from Spanish and Latin, also with a heavy smattering of Hebrew. Both languages are written in Hebrew characters, with minor variations in vocalization.

◄ **972** ► What is an *illui?* A child prodigy, usually one who at an early age masters the intricacies of the Torah and Talmud.

◄ **973** ► What is the Septuagint? According to tradition, Egypt's King Ptolemy II, in the third century B.C.E., asked Eliezer the high priest to have the Bible translated into Greek. Seventy scholars versed in both Hebrew and Greek set about to translate the Holy Scriptures, without any consultation between them, and produced seventy identical translations. Thus, their work is known as the *targum hashivim,* the translation of the seventy, or Septuagint.

◀**974**▶ What is meant by *marit ayin?* The concept that one should not do something that can be misinterpreted as sinful. Thus, a religious Jew who enters a non-kosher restaurant to make a telephone call should desist, lest he be thought of as breaking a commandment.

◀**975**▶ Of Moses' many attributes, which is traditionally regarded as his greatest? His humility.

◀**976**▶ What is a *herem?* Excommunication from the Jewish community, used rarely and always intended for the protection of the community and the safekeeping of Jewish law. (One of the most famous cases of *herem* was that of the philosopher Baruch Spinoza.)

◀**977**▶ What do the Hebrew words found on kosher butcher shops say? *Basar kasher,* or kosher meat.

◀**978**▶ The symbol of a "U" enclosed in an "O" is often found on kosher food (and detergent) products. What does it represent? The approval, in terms of Jewish dietary laws, of the Union of Orthodox Jewish Congregations of America, the nationwide group of Orthodox synagogues.

◀**979**▶ Is there a national American Jewish organization that speaks for all Jews on Jewish issues? There are scores of Jewish organizations, religious and secular, engaged in various programs. The two bodies that may be said to represent the overwhelming majority of American Jewry are the Synagogue Council of America, comprising the principal national synagogue and rabbinical bodies, and the Conference of Presidents of Major American Jewish Organizations.

◄ **980** ► What is the religious definition of a Jew? One born to a Jewish mother, or a convert to Judaism whose conversion was approved by a recognized rabbi.

◄ **981** ► Is it true that some Christian churches in Israel pray in Hebrew? Yes. It is the official language.

◄ **982** ► Who are the Neturei Karta? A tiny group of ultra-Orthodox Jews, largely confined to the Meah Shearim section of Jerusalem, who refuse to recognize the legitimacy of Israel, believing that Jews must continue to await the coming of the Messiah.

◄ **983** ► What is an *oleh?* An immigrant to Israel; literally, an ascendant. A *yored,* or descendant, is one who has opted to emigrate, usually for an easier economic life abroad.

◄ **984** ► What was Washington's famous letter to the Jews of Newport, Rhode Island? He wrote: "May the children of the stock of Abraham who dwell in this land continue to merit and enjoy the goodwill of the other inhabitants, while everyone shall sit in safety under his own vine and fig tree and there shall be none to make him afraid."

◄ **985** ► Who ruled that if "a woman says, 'My husband is distasteful to me, I cannot live with him,' the court must compel the husband to divorce her, because a woman is not a captive"? Maimonides.

◄ **986** ► Where does this line appear: "When a divorced man marries a divorced woman, there are four minds in the bed"? In the Talmud.

◄ **987** ► Which great rabbi and sage was virtually illiterate till the age of forty? Rabbi Akiva.

◄**988**► Who was the first Jew to receive a Nobel prize? Adolf von Baeyer, in 1905, for chemistry.

◄**989**► What are the "five Scrolls"? The Song of Songs, read in the synagogue on Passover; Ruth, read on Shavuoth; Lamentations, read on Tisha b'Av; Ecclesiastes, read on Sukkoth; and Esther, read on Purim.

◄**990**► Who was the first chief of staff of Israel's armed forces, after the creation of the state in 1948? Yaacov Dori, former chief of the underground Haganah (defense) organization.

◄**991**► Which country was first to recognize Israel? The United States.

◄**992**► Which President of Israel was both a socialist and a Hassid? Zalman Shazar, who served from 1963 to 1973.

◄**993**► What does the word *selah* mean? Although the word appears in the Bible, its true meaning is not known. It usually follows the word Amen, and signifies "may it always be so."

◄**994**► What were the cities of refuge in biblical times? Six cities to which perpetrators of accidental deaths could flee, to avoid vengeance by the victim's next of kin. There were three cities on each side of the Jordan River. When the high priest died, the refugees were permitted to return home to resume their normal lives.

◄**995**► According to Jewish law, may a rapist who married his victim ever divorce her? No.

◄**996**► In Jewish religious law, may a man ever marry his stepmother or stepsister? No.

Who? What? Where? When? Why?

◄**997**► In which country are Jews forbidden, in Jewish teaching, to settle on a permanent basis? Egypt, because of the enslavement of the ancient Israelites.

◄**998**► What is a blood libel? The totally false charge that Jews killed Christians (usually children) in order to obtain their blood for use in the Passover Seder ritual. Such libels have cropped up for thousands of years and were usually followed by murderous attacks against Jewish communities. One of the most notorious and recent such cases took place in Damascus in 1840.

◄**999**► Which American university specializes in Hebrew and cognate learning on a graduate level but is not a theological seminary? Dropsie University, in Philadelphia.

◄**1000**► Which country in Europe has the smallest Jewish population? Malta, with about fifty. The second-smallest Jewish community is found in Albania, with fewer than three hundred.

◄**1001**► How big was the territory of Israel prior to the Six Day War, in 1967? About eight thousand square miles, roughly the size of New Jersey.

SUGGESTED LIST OF READINGS

JUDAISM: BASIC BELIEFS

Kertzer, Morris. *What Is a Jew?* New York: Macmillan, 1971 (paperback).

Steinberg, Milton. *Basic Judaism*. New York: Harcourt Brace Jovanovich, 1965 (paperback).

Wouk, Herman. *This Is My God*. New York: Pocket Books, 1973 (paperback).

Birnbaum, Philip. *A Book of Jewish Concepts*. New York: Hebrew Publishing Co., 1975 (rev.)

Schauss, Hayyim. *The Lifetime of a Jew*. New York: Union of American Hebrew Congregations, 1976 (paperback).

Rosenthal, Gilbert S. *Four Paths to One God*. New York: Bloch Publishing Co., 1973.

PERSONAL LIFE

Siegel, Richard; Strassfeld, Michael; and Strassfeld, Sharon; eds. *The Jewish Catalog*. Philadelphia: Jewish Publication Society, 1974 (paperback).

Donin, Hayim Halevy. *To Be A Jew*. New York: Basic Books, 1972.

Kaplan, Sylvia; and Levi, Shonie B. *Guide for the Jewish Homemaker*. New York: Schocken Books, 1974 (paperback).

Abrahams, Israel. *Hebrew Ethical Wills*. Philadelphia: Jewish Publication Society, 1976 (paperback).

FAMILY LIFE

Dresner, Samuel H.; and Siegel, Seymour. *The Dietary Laws.* New York: United Synagogue Book Service, 1969 (paperback).

Schneid, Hayyim. *The Family.* Philadelphia: Jewish Publication Society, 1972 (paperback).

Kochan, Lionel; and Kochan, Miriam; text. Hubman, Franz; photos. *The Jewish Family Album.* Boston: Little, Brown, 1975.

Chill, Abraham. *The Mitzvot: The Commandments and Their Rationale.* New York: Bloch Publishing Co., 1974.

THE SYNAGOGUE

Eisenberg, Azriel. *The Synagogue Through the Ages.* New York: Bloch Publishing Co., 1974.

Kaploun, Uri. *The Synagogue.* Philadelphia: Jewish Publication Society, 1973 (paperback).

Millgram, Abraham. *Jewish Worship.* Philadelphia: Jewish Publication Society, 1969.

Dresner, Samuel H. *Prayer, Humility and Compassion.* Bridgeport, Conn.: Hartmore House, 1957.

HOLIDAYS AND FESTIVALS

Goodman, Philip. Anthology series: *Yom Kippur, Rosh Hashanah, Hanukkah, Purim, Passover, Sukkot and Simhat Torah, Shavuot.* Philadelphia: Jewish Publication Society, 1964–76.

Gaster, Theodore. *Festivals of the Jewish Year.* New York: Morrow, 1971 (paperback).

Suggested List of Readings

Schauss, Hayyim. *Guide to the Jewish Holidays.* New York: Schocken Books, 1962 (paperback).

CUSTOMS AND CEREMONIES

Ganzfried, Solomon. *Code of Jewish Law* (annotated). New York: Hebrew Publishing Co., 1963.

Roth, Cecil; and Wigoder, Geoffrey. *New Standard Jewish Encyclopedia.* New York: Doubleday, 1970.

Werblowski, R. J. Z.; and Wigoder, Geoffrey. *Encyclopedia of Jewish Religion.* New York: Holt, Rinehart & Winston, 1965.

THE SABBATH

Heschel, Abraham Joshua. *The Sabbath.* New York: Farrar, Straus & Giroux, 1975 (paperback).

Dresner, Samuel H. *The Sabbath.* New York: United Synagogue Book Service, 1970 (paperback).

Millgram, Abraham. *Sabbath: A Day of Delight.* Philadelphia: Jewish Publication Society, 1969.

ISRAEL

Hertzberg, Arthur. *The Zionist Idea: An Historical Analysis and Reader.* New York: Atheneum, 1969 (paperback).

Sachar, Howard. *A History of Israel.* New York: Alfred A. Knopf, 1977.

Meir, Golda. *My Life.* New York: Putnam, 1975.

Levin, Meyer. *The Story of Israel.* New York: Putnam, 1966.

Laqueur, Walter. *A History of Zionism.* New York: Holt, Rinehart & Winston, 1972.

Vilnay, Zev. *New Israel Atlas.* New York: McGraw-Hill, 1968.

JEWISH HISTORY

Baron, Salo. *A Social and Religious History of the Jews*, 15 vol. New York: Columbia University Press, 1952.

Dimont, Max. *Jews, God and History*. New York: New American Library, 1972 (paperback).

Margolis, Max; and Marx, Alexander. *History of the Jewish People*. New York: Atheneum, 1969 (paperback).

Ben Sasson, H. H., ed. *A History of the Jewish People*. Cambridge, Mass.: Harvard University Press, 1977.

WHO? WHAT? WHERE? WHEN? WHY?

The Holy Scriptures. Philadelphia: Jewish Publication Society, 1955.

Steinsaltz, Adin. *The Essential Talmud*. New York: Basic Books, 1976.

Noveck, Simon, ed. *Great Jewish Personalities in Ancient and Medieval Times*. New York: B'nai B'rith, 1959 (paperback).

Schwarz-Bart, André. *The Last of the Just*. New York: Bantam, 1973 (paperback).

Cohen, Mortimer. *Pathways Through the Bible*. Philadelphia: Jewish Publication Society, 1967.

GLOSSARY

ADLOYADA: The name given to the annual Purim parade in Israel, featuring costumed children celebrating the ancient victory of the Jews who thwarted Haman's plans to destroy them.

AFIKOMAN: The half of the middle matza taken from the Seder table early in the evening for "safekeeping" and usually redeemed at the conclusion of the service upon promise of payment of a suitable ransom.

ALIYAH: Referring to Israel, the term means the immigration of Jews to that country. The same word is used to describe the honor bestowed on a congregant when he is called to the reading of the Torah during Sabbath or holiday services. The literal meaning of the word is "ascent."

BENTSHING GOMEL: A mixed Yiddish-Hebrew phrase that refers to a special blessing recited by someone who has just recently come through a perilous journey and is safe and sound. It is usually recited in synagogue by a congregant who has recuperated from a serious illness.

FEER KASHES: The popular Yiddish phrase for the traditional Four Questions asked by the youngest child at the Seder table on Passover, which leads into the recital of the historic exodus of the Israelites from Egypt.

FRUM: A person who observes the Jewish religious laws with sincerity and conviction is usually described as *frum*. The implication is that he is not only fastidious about the details of the laws but that he also maintains about him an aura of gentleness in his daily life.

GABBAI: A layman who is honored in synagogue by being asked to serve as a keeper of decorum. It is usually poorly translated as "usher."

GOLDENEH MEDINAH: The catch phrase used by virtually all East European Jews who looked forward to the day when they would be able to emigrate to the United States, which they had heard was, from every standpoint, a "golden land."

HAGGADAH: The Passover Seder service, literally the "telling" (of the ancient story of the Jews' bondage in Egypt and their long trek to freedom). It is a miniature, family-oriented religious service, to which are appended traditional prayers, grace after meals, and songs.

HAMOTZI: A key word used in a blessing offered at the beginning of a meal, referring specifically to the "bread that God brings forth from the earth." Literally, it means "brings forth."

HAVDALAH: Literally, "separation." A special, brief ceremony performed at the conclusion of the Sabbath, separating the day of rest and peace from the rest of the mundane work week. The ceremony includes blessing of wine and sniffing of a spice box.

KADDISH: The mourner's special prayer, recited three times daily for nearly a year after the death of a parent or close relative.

KOSHER: Food that is ritually fit for consumption according to the Jewish dietary laws. It has in recent years also come to mean, in colloquial usage, adding a negative, something improper. To wit, "It doesn't smell kosher!"

LATKE: A potato pancake, associated with celebration of the Hanukkah festival.

MENORAH: A candelabrum, an ancient symbol of the Jewish people. Today the menorah is the official emblem of Israel and is also found in most synagogues. The special menorah for observance of the Hanukkah ritual is made up of nine branches—one each for the eight nights of the festival, and a ninth (the *shamash*) which is used to light the others.

NACHAS: An almost untranslatable term used extensively by Jewish parents. The word refers exclusively to the joys and pleasures that parents receive from seeing their children grow into mature, happy, productive adults.

NER TAMID: The Eternal Light, the small red lamp that is usually seen above the Holy Ark in most synagogues and that is supposed to be lit at all times, a remembrance of the menorah in the ancient Holy Temple.

PARNASAH: A livelihood. When asked, Jews will usually say that all they want out of life is *gezunt* (health), *nachas* (see above), and *parnasah*.

REFUAH SHLEMAH: The traditional wish extended to someone who is ill. It means "full recovery."

TZEDAKAH: Usually translated as "charity," the term is closely allied to the Hebrew word for "justice," indicating that Jewish tradition sees the giving of funds to the needy as nothing more than an act of justice for society as a whole.

YASHER KOACH: The traditional greeting offered to someone who has been honored by being called to the reading of the Torah in the synagogue. It may also be used as a general expression of congratulation.

INDEX

Index

Association of Orthodox Jewish
 Scientists, 221
Atonement, for living and dead,
 81
Aufruf, 49, 251
Autopsies, 126–27
Averah, 247
Avraham (Abraham), 23

Baal kriyah, 255
Baal Shem Tov, Israel, 37, 206
Baal tefilah, 254
Baal t'kiyah, 70
Baal t'shuvah, 247
Badchan, 49
Badge of shame, 201
Bar, Bat Mitzvah, where
 celebrated, 8; boy's use of *tallit*
 and *tefillin*, 24; boy counted in
 minyan, 24; synagogue
 celebration, 53–54; reading of
 haftarah, 247–48; ceremony of,
 57, 62; women and ceremony
 of, 57; definition of, 260; Friday
 evening, Sabbath morning
 service, 140–41
Bar-Ilan University, 161
Bar Kochba, 107–8; 189–90
Bar Yochai, Rabbi Shimon, 107–8
Baruch ha-ba, 250
Baruch ha-Shem, 251
Basar kasher, 268
Basar v'dam, 266
Bathia, 98–99
Bathsheba, 178–79
Beards, 27
Bechor, law of inheritance of, 243
Beitza. Egg. *See* Seder
Beni Israel, 264
Benjamin, Judah, 216
Bentshen. See Grace
Bentsher, 236
Bentshing Gomel, 228
Ben Yehudah, Rabbi Gershom,
 196–97
Besamim. Spice boxes. See
 Havdalah
Bet Din, 255

Bet Hillel, 226–27
Bet Knesset, 226
Bet Midrash, 226
Bet Shammai, 226–27
Bet Tefilah, 226
Bethlehem, 165, 261
BH. Hebrew abbreviation for
 B'ezrat ha-Shem, 259
Bialik, Hayyim Nahman, 214
Bible, definition and origin of,
 5–6; laws of, 9–10; reasons for
 commentaries, 13; teachings of,
 17, 27, 32–33, 123; ideal wife
 in, 41; sexual prohibitions, 42;
 rules on the aged, 43; laws on
 fruit trees, 93; Passover in,
 97–98; commandment on *omer*,
 101; pilgrim festivals in, 108;
 dietary laws in, 123; ban on
 eating blood, 124; Jews' claim to
 Israel in, 169; canonization of,
 187, 190; translation into
 English, 217; law of mezuzah in,
 227; law of inheritance in, 243
Bimah, 54, 191
Biro-Bidjan, 262–63
Birth, 250
Birth control, 28
Blessings, before meal, 25; of
 children, 118–19
Blintzes. See Shavuoth
Blood libel, 201; in Damascus,
 216, 266
B'nai B'rith, 12, 234–35
Boaz, 173
Brandeis, Louis D., 225
Brazil, 225
Bris, Brit, Brit Milah. *See* Brith
Brith, 11–12; ceremony of, 21,
 255; chair of Elijah at, 183;
 sandak at, 228
Bruriah, 189
Bukharan Jews, 235
Burial, laws regarding death and,
 126–29; of suicides, 237

Canaan, 11, 169; Joshua's
 conquest of, 172

282

Index

Canonization of Bible, 187, 190
Cantor, 14–15; table used by, 54; definition of, 62, 254–55
Caro, Joseph, 203, 256
Carpas. See Seder
Cedars of Lebanon, 179
Chanukah. *See* Hanukkah
Charity. *See Tzedakah*
Chayim, 22
Child abuse, 39
Childlessness, 39–40
Cholent, 144
Chutzpah, 243
Circumcision, 21. *See* Birth
Cities of refuge, 270
Cohen, Samuel, 234
Commandments, the 613, 10–11; charity, 17; *tallit* and *tefillin*, 24–25
Commentaries, Bible, 196, 197–98, 199; on Midrash, 195; Mishneh Torah codification, 199; methods of, 197–98
Compassion, 35
Conference of Presidents of Major American Jewish Organizations, 268
Confirmation, 110, 260
Conservative Jews, views on Halachah, 10; use of yarmulke, 26; view on birth control, 28; view on cremation, 29; use of *mikveh*, 42–43; synagogues of, 53; counting women in *minyan* by, 58; use of organ in service, 59; view of Sabbath driving, 143–44; U.S. movement of, 218; population in United States, 222
Contraception, Orthodox view of oral contraceptive pill, 45
Conversion, 7–8
Convert, naming of, 23; adoption of, 43; marriage restrictions on, 48
Convenant, 11–12; ceremony of Brith, 21; of Jews with God, 170
Creation, 12

Cremation, 29, 129
Cresques, Judah, 263

David, basic tenets in Psalms of, 15; descendant of Ruth, 173–74; chosen by Samuel, 175–76; conquest of Philistines by, 177; composition of Psalms by, 177–78; Bathsheba and, 178–79; length of reign, 179; grave of, 179; Shield of, 262
Day of Atonement, 5; as last of Days of Awe, 55, 70
Days of Awe, 55; visiting graves during, 71, 246–47
De Torres, Luis, 262
Death, 258
Deborah, 173
Decalogue, *See* Ten Commandments
Delilah, 174
Deuteronomy, law of *mezuzah* in, 115
Diaspora, 60–61; years of exile in, 149, 153, 258–59
Dibbuk, 11, 259
Dietary laws. *See* Kashrut
Divorce, 31; amount of, 39; childlessness as grounds for, 47; rapist and victim and, 270
Dori, Yaacov, 270
Drashah, 62
Dreidel, game of, 89; soldiers' use of, as ruse, 91
Dreyfus trial, 257
Dropsie University, 271
Duality of Judaism, 11
Duchanen, 253–54
Dvar Torah, 245

Eating, 15–16, 191
Ecclesiastes. See Koheleth
Education, 25–26
Egypt, ban on settling in, 271
Einhorn, David, 216
Einstein, Albert, 12, 241
El-Al airline, 159
El Maleh Rachamim, 259–60

283

Index

inscriber and sealer of man's fate, 71; how forgiveness is granted by, 73, 78; sanctification of, 121; charge to Joshua by, 171; martyrs who died for hallowing of name of, 239

Golden calf, 74, 77

Goldeneh medinah, 252–53

Golem, 228

Gomel, bentshing, 228

Goy, goyim (pl.), 260

Grace, 16, 121, 249

Graetz, Heinrich, citation by, 167

Great assembly, 185

Grogger. See Purim

Guide to the Perplexed, 198–99

Gut yomtov, 250

Ha-lahma anya. See Haggadah

Ha-Makom yenahem, 235

Ha-Tikvah, 234

Habad, 262

Hachnassat kallah, 233

Hadassah, 160; origin of name, 243

Haftarah, 57, 247–48

Hag habikkurim. See Shavuoth

Hag same-ah, 64, 250

Haganah, 270

Hagbahah, 55–56, 254

Haggadah, 99–100, 103; opening words of (*ha-lahma anya*), 105; story of four sons in, 105–6; art in, 106

Hagiographa, 233

Haifa, Sabbath transport in, 164

Hakafot, 256

Halachah, 9–10, 236, 256

Halaf, 124, 237

Halevi, Judah, 196, 198

Halitza, 48, 232

Hallah, Sabbath and Rosh Hashanah use of, 71, 119, 138, 242; tradition of two loaves, 120

Hallel, on Yom Ha-Atzmaut, 108

Halutz, 238

Haman. *See* Purim

Haman's sons, 97

Hamantashen, 96

Hametz, 98, 257; selling of, 101; burning of, 102; kinds of, 106–7

Hamotzi lechem, 25

Handkerchief dance, 239

Hanukkah, games played on, 30, 89–90; why so visible, 87; reasons for observance, 87, 184–85; menorah of, 88; non-biblical reference to, 89; gifts on, 90–91; contemporary celebration of, 92

Hanukkah menorah, description of, 88; miracle of cruse of oil, 88–89; lighting of, 90; Sabbath-eve kindling of, 90

Hanukkat ha-bayit, 122

Happiness, 34

Hara, 231

Haroset. See Seder

Hasidei umot ha-olam, 236

Haskalah, 214, 217

Hasmoneans, 184–85

Hassidic Jews, wearing of fringes by, 24; faith healing by, 32; *shmura matza* baking by, 103; haircuts in Meron by, 107; opposition to Israel by, 151; study of Kabbalah by, 229; hat of, 238; *shirayim* of, 248

Hassidim, historic group opposed to Hellenism, 186

Hassidism, rise of, 206–7; 214, 262

Hatan, 251

Hatan bereshit, 85–86

Hatan Torah, 85–86

Hatunah. See Wedding

Havdalah, 61–62, 122, 142, 229

Hazak, hazak, v'nithazek, 254

Hazzan, 62, 254–255. *See* Cantor

Head covering, 26–27. *See* Yarmulke

Hebrew, holiness of, 30–31; words for Scroll of Law in, 55; use of name in, when called to Torah

Index

reading, 56; words in, 116, 236, 241, 242, 243, 259, 268
Hebrew language, emphasis by Judah ha-Nassi on, 189; modernization of, 208
Hebrew Union College, 161
Hebrew University, 159, 161, 226, 234
Hebron, 176, 177, 261
Heder, origin of, 205
Hefker, 230
Hellenism, 9, 184
Hereafter, 8–9, 259–60
Heredity, 36
Herem, 268
Herzl, Theodor, 257
Heshvan, 262
Hevra kadisha, 127
HIAS, 217
High Holy Days, wearing white on, 26–27; liturgy on aged on, 43; synagogue seating during, 54; prayer book of, 58; wearing of *kittel* on, 72; new prayers on, 81
High priest, function of, on Yom Kippur, 77, 180
Hillel, interpretation of Judaism by, 10; attitude toward selfishness, 15; views on divorce, 31; teachings of, 186–87; followers of, 226–27
Hirsch, Samuel Raphael, 210
Hol ha-moed, of Sukkoth, 83; of Passover, 98, 260, 261
Holocaust, 7; memorial day for, 69; as stimulus for creation of Israel, 150; knowledge of, 218–19
Holy Ark, location in synagogue, 54; curtain of, 55; in desert, 171; contents of, 191
Holy land. See Israel
Holy of holies, 77, 180
Holy Temple, worship in, 10; glass-breaking ceremony in memory of, 47; rededication of, 87; first fruits brought to, 107;

building of, 179–80; contents of Holy of Holies in, 180; sacrifices and prayers at, 180; Western Wall of, 261
Homosexuality, 28–29
Hora, 238
Horeb. *See* Mount Sinai
Hoshanah rabbah, ceremonies on, 84; last day for use of four species, 85
Hoshanot, 84
Humility, 33–34
Huppah, 47, 250

Ibn-Ezra, Abraham, 196
Ibn-Ezra, Moses, 196
Ibn-Gabirol, Solomon, 196, 223
Idolatry, 253
Illui, 267
Im yirtze ha-Shem, 251
Imber, Naftali H., 234
Immortality, 9
Inheritance, 243
Intellectual dissent, 13
Interceders between man and God, 14
Intermarriage, 9
Isaiah, 183
Ish-Bosheth, 177
Israel, others names in Bible for, 11; bridal canopy in, 47; emblem of, 58; prayer for dew and rain in, 60–61; public Hanukkah menorah in, 88; Arbor Day in, 93; Passover in, 98; selling *hametz* in, 101; Sabbath in, 135; as haven for oppressed Jews, 151; religious situation in, 152; political allegiance to, 152; elections in, 152–53; conscription in, 154; civil rights in, 154; size, climate of, 155–56; economy of, 156–57, 162; Americans in, 157–58; marriage in, 159; organizations helping, 160–61; universities in, 161; alcoholism,

Index

drugs in, 162–63; Sabbath public transport in, 164; care for aged, 165; Law of Return, 233; Sabbatical year in, 240; Bahai in, 263; Socialist President of, 270

Israel Bonds, 161

Israel Declaration of Independence, 149

Israel Independence Day. *See* Yom ha-Atzmaut

Israel Museum, 159

Israelis, names of, 23

Israelites, early, 169–70; wandering in desert of, 171; conquest of Jericho by, 172

Jacob, 97; in struggle with angel, 124; as father of twelve tribes, 172

Jacobson, Israel, 209

Jaffa, 179

Jeremiah, Book of, read during mourning, 127–28; welfare of government, 261

Jeroboam, 182

Jerusalem, temple in, 10; interreligious peace in modern, 17–18; glass ceremony in memory of, 47; wall facing, 54; Sabbath desecration led to destruction of, 138; comparison with Washington, D.C., 159; Arab-Jewish relations in, 165; conquest by David, 177; meaning of word, 241; snow in, 264

Jesse, 173–74; sons of, 175

Jesus, 18

Jethro, 99

Jewish calendar, 69–70, 195, 241, 262

Jewish cemetery, oldest, 244

Jewish centers, 8

Jewish history, origin of, 169; early Israelites, 170; Joseph, Moses, Aaron, Joshua, 170–72;

Ruth, Boaz, Samson, Samuel, Saul, Jonathan, David, 173–77; Solomon, 179–82; loss of ten tribes, 183; Jeremiah, return of exiles, 184; Ezra, Nehemiah, Great Assembly, exile by Rome, Hillel, 185–87; Yavneh academy, Rabbi Akiva, Bar Kochba, 188–90; Babylonian Jewry, Talmud, Saadyah, rise of Spain, Jews in Christian countries, Moslem centers, 192–96; Halevi, Ibn-Gabirol, Maimonides, Ibn-Ezra, et al., 196–98; expulsions, blood libels, massacres, communal and educational agencies, *mitnagdim* vs. *hassidim*, emancipation, pogroms, waves of emigration, Haskalah, Zionism, Jewish settlement in United States and development of communal institutions, Yiddish, religious movements, 199–218; contemporary situation of U.S. and other Jewish communities, 219–22

Jewish museums, 241

Jewish National Fund, 93; work of, 161; trees planted, 252

Jewish Nobel Prize winners, 270

Jewish population, state with smallest, 241; before destruction of Temple, 264, 265; in China, 266; smallest in Europe, 271

Jewish science, 32

Jewish sports, 248

Jewish star. *See* Magen David

Jewish Theological Seminary, 161, 218

Jew, religious definition of, 267

Jezebel, 182

Job, 14; reading of during mourning, 127

Jonah, Book of, 78

Jonathan, 175–76

Index

Index

birth control, clothing, shaving, 27–28; family purity among, 42–43; views on sterilization, contraception, 45; *aufruf* custom among, 49; synagogues of, 53–54; use of *mehitzah*, 58; use of *kittel*, 72; resurgence in United States, 221; *aliyah* among, 221–22; population in United States, 222; *eruv* observance, 247; *shatnez* prohibition observed by, 249–50

OSE, 232

Paitanim, 195
Palestine, 184, 238–39, 244
Parental responsibility, 26
Pareve, 237
Parnas, 231
Parnasah, 267
Parochet, 55
Parsha. See Sidrah
Partition, 158
Passover, 23, 60–61; as pilgrim festival, 82, 97–107; dishes, 123, 241, 257, 258, 260–61, 270
Payot (also *payos*), 249
Pentateuch, 5–6. *See* Torah
Pentecost, 110
People of the Book, 265
Peretz, I. L., 214
Pesach (Passover), 23
Pesachdig, 257
Pharisees, 186
Philanthropy, 17
Philo, description of ancient Yom Kippur in, 80
Phineas, 173
Phylacteries, 24
Pidyon ha-ben, 23, 252
Pikuach nefesh, Yom Kippur and, 78, 239
Pilgrim festivals, 82, 98, 108
Pioneer Women, 160–61
Pitah, 244
Piyutim, 195
Plagues, 97–98. *See* Passover

Pleasures, 15
Pogroms, 150
Polygamy, Jewish view of, 30; ban of Rabbi Gershom, 197
Pornography, 30
Prayers, 23–25; memorial service, 60; for rain, dew, 60–61, 74, 81, 109–10; for deceased, 259–60; for welfare of government, 261
Predestination, 4
Pride, 15
Priesthood, 23; task of, 171
Promiscuity, condemnation of, 40
Promised Land, wandering in wilderness before entering, 171; Moses' view of, 171
Prophets, portion of, 57, 145; as section of Bible, 233, 247–48; early and later, 256
Proselytizing, 8
Prostitution, condemnation of, 40; in Israel, 166
Proverbs, Book of, view of God in, 13; monogamy as ideal in, 30; view of child rearing in, 35–36; verses from, 181
Psalms, Book of, 10–11; verse on aged, 43; view of life and death in, 126; composition of, by David, 177–78, 251
Pshat and *drash*, 197–98
Punishment, 26
Purim, games of chance on, 30, 94–97, 236, 256, 257, 258, 270

Rabbi, role of, in congregation, 14–15, 48, 62; ordination of, 233
Rabbinic rulings on divorce, 31
Rabbis, views on faith healing, 32; interpretation of divine spark, 33–34, 39–40, 44; selection of, 188; mothers' views, 261
Rachel's tomb, 261
Rachmanim bnai rachmanim, 265
Rape, 268
Rashi, 196–98

291

Index

Shabbat Hagadol, 72–73
Shabbat Shalom, 64, 118
Shabbat Shabbaton, 77
Shabbat Shuvah, 72–73, 246–47
Shabbes goy, 257
Shabbetai Tzvi, 203–4
Shacharit, 24–25
Shadai, 227
Shadchan, 46, 238
Shalach manot, 257
Shalom, 236
Shaliach tsibur, 15
Shalom aleichem, 236
"Shalom Aleichem," 119
Shalom bayit, definition of, 39;
  role of parents in, 41
Shalom zachar, 252
Shalosh seudot, 63–64, 142
Shammai, on grounds for divorce,
  31; followers of, 185, 226–27
Shammus, 243
Shamash, 88
Shankbone. *See* Seder
Shatnez, 249–50
Shavua tov, 142
Shavuoth, pilgrim holiday of, 82;
  harvest, 82; *omer* and, 101, 107;
  definition of, 107–10;
  confirmation on, 260, 270
Shazar, Zalman, 270
Shechem, 182
Shechinah, 240
She-he-che-yanu, 246
Shehitah, meaning of, 123; laws
  governing, 123–24
Shekel, 243
Shemitah, 240
Shevah b'rachot, 47
Shield of David. *See* Magen David
Shiloh, 172–73
Shirayim, 248
Shiva, 127–28, 235
Shloshim, 128
"Shma Yisrael," idea of
  monotheism, 4; proper attire
  for, 29; in *mezuzah*, 115, 227
Shmad, 249

Shmini Atzeret, 84–85, 254
Shmoneh esray, 60, 245
Shofar, significance of, 70;
  sounder of, 70; meaning of
  sounds of, 70–71, 74, 75, 172
Shohet. *See* Shehitah
Shomrim, 244–45
Shtadlan, 231
Shtetl, 226, 232
Shtibel, 53
Shtreimel, 238
Shulhan Aruch, 203, 256
Shulklapper, 74
Siddur, 58, 116, 117, 187
Sidra, 61, 144–45, 253
Simcha, 246
Simchat bat, 121, 252
Simhat Torah, 61, 85, 86, 87, 145,
  256
Sinfulness, 32–33
Sins, three cardinal, 253
Six Day War, 150–51, 159
Six Million, memorial and kaddish
  for, 125–26, 150, 225
S'micha, 233
Social service agencies, 202
Sodom, 29
Sofer, 243
Solomon, 179, 180, 181, 182
Song of Songs, 190, 270
Soul, 34
Soviet Jews, 158, 164, 165–66,
  219, 241
Spinoza, Baruch, 268
Sterilization, 45
Straus, Oscar, 225–26
Strauss, Levi, 244
Suffering, 14, 44–45
Sufganiyot, 91, 233
Suicides, 237
Sukkah, 82, 83
Sukkoth, 6–61, 82, 83, 84, 243,
  254, 260–61, 270
Superstitions, 44, 115
Sura and Pumbedeitha, 192
Synagogues, definition of, 8,
  21–22; origin of, 53; number in

293

Index

Yeshiva, in Poland, 205; in United States, 217, 221, 245
Yeshiva University, 161
Yiddish, 8, 26, 47–48, 50, 64, 72, 214, 217–18, 263
Yigdal, 199
Yihus, 262
Yimah shmo, 262
Yisrael, when called to Torah, 56; at Seder, 103
Yizkor, 60, 85, 229
YM-YWHA, 8, 215–16
Yocheved, 98–99
Yohanan ben-Zakai, 188
Yom ha-Atzmaut, 108
Yom Kippur, 21, 24, 59, 60, 71, 74, 246

Yom Kippur War, 239
Youth Aliyah, 160

Zemirot, on Sabbath, 120–21; 139–40, 234
Zion, prayer for, 54
Zionism, aims of, 150–51; development of, 213–14; in United States, 217; effect of Holocaust on, 219, 234, 238–39, 257, 263
Zipporah, 99
Zivig, 48
Zohar, 131, 229
Zoroastrianism, 9

ABOUT THE AUTHOR

DAVID C. GROSS was born in Belgium and came to the United States as a small child. He spoke Yiddish exclusively until he was seven, and then struggled to master English. Writing and the welfare of the Jewish people have remained his twin lifetime interests.

A graduate of Herzliah, a Hebrew teachers seminary, he at one time planned to enter the rabbinate but opted instead to work in the world of letters. After a stint as a reporter for the New York *Post,* he became an editor of the Jewish Telegraphic Agency, the world-wide Jewish news agency, where he conducted a weekly column, for more than fifteen years, that appeared in more than one hundred newspapers around the world.

Later, he became a publicist for various organizations aiding Jews and supporting Israel: the Joint Distribution Committee, United Jewish Appeal, Palestine Economic Corporation, and the American Technion Society. He has visited Israel more than a dozen times since 1952, where he wrote and directed documentary films and instituted public-relations programs.

In 1967, after having had two books that he edited and translated from Hebrew and Yiddish, respectively, published by Doubleday, he was named editor of the American-Israeli Book Co. He then became vice-president of Keter/Encyclopedia Judaica, helping to introduce this massive Jewish cultural enterprise, published in Israel, to the American market. Subsequently he became executive vice-president of the Jewish Publication Society of America.

Mr. Gross is married, and his wife, Esther, teaches in a Jewish religious school. Their daughter, Laura, is a professor of history; their son Joel is a novelist and screen writer, and their son Marc is a student.

THE JEWISH CALENDAR, HOLIDAYS & FESTIVALS

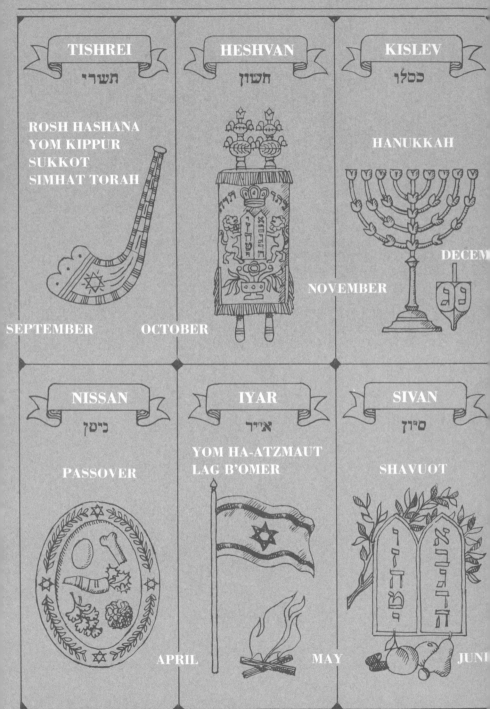

TISHREI
תשרי

ROSH HASHANA
YOM KIPPUR
SUKKOT
SIMHAT TORAH

SEPTEMBER   OCTOBER

HESHVAN
חשון

NOVEMBER

KISLEV
כסלו

HANUKKAH

DECEM

NISSAN
ניסן

PASSOVER

APRIL

IYAR
אייר

YOM HA-ATZMAUT
LAG B'OMER

MAY

SIVAN
סיון

SHAVUOT

JUNI